D0883313

CONSERVATION
OF BUILDINGS

Other books by John Harvey

Henry Yevele
Gothic England
The Plantagenets
Dublin
Tudor Architecture
The English Cathedrals
The Gothic World
English Mediaeval Architects
The Cathedrals of Spain
The Master Builders

BIBLIOGRAPHIES

English Cathedrals – A Reader's Guide
Conservation of Old Buildings

EDITED WITH TRANSLATION

William Worcestre: Itineraries 1478–1480

CREATIVE CONSERVATION

York Theatre Royal after removal of excrescences and the building of
its dynamic extension in 1967.   *Architect: Patrick Gwynne.*

CONSERVATION OF BUILDINGS

JOHN HARVEY

4, 5 & 6 SOHO SQUARE LONDON

First published in 1972 by
JOHN BAKER (PUBLISHERS) LTD
4, 5 & 6 Soho Square
London W1V 6AD

ISBN 0 212 98420 9

Printed in Great Britain
BY W & J MACKAY LIMITED, CHATHAM

Contents

Illustrations

Frontispiece YORK, Theatre Royal after extension, 1967

Illustrations

Acknowledgments

The author and publishers here express their indebtedness to the following persons and institutions for the photographs named: Mr. B. J. Ashwell for 18, 19 (by Peckams, Stroud); Mr. Patrick Gwynne for Frontispiece (by Henk Snoek); the Leatherhead & District Countryside Protection Society for 16 (by Austin Youell) and 17 (by *The Leatherhead Advertiser*); the National Monuments Record for 12, 13, 45; Messrs. Norman & Underwood Ltd. for 30–33; the Tewkesbury Abbey Lawn Trustees for 10, 11 (by S. P. Hamill); Messrs. Thomas-Photos, Oxford, for 1–9; the Warden and Fellows of Winchester College for 14, 15, 20–29, 34–43, 46–51 (21 by A. E. Rice; 14, 15, 20, 22, 24, 25, 42, 51 by Sidney Pitcher; the rest by E. A. Sollars).

Preface

Conservation has become one of the keywords or crucial concepts of our time. It is easy to see why this is so. We live in an age of almost unparalleled destruction, both in regard to the amount of what is destroyed and the rapidity of dissolution. To those who were born before 1939, even more those born before 1914, it must seem that the foundations of the earth are out of course. Just as the Lisbon earthquake of 1755 rudely shook the complacent faith of those who held that all was for the best in the best of possible worlds, so the discovery of atomic fission and all that it implies has raised in agonizing form the question of whether anything can or will survive.

This is not the place to discuss philosophical and metaphysical concepts of time and eternity: it is fundamental to conservation of every kind that it concerns material things existing in time. The essence of the subject lies in duration. Put crudely, the basis for any theory of conservation lies in the view that material objects can have value; and that it is therefore desirable that those things which have relatively greater value should last. Nor is the relativity of the proposition limited to the value put upon particular objects. The duration of 'life' of a given object is itself relative, since it must be accepted as axiomatic that neither any natural object or living creature, nor any work of man (himself in fact a part of nature), goes on for ever, even if we deliberately limit the sense of 'ever' to the extreme duration of Time itself.

Everything known to us has a longer or shorter period of existence and then, whether suddenly or by a process of slow and perhaps extremely protracted decay, comes to an end. In the so-called world of nature, i.e. exclusive of the works of man, there is an important qualification of this proposition. Though it still remains true in regard to all individuals, whether a single boulder, a tree, or an animal, there is a gigantic disproportion between the life of the single object and the total extension of the species (e.g. granite, oak, elephant) of which the single individual forms a part. It is probably because of our awareness of this rule of the enormously long life of the species that modern alarm has been particularly aroused over the conservation of nature: of the landscape and of all the living species which inhabit it. To us it is inexpressibly dreadful to contemplate the approaching doom of a whole species, or retrospectively to contemplate the final end of a race, whether that of the natives of Tasmania in 1876 or of the North American Passenger Pigeon, totally extinct by 1915, yet so numerous as to have blackened the sky in flocks of millions less than a hundred years before. Faced with many other species threatened, man belatedly expresses concern and begins to pay rather more than lip-service to Nature Conservancy.

It has already been insisted that man himself is a part of nature, and man's artefacts also are 'natural'; but by custom they are regarded as in a separate category. Whereas ants make nests and bees form waxen cells, while birds construct nests, all these are as it were inevitable extrusions of the species as a whole. In these instances there is no significant difference between one cell or nest and another made by the same species. What they lack is a quality present in the works of man, namely design. Animals may often have individuality, as anyone who has had to do with many cats, or horses, or even domestic fowls, can testify. But their personal equation is not, apparently, ever expressed in those works done by them as part of their natural activities. With man, or at any rate with a good many men, it is otherwise. To a greater or a less extent the individuality of design marks out every original product of men's brains or hands.

The recognition of this private quality of each single work of art or prototype of any given human product has given rise to the world's museums and collections, and to many legal provisions such as those of deposit of copies of all published literature in certain libraries. Underlying all this activity and legislation is the idea that each single object fashioned by man – whether a jewel or a poem – is stamped with the unique. Each of these items never happened before, and never will again; it must therefore be preserved now. It will be noticed that in this context the word used is 'preserved', rather than 'conserved'. As we shall see, there is need for both words as distinct in usage; the point here is that the continued existence, unchanged as far as may be, of an object in a museum, a painting in a gallery, or a book or manuscript in a library, constitutes *preservation*. In itself this is negative and merely allows continued study of the object for aesthetic or intellectual purposes. Taking an extreme instance, a precious cup wrought by a goldsmith as a drinking vessel for a king, and at first actually used as such, has eventually come to rest in the glass case of a museum. With very rare exceptions, any object preserved in this way has come to the end of its working life. Never again will a king, or anybody else, drink from the cup. Normally it will only be things kept in personal collections that will continue to be used, cherished, passed from hand to hand, or bought by some other collector for the like use.

The case of Buildings is very different from that of most other man-made objects, and that for several reasons. In the first place they are too large, extremely rare exceptions apart, to be portable. They are fixed to the soil irrevocably and in their first position they must live or die. (Something will have to be said later of the special and unusual problem of the preservation of buildings by removal; see p. 191). Secondly, this factor of their grand scale makes them the dominant feature in all the artificial aspects of human environment. It is only tribes or nations living in nomadic conditions and without fixed settlements who remain free of this domination by their own artefacts; and by definition these people have no buildings. Thirdly, buildings are not merely made for use, as are many tools and devices, but their use is highly complex and continually subject to change, interpenetrating the lives of the dwellers within them. Because of this last factor, almost every building takes on a kind of transferred life of its own, and this cannot, without serious difficulty and strain, be turned into a radically different channel.

It is then the factor of changing and developing use, on a site already fixed and permitting no alteration, and upon a scale of at least such significance as to bring in the factor of comparative site values, that gives to the continued existence of buildings a special character. Mere negative preservation of a building, that is to say preventing change of any kind so far as this is technically possible, is not only not enough, it is not within the realms of practical possibility at all. Unless the building is to be kept as a 'dead' specimen of a type now extinct, it must be so maintained as to keep it fit for living use within its potentiality. It is maintenance of this sort, including repair of decayed buildings to bring them back to a state of technical good health and utility, that constitutes conservation. This in turn is the subject of the present book.

The author's qualification to deal with the subject rests simply upon the experience of a working career in dealing with many aspects of building conservation. Until quite recent times there have been no academic qualifications in the subject available; but when the first British course of this kind was planned by the Bartlett School of Architecture at University College, London, in 1950, it was a source of great pleasure to be asked by the late Professor Hector O. Corfiato to take part. That I was able even to attempt this was due mainly to the fact that my childhood and upbringing had been in the midst of the architectural practice, mainly in the field of conservation, of my father William Harvey. From frequent visits in his company to such monuments as Westminster Hall, St. Paul's Cathedral, Tintern and Rievaulx Abbeys, and innumerable churches and houses; from holding the tape and steadying the plumb-bob in survey work; from later extended periods as his professional assistant, I was gradually and naturally initiated into the knowledge of a sound way of treatment for old buildings in a state of decay. It was not necessarily the only sound way, but it had the great merit of springing from my father's devotion to good craftsmanship and his love for art. Above all, he cared for buildings as possessing individual 'lives', derivative it may be, of their own. He viewed the duty of the architect-conservator as precisely analogous to that of the physician: to preserve life, and above all to conserve health.

From what has been said it will be manifest that this book owes most to the example and encouragement of my father, to his knowledge, and to his skill in imparting it. It also derives much from the good fortune of being brought into contact from my earliest years with a circle of my father's friends and acquaintances, architects, antiquaries, artists and archaeologists: notably, for the past fifty years, Sir Archibald Creswell. Others of the circle, now gone from the scene but living in memory were T. F. Amery, David Black, F. V. Blundstone, F. R. Hiorns, A. M. Hocart, A. R. Powys, E. T. Richmond, and J. F. Wilson. A special tribute of admiration and affection is due to the master under whom I trained, Sir Herbert Baker, great man and great architect as well as an outstanding expert upon the Wealden house of Kent, the county of his yeoman origins and his first love. Among the very many friends with whom I have discussed problems of conservation and architectural history were the late T. D. Atkinson, P. B. Chatwin, G. H. Chettle, Sir Alfred Clapham, Sir Cyril Fox, H. L. Honeyman, R. P. Howgrave-Graham, H. A. James, Jean Maunoury, the late Lord Mottistone, the late Lord Raglan, L. F. Salzman, and Colonel B. C. G. Shore.

My special thanks go to Messrs. W. Godfrey Allen, Bernard J. Ashwell, Frank Benger, J. A. Farmer, S. J. Garton, Dennis G. King, Dr. T. L. Marsden, Dr. H. J. Plenderleith, Mr. E. Clive Rouse, Dr. R. J. Schaffer, Mr. W. J. Carpenter Turner, and Dr. Raymond B. Wood-Jones; as well as to Mr. James C. Palmes, Mr. H. V. Molesworth Roberts, and successive librarians and staff of the library of the Royal Institute of British Architects; to Mr. John Hopkins, Librarian of the Society of Antiquaries; and to the York Institute of Advanced Architectural Studies. In a category by himself stands Mr. Ivor Bulmer-Thomas, to whom I owe gratitude not only for the example set by his lion-hearted defence of worthy buildings, but also for his incisive discrimination over the moral values of conservation.

A book based largely upon professional experience necessarily owes much to a large number of clients, whom it is impossible to name individually. It will be obvious that text and illustrations are indebted to the Warden and Fellows of Winchester College, who have afforded me a continuing opportunity through the past twenty-five years to work both upon their buildings and their historical documents. For permission to reprint the extract on pages 16–17 I am indebted to Messrs. Constable & Co.; to the Society of Antiquaries of London for allowing me to quote the document in Appendix II; and for Appendix IV to the Ancient Monuments Society. To the late John Baker I owe not merely the suggestion for this book, but also the benefit of his knowledge of and concern for old buildings and the countryside; my thanks go to his colleagues for their care over design and production. My wife, who has been deeply involved in a great deal of the conservation work described, has also earned my gratitude as critic and as proof-reader.

JOHN H. HARVEY
27 February 1972

Note: references for important facts will be found in the Notes to the text, pp. 223–6. A key-word is given in each case.

Introduction

It is essential to the proper understanding of any subject that it be discussed in clearly defined terms. In the present case there is need for definition of the two words: 'Conservation' and 'Building.' As has been remarked in the preface, there is a distinction to be drawn between preservation and conservation: the former describes the static maintenance of an object in unaltered condition, analogous to that of a museum specimen in optimum surroundings. The latter, while including maintenance, takes on a dynamic character by being concerned also with needed adaptations. These adaptations, of any utensil but here of the complex artefact to be described as a 'building', are not limited to the thing itself, but concern also alterations of the scene in which it is set. Conservation thus embraces not merely questions affecting a single structure, or a group of structures related to each other, but is also concerned with the environment of the isolated building or group of buildings. Questions of visual appearance from viewpoints near and far, the effect of new and possibly much larger adjacent structures upon apparent scale, and the blocking of views or approaches, all arise in the general context of conservation. It may, in short, be said that conservation consists of the cherishing of existing structures so that they may not merely continue, but may also receive a more abundant life from the changes and fresh associations which occur.

The definition of 'building' might seem to be so simple as hardly to deserve a mention. Yet, as so often happens once a term is scrutinized, this is not quite as straightforward as it looks at first sight. To many, it might seem that 'building' is a synonym for 'work of architecture' or, as in some dictionaries, for 'edifice'. The importation of the concept of Architecture must be firmly rejected, for this introduces the vital element of creative design, present in very many buildings but not, for example, in many traditional (or 'vernacular') structures which are the outcome of ready-made solutions already reached in certain fields of craftsmanship. To us a building must include both the architectural and the vernacular, for the structural problems of their maintenance are fundamentally similar, and both types are commonly found in association with one another in the same group. But beyond the structures themselves, the output of craftsmen concerned with stonemasonry, bricklaying, carpentry, cob-walling or concrete, 'building' will also cover the artificial terrace on which the structure is set; not merely a bridge or viaduct but also the earthen embankments leading to it; not just the watermill but the associated artificial pond and leats.

We have then the conclusion that the subject of this book must be not merely the conservation of buildings in the obvious and more limited sense, but must include all those ancillary interferences of man with the 'natural' (i.e. non-human) landscape that are left over when the limits of Nature Conservancy have been reached. Nature Conservancy and the Conservation of the Human Environment are indeed closely linked parts of a single whole. The separation here implied is one of convenience only, and is due partly to limitations of space, but also largely to the different techniques involved in the conservation on the one hand of natural landscape and on the other of the structures with which man has punctuated or altered the scene. In practice it may often be necessary to trespass some way beyond the boundary between the two aspects of conservancy, in order to do justice to the inter-relationship between 'scenescape' or landscape, and cityscape, town-scape, or the rural setting of isolated churches, houses, castles or monuments.

As will be apparent, the conservation of buildings is opposed by material interests of certain kinds, and this opposition is often justified by what purports to be a philosophical argument. 'Preservationism' is itself criticized as a materialistic cult which seeks to set the value of mere artefacts above what are claimed as transcendent values. According to the opinion of the individual critic these values differ: to some, human life is regarded as transcending all or most other considerations; others may add health, happiness, freedom, and other desirable states; sincere Christians have been known to quote the Gospels (Luke 21.5–6; cf. Matthew 24.1–2 and Mark 13.1–2) as proof that buildings and their enrichments are mere dross, destined in any case for destruction. Yet there is another aspect to this, a viewpoint most poignantly expressed in connection with the deliberate burning of the Dublin Customs House in 1921.

In a moving passage in her book, *Bricks and Flowers*, Mrs. Katherine Everett thus succinctly expresses the paradox of values: 'One day, having heard that the lovely Customs House had been set on fire after street fighting, I went into Dublin to see, and found a shrieking crowd watching flames lick up towards the dome. It was utterly horrible that these savages should enjoy such vandalism. A loyalist whom I met reproached me for feeling the loss of any building so bitterly, implying that by doing so I minimized the much more important loss of life the movement had cost. It was impossible to explain in that crowd that it was not a matter for comparison, for I felt that any real great work of art represented one of the highest expressions of man's spirit which remained to rejoice the heart and inspire countless numbers of those who had eyes to see, long after the bones of the creator had turned to dust. The value of human life is a totally different thing, and cannot be assessed in the mass; the death of certain people might be a good thing, and a great saint might be of more value than any great work of art.'*

This discriminating and balanced viewpoint brings up another aspect of conservation, that of relative value and the need for approaching cases upon their individual merits. Destruction by the deliberate vandalism of a mob is an extreme case; but in its effects all destruction comes to the same thing: whatever values the work had are annihilated. If men have different values, so have buildings; and while it may be highly desirable that many unworthy or ugly buildings should perish, the decision to destroy is always a serious burden. It must always be for the would-be destroyer to justify his action by showing that positive and not merely imagined benefits will accrue. This applies with great force to all kinds of rebuilding and redevelopment, where it should rest with impartial judges to decide that the positive value of the new works intended outweighs the loss of what is to be destroyed. If those buildings which are of high value are to survive it is imperative that their fate should not depend upon decisions taken by those who have a material or financial interest in the matter. Such an interest does not have to be a personal one; it may be entirely altruistic and inspired by local patriotism or by a sense of duty. For example, the officers of a municipality whose revenue depends upon Rateable Value are simply acting as loyal servants of their authority if they favour a scheme of redevelopment which will increase this value, or if they press for the demolition of one group of properties rather than another because the costs of compensation will be less. Yet it may well be that an outside judge, with no local interests, would decide that the

* *Bricks and Flowers* (London, Constable, 1949), chapter 19.

conservation of the older properties would, in the longer term, be the right course, and that the proposed redevelopment would on balance be a loss to human values and to the body politic as a whole. It will be seen that such considerations lend point to the view that all decisions affecting the destruction of existing buildings should be taken out of the hands of those locally concerned. To this and related problems involving future legislation we shall return towards the end of this book (see pp. 198–9).

Before leaving the general question of values, however, it is desirable to consider the different kinds of positive value contributed by old buildings to society. The value of the great or exceptional building as a work of art as 'one of the highest expressions of man's spirit' has been stated by Mrs. Everett in the passage quoted above. This value, as of great even if not transcendent importance, will probably be granted by most persons of culture. It is one of the most remarkable aspects of the Conservation of Buildings that, though it is a common feature of revolutions that great buildings are destroyed by ignorant mobs, as much if not more pains and expense are put to the maintenance of historic structures and scenes in Communist as in Capitalist countries. Even if some of the ultimate aims involved may be different, there is sufficient common ground for it to be said that political ideology plays little or no part in this field. This is borne out in countries which, like Britain, are governed by a party-political system: what may be termed the 'Conservation Lobby' cuts across all party affiliations.

In the second place, and in no way limited to buildings which are exceptional as works of art, is the quality of permanence given to the environment by the survival of a high proportion of old buildings. Permanence is, of course, a relative term, but in relation to the normal span of human life it implies a duration of several lifetimes. It is noteworthy that in newly developed countries even buildings of the mid-nineteenth century are regarded as 'ancient monuments' suitable for preservation. The fundamental reason for this is not mere worship of age for its own sake, but the fact that a building which has existed since before the memory of those now alive provides an anchorage. It is part of an environment which conveys a sense of stability and repose, a fulcrum which will serve (in a metaphorical application of the Archimedean sense) for moving the world. Without a fixed environment, at least relatively permanent in the context of the ebb-and-flow of life, man is unable to exert to the full the energy of which he is capable. Even the apparent exception of the great historic feats performed by nomadic tribes such as the Turks and Mongols proves the rule: for the nomads who lacked settled cities had the perpetual natural environment of the Steppes. In point of fact even the nomads came to accept the virtues of the city and to derive benefit from such settled centres as Samarkand, Peking, Kabul, Konya or Istanbul.

The third value might best be expressed as Consonance. All buildings put up before c. 1900 tended to vary largely according to local materials used and to display regional qualities in their design. This applied to works of architecture and not merely to the vernacular products of continuous tradition. The resulting phenomenon of local style, a feature of the building of all lands, provides a great part of the variety which is the charm of travel. Each human environment produced its own characteristic shell or incrustation of buildings peculiar to itself. Types of plan, both of town and of house, of material, style, climatic adaptation, all varied and, in this variation, lent interest to the scene. The traveller in search of such differing qualities is in a sense a collector; though unable to carry whole villages or even cottages away with him, he stores his memory, his sketch-book or his album of photographs with their forms. It is this harmless and indeed beneficial form of collecting that gives zest to international tourism and provides one of the main incentives to expenditure by tourists. Thus the value of old buildings, besides providing a healthy and firm background to life, turns out to be also a cash value in bringing a large financial return.

If, as some hold quite seriously, all values have to be assessed quantitatively and expressed in monetary terms, then the values of old buildings are very real. Spending by tourists in the world's cities of art is on an enormous scale, and merely from a budgetary viewpoint it would be a shortsighted national or local administration which neglected this aspect of the matter. Hardly anyone visits as a tourist the 'new towns' developed, in Britain and in other countries, in recent years. It is not likely that the stereotyped small towns, or even middling cities, of the vast area of the United States will ever become tourist attractions. In such localities the yardstick of Rateable Value is and will for ever remain the only one. But any city, town or village consisting largely of old buildings possesses a capital asset of the first importance, which yields a rich harvest from visitors year in and year out. The progressive reduction of this asset by demolitions, or the cancelling of its impact by encircling it with unworthy modern development or with an overdeveloped mesh of traffic arteries, is not only a crime against humanity and taste but also spendthrift folly leading towards bankruptcy.

Even expressed upon this lowest level, that of financial gain, there are sound reasons for keeping every old building that has, either in its own individual right or as part of a group, the qualities of pleasing design, sound materials, and a reasonable fitness for continuing use. We should beware of accepting this purely materialistic assessment, but it has genuine importance. The capital investment in buildings over the centuries has been enormous, and cannot be disregarded by any community except at its peril. Until quite modern times there was no mathematical theory of structures governing structural design, but only empirical rules deduced from trial and error. For this reason the amount of material used in old buildings is considerably in excess of what is strictly required: that is to say, the factor of safety is far greater than would be demanded by modern building regulations. This does not merely mean that old buildings, contrary to general supposition, are actually stronger and safer than most modern structures; it also means that they are for the most part better insulated, warmer in winter, cooler in summer, provide better protection against noise and vibration. The idea that old buildings are automatically less comfortable and less convenient than new is false; and it is a falsehood that has been deliberately fostered as a superstitious article of belief by those with vested interests in redevelopment of many kinds.

Common sense rightly tells us that it is not, and cannot be, cheaper to demolish a sound old structure lavishly built of good materials, and to erect from the foundations a new building even of flimsier construction, than to make full use of the old work by careful rehabilitation and, if necessary, conversion to new uses. So long as like is compared with like, and the amount of accommodation provided is taken into account, the answer will always be in favour of maintenance of the old and conservative adaptation. The only proviso is that the building must have been of sound construction from the start (not all old buildings were necessarily well built), and that it should not have been so seriously neglected as to have fallen into general structural decay. In fact it takes a long time for a building which has been well maintained to fall to decay through mere neglect; but once structural ruin has set in, or major infestations with rots or woodworm, the last stage to downfall can be disconcertingly rapid. This is why every owner or occupier of a building concerned with its upkeep should deal with it on the principle that 'a stitch in time saves nine', and do something quickly, as it were on account. Neglect of simple precautions such as the periodic cleaning of gutters and rainwater downpipes is responsible for the loss of many buildings worth hundreds of times more than the very small outlay involved.

Consideration of the values involved in conservation has shown that they are of two main kinds: the transcendent or spiritual, to be appreciated by all men and women of culture; and the material and financial, appealing to instincts of economy and thrift. Throughout recorded history both these factors have played their part in conservation and have been discussed in all controversies upon the subject. Even where they have not been overtly considered it must be admitted that, behind the appearances of any given case, a struggle has been in progress between crassly materialistic motives of short-term interest on the one hand, in favour of destruction; and, on the other side, the conservative force of a combination of factors expressing the values we have been considering. Undoubtedly the leading factor, often unacknowledged, is reverence: that is to say, human regard for the sanctity of existing institutions which have stood the test of time. It is not simply aesthetic pleasure which we feel on visiting the Acropolis of Athens; agnostics and even professed atheists are likely to feel that they stand on holy ground, even if they are not sure what is holy, or that holiness exists. Whether we like it or not, the whole human race has been conditioned over many centuries by a series of half-formulated beliefs.

The study of the patterns formed by groups of human beings in accordance with their particular beliefs is the province of the anthropologist. The fact that most anthropologists carry out their researches among so-called primitive or barbarous peoples has tended to conceal from the layman that the findings of comparative anthropology have universal application. The way the human being reacts, what 'makes us tick', however much it may differ in details and in outward appearance, is fundamentally one and the same throughout history, and among sophisticated nations of ancient and modern times, as well as among tribes whose material culture is still in the Stone Age. This basic fact was clearly enunciated by A. M. Hocart in his essay on the comparative anatomy of human society, the great book *Kings and Councillors*.

In all parts of the world, and in ancient and modern times, Hocart sought and found the fundamental purposes and analogies of human ritual. As he put it: 'All men wish to control nature in order that they may live.' Ritual has been the universal means by which they sought to obtain this control; and in general ritual consists of the imitation or impersonation of nature, not 'nature as it is, but as they want it to be.' What specially concerns us here out of Hocart's far-reaching survey is his study of the City. Reminding us that 'king, priest, animal, tree, corpse, idol, all represent things it is desired to control', as do 'the temples and palaces in which these cult-objects or principals are housed', Hocart continues: 'So does the city in which stand the temples and palaces: it is sacred in the same sense as they are, that is they are equivalent to that on which the life of the people depends. Only the city never stands for anything specific; it is never less than the whole world . . . That is indeed the purpose which has brought cities into existence . . . Population first condenses round the centre of ritual, not round shops.' The point is brought home by mentioning that 'in the West of England they talk of "church towns," not of "shop towns," . . . because the church is the primary fact.'

The city, whether round or square, is divided into quarters – the 'Four Quarters of the World' – by great thoroughfares leading from gateway to gateway; the quarters may be deliberately occupied for different specific purposes, as in an Indian precept which laid down that the royal caste should be to the East, the mercantile to the South, artisans to the West, and priests to the North. The gates are sacred; and this is exemplified even now in England by the existence of city churches actually over gates, or set just beside them. At Winchester Little St. Swithun-upon-Kingsgate, at Bristol St. John's, at Langport in Somerset the Hanging Chapel exemplify the first type; the latter is widespread and exists, for example, in the three London churches of St. Botolph without Aldersgate, Bishopsgate, and Aldgate, as well as St. Giles, Cripplegate, and St. Martin within Ludgate. It is not for nothing that in English we accord by tradition the name of 'city' only to such towns as possess a cathedral church and among them only to those which have an ancient cathedral. It is the age-old continuity of custom that counts.

In his comparison of human cities the world over, Hocart goes further than this, and remarks that in Polynesia the village has the crossed streets of the ideal city, and at the centre of the cross the '*malae*, the common term in Polynesia for a village green or sacred enclosure. . . . The temples stand on the green . . .' One might add from England a former exact parallel to this arrangement in the early layout of the city of York, where two main roads crossed in the middle of a wide green, and at the point of intersection stood the church dedicated to the Holy Cross, St. Crux. It is a sad commentary on the recent break-up of immemorial tradition that St. Crux was the first of York's churches to be destroyed in modern times, in 1886.

Whereas it might be thought that the concept of a Heavenly Jerusalem as pictured in the Book of Revelation was based upon the glorification of a material, earthly city, the probability is that the truth is the exact converse. Revelation simply embodies a far more ancient concept, at the centre of man's religious ideas, and the physical Jerusalem – or any other city – is an attempt to realize this symbolic and celestial city upon earth. We are not here concerned with dogmatic religions or with the specific faith of given creeds in the truth of matters beyond physical verification. The fact which emerges from the investigations of anthropologists is that there has been in general terms a universal human belief, through all recorded periods, and among all peoples, identifying the human city built of materials – stone, brick, timber – with a celestial macrocosm identical with the whole universe through symbolism. The rituals of the human city ensure its prosperity by identifying it with the eternal life and continuity of the Universe itself.

The rationalist may, if he cares to, say 'Stuff and Nonsense', regarding the whole history of human thought as simply untrue and not corresponding to any objective reality. He may say that it is impossible to demonstrate any connection between the continuity of civic rituals and human prosperity; that, regarding the value of a superstitious and non-factual doctrine as $= 0$, its multiplication by ritual performance 1000 or 50,000 times will still leave it valueless. Carried to its logical conclusion this view will eliminate not merely the numinous value of the city and its monuments, but also its alleged aesthetic value. For all aesthetic values reside in the beholder, which is to say that they are subjective. By hypothesis, our rationalist is prepared to reject a consensus of opinion, even one involving the common practices of almost the whole of the human race; hence the consensus of opinion on beauty, coming from any group however well informed, will still have no evidential value.

It has seemed worth while to explore this critical opposition of views to its extreme in order to show precisely where we are led by outright rejection of the traditional view. Rejection in the interests of a theoretical rationalism really does mean throwing the baby out along with the bath water, and our criteria would have to be exclusively utilitarian and based upon solely material facts which could be quantitatively assessed. Quality, as a factor subjectively appreciated, would cease to exist, except in so far as it was given arbitrary value by linking it to quantity: as to duration, to yield or fertility, and the like measurables. Now it is quite possible to justify conservation exclusively upon the criteria of enlightened materialism. The quantitative data derived from statistics of physical and mental health would, alone, suggest that the provision of open spaces in towns, green belts to break up larger conurbations, and quiet zones or 'cities of refuge' from the noise and stresses of modern life are all sound investments. In dealing with future policy more will have to be said of this (see pp. 45, 195), but it is important to keep in mind that there is even on grounds of material benefit a valid argument for saving substantial areas of town and country.

Although an extensive programme of conservation in Britain is implicit in the legislation of the last twenty-five years, reflecting a substantial body of public opinion, rapid losses of buildings listed as worthy of preservation show that short-term expediency all too often wins. This is evidenced even more in the destruction of group-values and 'townscape', especially by street-widening and the construction of new roads and motorways. In many cases the decisive factor has been the relatively low cost in compensation payable for old properties acting as a positive inducement to planners to route traffic through areas which called for overall rehabilitation of the kind now normal in France and Holland, for example. The recent legislation requiring the declaration by local authorities of Conservation Areas, though an important step in the right direction, is not yet enough to give adequate protection to all of the historic districts which deserve to be kept.

The very slow movement of public opinion in Britain is well exemplified by the fact that this very distinction between 'the few outstanding monuments' and 'the general physiognomy of the place' was already fully recognized in Germany more than two generations ago.

The late Professor Baldwin Brown, in his fundamental book *The Care of Ancient Monuments* (1905), devoted to this subject a lengthy discussion in which he instanced the care of the Germans, by 1904, for *'das Stadtbild'* – the general townscape produced by the large number of humbler domestic monuments rather than those outstanding buildings 'of which every inhabitant could give off-hand a general list.' It is a tragic irony, in the light of the destruction in this country *since* the end of the *second* World War in 1945, that twelve years before the start of the first, the then Burgomaster of Hildesheim should have laid down the classic expression of principles in a congress held in Düsseldorf in 1902 on the care of monuments. In the burgomaster's speech, translated by Baldwin Brown, vital questions are posed: 'Does a civic administration exist merely for the sake of enabling the people to fulfil the needs of daily life as well, as cheaply, and as completely as possible? Is the City Council there for this alone? . . . Does the well-being of men consist only in bodily things, or is there not something far higher, the spiritual well-being of men, and does it not contribute greatly to this when they feel in close relation to the past, and take delight in realizing how the city has gradually built itself up, and how not only the streets, but every single public building, each individual house, even each piece of carved ornament, has grown in the course of time to be what it is. To make this feeling real is the task of the civic authorities . . . It is a matter of intimate duty, of conscience on the part of city governors, to care for the older monuments, not in amateur fashion as a by-work, but of set purpose as one of the most important objects of civic administration.'

Britain, in so many ways a country of tradition, has certainly lagged behind in this field. The price paid for primacy in the Industrial Revolution has been heavy, and the lesson has not yet been learned. Though the wave of general interest in the subject which led up to Baldwin Brown's book was able within a few years to effect the setting up of Royal Commissions to take inventories of our ancient and historic monuments and the passing of an effective Ancient Monuments Act, destruction of our heritage has proceeded for sixty years with only the slightest of checks. The contrast between photographs of the same areas of town or country in the first and the seventh decades of this century is horrifying. It is not merely the enormous losses of individual buildings, but the incongruity of new intrusive structures built next to what is left, the proliferation of unsightly road-signs and the impedimenta of electrical transmission and of the craze for television. In very many places, though fortunately not in all, it seems as though all sense of beauty, of fitness, and even of civic pride had been lost. Whatever the reasons may be, this sad decline contrasts unfavourably with the active steps taken in France, Germany, Italy, Spain and other continental countries to safeguard their remaining monuments and historic towns, and in many cases to improve their condition.

The fact of the matter is that, though much of the private wealth of Britain was laid out upon the collection of portable works of art between the reigns of Elizabeth I and Victoria, the active care of buildings aroused relatively slight interest and received little official encouragement. There had been an active society of antiquaries in Elizabethan and Jacobean England, and the train of antiquarian thought remained active, to spring forth with renewed vigour in the new Society of Antiquaries of London from 1707, yet the preservation of buildings lay only on the margin of this activity. The care of fixed monuments as opposed to that of portable objects, already of concern to mediaeval Italians, did not strike root on British soil until most of the other nations of Europe had taken serious steps towards conservation. Gustavus Adolphus and Charles XI of Sweden, in the seventeenth century, John V of Portugal in 1721 made ordinances for protection, and during the latter part of the eighteenth century it was the rulers of various German states who began to widen the scope of this interest from ancient and prehistoric remains to those of the Middle Ages. It is highly to the credit of the princes concerned with these pioneer steps that they were taken before the massive destruction of the Revolutionary and Napoleonic Wars had awakened public opinion to the devastating losses suffered by the monumental heritage of the Continent.

The results of revolutionary destruction in France were to arouse responsible and courageous men to defend great buildings threatened, but their efforts remained unco-ordinated for more than a generation. It was in Germany, where Goethe had aroused a spirit of national pride in history and monuments of art, that damage by the French armies provoked the first really effective measures leading towards general conservation. The crucial date is, significantly, the year of Waterloo, 1815, when the Prussian official architect Karl Friedrich Schinkel (1781–1841) appealed, in a report on the war-damaged state of the church at Wittenberg, for a campaign to save the mediaeval monuments of Germany. In the following year he inspected Cologne Cathedral. The honour of producing the first general decree dealing with the whole problem of architectural monuments seems to belong to Louis X, Grand Duke of Hesse-Darmstadt (1753–1830). This decree, masterly in its succinct handling of all aspects of the subject, may owe something to Georg Moller (1784–1852), architectural historian and Director of Buildings to the Grand Duke. Moller it was who gave wide publicity to the decree by inserting it as a footnote in his important book *Denkmäler der deutschen Baukunst*, and who commented upon it that the publication of buildings would act as a protection against vandalism. His estimate of human nature was perhaps somewhat optimistic, for he held that, once a building had been brought to notice by published drawings and description, fear of public ignominy would prevent ignorant officials of low rank from treating it as a stone-quarry, as had hitherto been the case.

The Hessian decree of Louis X, dated 22 January 1818, is of such fundamental importance that it must be quoted in full:

'Louis, by the grace of God Grand Duke of Hesse and the Rhine, etc., etc.

Whereas the surviving monuments of architecture are among the most important and interesting evidences of history, in that from them may be inferred the former customs, culture, and civil condition of the nation, and therefore their preservation is greatly to be wished, we decree as follows:

1. Our Higher College of Building is charged with bringing all the discoverable remains of ancient architecture in the Grand Duchy of Hesse, which are worthy of preservation on historical or artistic grounds, into a correct inventory wherein their present condition is to be described and the ancient works of art to be found in them, such as paintings, statues and the like, are to be noted.

2. For the compilation of the historical part of this inventory the aforesaid College is to invite such as are most learned in the history of every province to collaborate in this patriotic purpose, and these are to communicate to that end the necessary information from the archives.

3. The most distinguished of these works, or the most ruinous, are to be completely and accurately surveyed and the drawings deposited with their description in our Museum.

4. Our Higher College of Building is hereby charged: to lay before us the inventory of these buildings considered worthy of preservation or illustration for our approval, in order to put in hand the preservation and repair of the same in conjunction with the various authorities; and to give us the appropriate advice thereon.

5. If it should seem necessary to put in hand alterations of one or other of these buildings, or to demolish one entirely, this is to be done only with the previous knowledge of the said College, and in appropriate cases after it has obtained our supreme approval.

6. If in the course of excavations or on other occasions antiquities are discovered, our officers are to take care that if possible they should be preserved, and notice thereof is to be given immediately to our Higher College of Building or to the Directorate of our Museum.

7. It is the duty of all public authorities to take the greatest possible care of the monuments made known in the aforesaid inventory, to which end the same shall be printed and communicated to them.

Darmstadt, the 22nd of January 1818.
Louis.'*

It is hard to imagine how the essentials of the whole subject could have been better expressed; certainly their compression into less than four hundred words is little short of miraculous. The principles and practice of listing, recording, repair and future preservation of monuments are all included, as well as the main problems involved. The brilliant intuition which grasped this and set it down puts to shame the long-winded legislation and regulations which beset the subject more than 150 years later. The bitter experience and the long-winded argument, in many countries and parliaments, could almost all have been saved had this decree simply been adopted in all parts as containing what was needful.

As an explicit programme and directive for conservation this seems to be the first in the world, and enough is known of the later development of the subject in Europe to say that it stemmed directly from the work of Louis X. In 1818, and for that matter until 1871, Germany was a geographical concept, the area of a great language and of a spirit of patriotism; but it was not a nation. Intense though petty rivalries made it impossible for the initiative of a single one of its

* For the German text see Appendix I.

princes to be adopted elsewhere. It was thus, by a paradox, that the whole subject of protection of monuments was first explored on a large scale in France. There the impetus came from a private individual, Arcisse De Caumont (1801–1873), the founder in 1823 of the regional Société des Antiquaires de Normandie. De Caumont went on to publish from 1830 to 1841 his *Cours d'antiquités monumentales*, and by 1831 in its fourth volume he gave a survey of the international literature on the subject, proving that he was well acquainted with the work of Moller. The text of the decree of 1818 therefore was certainly before him at the time that he was pressing upon the French government the need for a positive programme of conservation with finance provided out of taxation. A French financial credit for the upkeep of monuments was actually set up as a result of De Caumont's pressure, and in 1837 this was followed by the formation of the national Commission des Monuments Historiques. In the meantime De Caumont had also organized on a private basis the two great complementary series of the *Congrès archéologiques* meeting yearly in different centres, and the periodical the *Bulletin Monumental*. Both of these started in 1834, as aspects of the *Société Française d'Archéologie pour la Conservation et la Description des Monuments Historiques* with headquarters at Caen.

The fact that De Caumont, a Norman, based his societies on Caen rather than on Paris was part of a conscious protest against the tendency to over-centralization in French government. Five years after the founding of his national society De Caumont inaugurated an auxiliary Institut des Provinces with local correspondents in every part of France, reporting back to the national society (at Caen) the state of monuments and any threats to their well-being that arose. From the start these bodies inspired by De Caumont attracted as members many distinguished individuals from the older families of the French provinces. These families, based upon the Ancien Régime and deeply traditionalist, looked with suspicion upon, and in turn were suspected by, the governmental agencies of French conservation over a long period. This rather unfortunate dichotomy did not, however, prevent France from getting the best balanced system of conservation so far available.

It is unnecessary to follow the history of European care of monuments through the nineteenth century, for this was done in great detail by Baldwin Brown. The parallel development of opinion in Britain has also in some measure been covered by the relevant chapters of the late Paul Frankl's study, *The Gothic*, in which the intellectual attitudes towards ancient architecture are thoroughly described and analysed. It must be said, however, that Frankl's knowledge of the English material fell short of his mastery of both the German and the French sources, and that he did something less than justice to several of the formative minds of the late eighteenth and early nineteenth centuries in Britain. At a later stage a reassessment will be attempted to show how far there was an independent movement of opinion in this country, distinct from the continental activities derived by direct descent from the initially German impetus given by Schinkel, Moller and the Grand Duke of Hesse (see Chapter 9, p. 157 ff.).

What emerges from this general survey is that conservation, with the care of monuments, in the modern sense, has developed within the last two centuries and in western Europe. It has earlier roots in antiquarian interest in buildings, traceable in England, for example, to the travels of William Worcestre in 1478–80, and in Italy to the protest of the poet Petrarch (1304–1374) against the destruction or exportation of Roman works of art. Interest of this kind was sophisticated and essentially modern in outlook; but long before this concept of conservation had made its appearance there had been *de facto* conservation – and preservation – for different reasons. In earlier times the chief reason for the preservation of a particular building or work of art was its sanctity. The world's museums contain many early cult images which have been carefully preserved over long ages because they were regarded as sacred, although their continued existence depends upon the modern and sophisticated frame of mind which keeps them for supposedly 'rational' and not 'superstitious' motives.

It is probable that the two main types of motive for preservation have always to some extent coexisted. Ashur-bani-pal, king of Assyria in the seventh century B.C., was one of the earliest known antiquaries, and founder of a great library and museum. It is obvious that his motives were at least in part sophisticated and that his treasures were not collected and kept simply for their holiness. On the other hand, he was surely to some extent the possessor of relics, proud to keep them in safe custody, as was St. Louis proud to build the Sainte Chapelle as a reliquary for the Crown of Thorns two thousand years later. The regard of the Old Testament Hebrews for the Temple, and their care to rebuild it, was primarily founded on a superstitious awe; but this did not imply that other factors were not present too. On several occasions stones were set up as memorials; of events of religious import, it is true, yet human affection for the old and the traditional may be assumed as well. The desirability of memorials of famous men and their worthy actions in the past is implied in the well-known chapter of the Apocryphal book of Ecclesiasticus.

Due conservation of religious buildings was a notable work of piety in ancient China, where Confucius praised King Wu and the duke of Chau for having regularly, in spring and autumn, repaired and beautified the temple halls of their fathers. Here the motive was evidently religious; but in Confucius's own time there was a proposal to pull down and rebuild the Long Treasury of Lu. The disciple Min Tzu-ch'ien asked why it could not be repaired after its old style, and this was endorsed by the Master as the right thing to do, evidently on grounds of economy, but doubtless also because of regard for tradition and things venerable with age. In the Middle Ages too there was some disapproval for the mania for change in fashion which led to re-development: Alexander Neckam took up the special case of buildings, and in describing the craze for demolition and rebuilding quoted the tag of Horace: *Diruit, aedificat, mutat quadrata rotundis.*

In the long run conservation has always depended, and will depend, upon the existence of a current of informed opinion favourable to the worthy monuments of past ages. Again and again officials charged with preservation fail in their trust, and some precious work is lost: we must ask frequently: *Quis custodiet ipsos custodes?* The answer is, ourselves. It is only by constant vigilance and by preparedness for the arduous fight against vandalism and short-term profits that we can save what is left and hand down, as little diminished as may be, to the next generation the inheritance that we received.

Part one

WHAT TO SAVE AND
HOW TO SAVE IT

[1]

The Town

The cardinal principle in the selection of what buildings to save must be discrimination. Obviously it is neither desirable nor practically possible to keep all old buildings. The overall problem has to be kept within bounds by limitations of various kinds, the main criteria being quality, date, and position. It will probably be agreed by all who accept the preservation of works of art as a valid social activity that there are some buildings which, on grounds of their exceptional artistic quality, or their historic interest, or both together, deserve to be kept in perpetuity: that is, for as long as they can physically be maintained. Except for marginal cases where there is dispute as to the rank of the building, this group presents little or no difficulty. On the other hand, the great size of many buildings in this category does mean that their maintenance is likely to be costly, and that unless appropriate measures are taken they will get the lion's share of all funds, both public and private, made available for conservation. The question of fund-raising will be dealt with later (see p. 199).

Much greater difficulty in selection occurs in regard to buildings which are clearly of high quality, or of outstanding historic interest, but which cannot match those in the exceptional class. It is over such cases that a disproportionate amount of time and energy is spent in discussion at all stages of every threat to their continued existence. Whereas no responsible person would dream of suggesting the demolition of Westminster Abbey, the Tower of London, or Durham Cathedral, simply because of their surpassing fame, serious applications for demolition and redevelopment are constantly being made in respect of buildings of equivalent aesthetic or historical importance. The fact that there is a great disparity in fame between works which essentially belong to the same category in quality has to be faced. The waste of time and energy just mentioned provides a *prima facie* case for enlarging very widely the scope of legal protection given: a much greater number of buildings than those of first-class *fame* should be debarred by legislation from even proposals to demolish or to degrade by any form of neighbouring 'pernicious development.' In this case 'pernicious' would have to include many kinds of aesthetically undesirable change, not necessarily objectionable elsewhere.

Setting aside these two sections of the highest class of building, both of which should be given absolute and unqualified protection, not merely from demolition or damage, but from even the threat of such spoliation, there is left the great mass of buildings in existence. British practice in the past quarter-century, that is since the Town & Country Planning Act of 1947, has been to attempt grading, building by building. Experience has shown that this method of assigning a qualitative value was fundamentally unsound, and that it results in serious and widespread losses. There are two distinct reasons for the failure of this method. In the first place is simply the fact that, to compile an adequate list of 'interesting' buildings in measurable time, inspection cannot be other than superficial. Even the best investigator, adequately trained to use a considered judgment on each case, is unable to make a true assessment when all interior features are unknown to him, and he has no information on the documented history of the property. The degree of inaccuracy and of inequitable discrepancy is too great for this to be an appropriate legal criterion of protection.

The second reason for the failure of the system is inherent in the underlying legislation. The lists, when compiled and divided into grades by the superficial method described above, provided a basis for conservation sharply divided into two: a higher category comprising buildings awarded statutory protection; and a lower class ('Grade III' in the Provisional Lists drawn up under the 1947 Act) merely recommended to the consideration of local authorities. Considered by the standards which were undoubtedly in the minds of the authors of the relevant Acts, this listing of buildings which were not given any degree of legal protection has been contraproductive. In many areas there can be no doubt that the listing has been misused as an indication of buildings that were both old and of relative unimportance, and probably of slight financial value for purposes of compensation. Their vulnerability was actually increased without any form of safeguard having been imposed. The unprotected category has, in the light of this experience, now been dropped.

A further disability, inherent in the original arrangements made in 1947 but since removed in the light of experience, was the method of dealing with each building as an isolated unit. The value of groups of buildings, subsequently recognized, was not at first given official acknowledgement. Yet it is precisely this 'group value' that constitutes the '*Stadtbild*' already recognized in Germany by 1904 as transcending in importance the individual works regarded as famous by every inhabitant. After appalling losses of smaller buildings, altered and demolished piecemeal in all parts of the country for years, and in the teeth of a sound and awakened public opinion, the stable door has been pushed to, though not yet shut and bolted. This is in itself a good sign, but it needs to be followed up by far more radical improvement of the basic methods of selection.

At the start of this chapter the limiting criteria on selection were named in order: quality, date, position. We have seen that works in the upper sector of the highest grade in quality are more or less automatically safe: their renown protects them, and for that reason they need not here be matter for further concern. As far as date is concerned, it is an obvious rule-of-thumb that there are more buildings that survive from any given century – or other equal period – as we approach the present time. Mere common sense indicates that a good deal more trouble and expense is worth while to save a work of comparative rarity than one extremely common. The total cost of conserving all of the very few English houses of the fourteenth century would not go far towards solving the economic problem set by the many eighteenth-century houses of comparable quality and interest. Hence, on grounds of rarity alone, there is an economic justification for accepting a lower aesthetic quality and a poorer state of physical condition in older buildings than in those of more recent date.

We cannot accept relative age as a simple yardstick of value, for the artistic output of different periods is highly unequal in aesthetic quality. Although the extremely small number of surviving Anglo-Saxon buildings, mainly churches, may be worthy of preservation for their age and rarity alone, they are clearly of far lower intrinsic quality than most of the Norman and Gothic churches which succeeded them. Exceptions apart, the quality of Victorian buildings of the fifty years 1840–1890 is a great deal lower than that of works of the succeeding twenty years, 1890–1910, as well as being lower than that of the 'Regency' generation of 1810–1840. In sheer numbers the amount of Victorian housing is overwhelming, but in quality a large proportion of it is negligible and a good deal consists of unworthy industrial slums which ought never to have been built and should be cleared with relief at the disappearance of a shameful blot on the English historical scene.

To some extent, then, the problem solves itself by the small numbers of surviving buildings of the earlier dates, and by the poor quality of much of the multitudinous output of Victorian times. Sentimentality and passing whims must not be allowed to exaggerate the importance of the architectural output of a period which was truly distinguished for its feats of engineering. Thus a great deal more attention should be paid to nineteenth-century bridges, railway works, factories and even warehouses than to housing or to the general run of churches. At the same time it must be recognized that there are exceptions to every rule, and that some few streets and layouts of the period genuinely deserve permanent conservation, while others might well survive for another century, as being fitter for their purpose than any of the proposed redevelopments now offered. A serious and *unbiased* consideration is the due of every case, and the leading principle of English criminal law, that of innocence unless guilt is proved, should be applied before destruction is decreed.

So much for quality and date as criteria. The third, that of position, is left for consideration. Instead of being left until last, this ought to have been the first to be dealt with when national legislation was in prospect. It is the overall living character of certain cities, towns, villages or districts that is the nub of the question. Conservation is not primarily a matter of saving individual specimens, even if they are to be maintained *in situ* rather than transported to a museum or to an open-air folk-park. Now this was not merely realized on the continent at the opening of this century, and endorsed by Baldwin Brown in his book of 1905. It received due emphasis from all serious planners in the 1920's, was taken up by the series of *Cautionary Guides* issued by the Design and Industries Association in 1929–31, and underlay the Town and Country Planning Act of 1932, which was a serious beginning. The inroads made upon the rural scene by the condemnation of old cottage property, and upon towns by street widening, caused grave concern to local amenity and antiquarian societies and to national bodies such as the Council for the Preservation of Rural England. Well before the end of the war of 1939–45 campaigns of action on these dangers were planned, yet serious national realization was not to come until after the publication of the Buchanan Report on *Traffic in Towns* in 1964. This time-lag of some twenty years was, from the viewpoint of conservation, the most tragic episode in our history since the dissolution of the monasteries in 1536–40.

At long last, and far too late, came the vitally important memoranda on historic towns published by the Council for British Archaeology in 1964 and 1965. Two lists were prepared, of which the more comprehensive aimed at including every urban area in Britain whose *historic quality* required careful treatment in any planning or redevelopment proposals. A number of towns of undoubted historic quality, but which had in the view of the compilers already been injured beyond recovery, were deliberately omitted in order that the list might not be overloaded or suffer from appearing unrealistic. None the less, it comprised 324 towns (232 in England, 57 in Scotland, and 35 in Wales). Out of this total enumeration a more concise list of fifty-one towns (40 in England, 8 in Scotland, 3 in Wales) was prepared as being cases of *national* concern. Belatedly, a measure of Government support was given to four pilot surveys chosen from this list, and further legislation on Conservation Areas and upon the care of monuments generally has followed. In theory, it might seem that further insistence upon the risks to old buildings would be superfluous.

Regrettably, the facts of the matter differ greatly from the theory. It is true that four pilot surveys by independent experts have been made and published, and that to a greater or less extent the proposals in these surveys have been approved by the four local authorities involved. Yet, seven years after the publication by the C. B. A. of its first memorandum, and six years after the appearance of its two definitive lists, destruction still proceeds. Conservation areas have, it is true, been defined and published in many places, but just as relegation to 'Grade III' cast a special blight upon smaller housing for many years after 1947, so there is a marginal penumbra surrounding the areas to be conserved. The specific limitation of something which is to be maintained with assistance from public national or local funds has proved in practice to increase the risk to everything else not specifically within the designated boundaries. The argument in the minds of most laymen is perfectly clear and logical: the experts have laid down that what is within this line deserves to be kept; therefore, what lies outside the line is of little or no account.

While it is easy in extreme cases to convince almost everyone that there is a serious case for spending money on maintaining the historic character of Oxford or York, but not of Reading or Leeds; or to single out certain showpieces as individual streets or areas where a consensus of reasonable men would be against change; it is very difficult to convince the ordinary man that devastating change is not inevitable. It is indeed a truism that change is inevitable; but the character of change is – apart from natural disasters and warfare – subject to human control. What has been happening throughout the period of ostensible public concern for conservation of values is piecemeal destruction. As was strongly emphasized by Baldwin Brown in 1905, with particular reference to the admission of the railway into Princes Street Gardens at Edinburgh, the demolition of part of the walls of Avignon, and the comparable inroads on the fortifications of Berwick-on-Tweed, it is a hazardous policy 'to introduce the thin end of the wedge, under the condition "that it is not to go in any further".' This is exactly what has gone on *and is going on now*. The whittling away proceeds apace and has often left little that is worth saving.

There are two main enemies, acting in unholy alliance against all the traditional values of the urban and rural scene: Transport, and Redevelopment, the latter including the siting of New Towns. The false assumptions commonly made on both subjects must be challenged and relentlessly exposed. Let us first consider the problem posed by modern transport in Britain, so far as it affects the conservation of worthy built-up areas. The first thing to note is that Transport has been allowed to arrogate to itself a position of national priority over almost any other consideration. This is sheer nonsense. Nobody denies that adequate communications are a national necessity, but their planning requires the utmost care of antecedent rights and interests, not least the right, however much qualified, to quiet and peaceable possession of property and in particular of the citizen's own home. The excessive rights of compulsory purchase granted by recent legislation need to be strictly curbed.

In regard to the routing of communications this problem ought never to have arisen in its present acute form. Britain has had, in the

course of the past two centuries, two major campaigns of expropria-
tion of routes in the national interest: for the Canals, and for the Railways. Before the onset of the third campaign, for modern roads and
motorways, the unnecessary waste, duplication and reduplication of
routes by the construction of canals and railways were obvious. The
lesson was taught, but was not learned. Compared to the expanding
economy of Britain throughout the period of the Industrial Revolution,
this is now a poor country, and a first consideration should be: how
much of the contemplated expenditure (to say nothing of the destruction) is *really necessary*? Is road transport in its present form likely to
last more than, say, one more generation? Will the provision of even
the most elaborate mesh of motorways, links, bypasses, relief roads
and widenings enable road transport on its present lines to fulfil a
permanent need? Is there not a very real likelihood that within a single
century the vast outlay in terms of capital expenditure and in utter
devastation of our historic towns and countryside will prove to be out-
dated and largely if not wholly superfluous?

The old gibe that the British General Staff was always ready to win
the last war – or the last but one – seems, *a fortiori*, to apply to Britain's planners. It is essential that future, rather than present needs
should be envisaged, and with an awareness of the possibility and
probability of completely revolutionary changes in means of trans-
portation. If some surgery is needed, at least let there be thorough
diagnosis first. The pace is too good to inquire; and what is needed
first is a moratorium of several years upon all fresh schemes for roads
or road widenings. Adequate time for a proper assessment of all the
factors involved has never yet been given, and proposals of fantastic
extent and cost are adopted before those most affected by them have
realized even their possibility.

In a more limited way, the needs of conservation in urban areas can
be served by insisting upon a special re-survey of all routes that
involve any of the 324 towns on the C.B.A.'s larger list, or which come
close to – say within a mile of – the 51 places listed as of national
concern. Buildings in rural areas should be given high priority among
the negative conditions set for the transport planners: that is, a basic
map showing all the buildings listed under the 1947 and subsequent
Acts should be a necessary prerequisite of the first stage of planning
any new route, and avoidance of listed buildings, except in cases of
absolute necessity, should be a condition imposed at the highest level.

It need hardly be added, in the light of recent events in the field of civil aviation, that the siting of new airports and their access routes needs if not more stringent controls. Again, the first question that must be asked is not: where should an airport be placed? but, is an airport really essential?

The principle of the moratorium needs to be applied, not only to transport routes, but to redevelopment. A pause for thought and for adequate survey of all the problems involved in each case is the most urgent requirement for every one of the 324 listed towns. These towns, at least, should be the subject of special protective legislation which would ban, for an initial period of five years, all new road-works and all schemes of comprehensive redevelopment. A fresh planning procedure, complying with the needs of conservation, should be instituted to deal with individual applications for demolition, alteration, or new building within each of these areas. The rest of the country would be unaffected except in so far as it is already covered by existing legislation. In view of the terrible onslaught made on many other historic towns within the last twenty-five years – an onslaught which has already removed them from any possibility of inclusion in the special category – such a sorting of the sheep from the goats is a modest minimal measure to demand. The time has come, is long overdue, to say 'Halt!' This time the stop must be definitive; not in the sense that the 324 towns, or any one of them, would become sterilized museum specimens, but in order that their historic character may be given a chance of surviving at all.

We now approach the most difficult part of the whole problem. Whereas any government of good will and determination could within a few months pass legislation of the kind outlined above, to give an adequate measure of protection for the time being, it is far from easy to lay down rules as to the best kind of conservation. Although there may, in a few highly exceptional cases, be room for the preservation of a village or small town *in statu quo*, as an unspoiled and untouched specimen of a period, this will in almost every case lead to a death-in-life. This is not conservation in any true sense, and the continuing vitality of the human social scene is lost for ever. The phenomenon of Venice is, on the grandest scale, an example of this risk becoming an imminent danger; and the strict preservation from all change of, notably, the little town of Santillana del Mar near the north coast of Spain provides a valuable object lesson. Santillana is a paradise for the photographer: the surface of the streets remains cobbled, there are no modern road-signs, nor are there obtrusive lamp-standards or over-head wires. All that the tourist has sighed for, in regard to the picturesque view of antiquity, completely unaltered, is there. Yet Santillana is practically unique in Spain in having no sense of human life. Real life once went on in its streets and houses, but it is impossible to feel that it does so any longer. A similar impression is given by Lacock, Wiltshire, though the effect is less extreme.

What has just been said is not intended as an adverse criticism of the very remarkable works carried out at Santillana by the Spanish authorities since the whole town and its surroundings were declared a monument of historic-artistic value in 1943. On the contrary, they are a model of what such technical work should be, worthy of imitation everywhere. It may well be that in this particular case the policy was the best available, and that the conversion of Santillana into a museum-town is justified for its interest as a total sample of the past. Not every visitor will feel the same about its human atmosphere; it certainly does provide a welcome haven of rest from the speed and noise of con-temporary life. Within the total field of conservation, on a world-wide scale, there may perhaps be room for the strict preservation of a few specimens comparable to Santillana. What seems certain, how-ever, is that this method does not offer a solution applicable to the great majority of towns of historic interest; in Britain it is pretty certainly inapplicable to any city, town, or village that now survives in a state relatively worthy of conservation.

If the method so well adopted at Santillana be rejected as unsuitable for general use, what can be put in its place? The opposite end of the spectrum is represented by unharnessed change of individual units, a process all too common in our old towns at the present time. Some planning authorities, more enlightened than others, do impose effec-tive checks upon height, materials and the character of design; but even in such places the results are seldom happy. This is because no planning committee nor advisory panel, exercising a negative control, can put into the new building a positive quality which it does not possess. In other words, comparatively few of the designs for new buildings in Britain are satisfactory as fresh designs. At best they are anodyne, and have the mild virtue of imitative secondary art. It is otherwise in parts of the Continent, where good new buildings of excellent material, colour and surface texture have gone up in the last quarter-century, without clashing unduly with the atmosphere of old streets and buildings in course of change. The answer to this discrepancy is undoubtedly that Architecture in Britain, as a creative art, is at a low ebb. Here is one more reason for declaring a moratorium, and hoping that at a not too distant date, architectural values may revive.

The best cases of modern redevelopment are unsatisfactory; but we learn more, in a negative way, from the worst cases. Of all faults, that of overpowering scale is probably the worst. To permit the erection of a towering block of as little as five stories in a traditional street where three is the rule and the older houses have only two, is to ruin the scene for ever – or for as long as the new building stands. In conservation areas certainly, and it is to be hoped throughout the fifty-one if not the 324 towns, a 'ceiling' on all new construction should be placed at a level not higher than the cornice or eaves of the tallest existing street fronts. This is not only necessary within the core of an ancient town; it is also of the highest importance that the view of the town from without, as it is approached by road or rail, should not be obscured by masses of overweening and arrogant modernity. In determining the limits of the protected zone in any given case the configuration of the ground must be considered, but in general a belt of low-level building and open spaces should surround the nucleus in depth. The clear space which surrounds most of the walled city of Ávila is responsible for its almost unique impact.

The second of the serious faults common in most of the new buildings scattered through our old towns is the use of unsuitable materials. In a town almost entirely of old brick, probably for the most part made locally, an occasional front of natural stone will provide a satisfactory punctuation. This is rarely the case with exposed concrete, almost invariably the most unsympathetic of permanent materials. Yet even concrete *can* be given an attractive surface (for instance, by hammer-dressing) or improved in colour by suitable mixes. If concrete buildings are allowed cheek-by-jowl with traditional buildings in the same street or group, the strictest supervision of the proposed, and executed, colour and finish is essential. This should not be a matter of imposed control, but one of natural good manners on the part of developer and architect, in whose hands the fate of the whole environment lies. Where concrete buildings of unsuitable texture already exist it should be made obligatory to use surface coatings or paints of an approved type, analogous to the painted stucco of the Regency.

Certain technical problems would have to be overcome in each case, but they are not insuperable and should be welcomed as the simplest and cheapest way of undoing at least a part of the harm already done.

It may be objected that the degree of planning and design control implied by the suggestions made above is unacceptable. This is to beg the question: if our aim is to be adequate conservation of what should be conserved, then the means adopted must necessarily be accepted by the public opinion on which all conservation rests. As has been indicated above, there is a radical way to deal with this problem of the conservation of towns: they (at any rate a selected number such as the fifty-one of the C. B. A.) should be removed altogether from the general system of planning controls and subjected to a different series of legal sanctions. Each of these towns would then automatically become a 'city of refuge' from the pressures of modern life and, without being sterilized, would obtain special safeguards and would live in a special 'climate'. Like any other form of zoning, a practice fully accepted already, this would have the effect of causing types of business and industry which were unsuitable to remove themselves elsewhere. Conversely, residential use and various kinds of light industry, craftsmanship and retail trade would be encouraged to settle. The individual moves made would in no sense be made under compulsion; they would be a natural outcome of the altered status of the place.

All this would, in the towns concerned, amount to a considerable change; but it is illogical to regard change in one breath as inevitable and to object to it with the next. What is proposed should be accepted as a particular aspect of modern change made desirable by the pressures set up by other changes elsewhere. A welcome outcome of the altered status of conservation towns would be that the *demand* for premises of unsuitable scale would diminish and finally cease. At least within designated conservation areas, if not throughout the whole of such towns, it should as a normal rule be made legally impossible to apply for permission to demolish and redevelop a site from the ground. On the other hand, suitable kinds of conversion of existing premises should be encouraged by financial grants and otherwise. Remaining traditional users of town properties, and incoming new users attracted by the conditions, would thus have an incentive to improve and maintain the buildings and to make adequate use of them. Special encouragement ought to be given to traders and business men occupying urban property to 'live over their shop'; or, failing that, to provide suitable access to upper floors not needed for commercial purposes, so as to increase the number of residential units available. This could within a short time remove one of the main sources of decay in urban areas: the phenomenon of partially derelict property left without adequate maintenance because unoccupied.

A great deal of suitable conversion and improvement could be spread over a number of years on a voluntary basis, in accordance with free accommodation of individuals to the new circumstances; at least this would apply in some instances. In others, where the scale of necessary works in a given town or area was large, and involved substantial amounts of clearance and redevelopment of intrusive buildings not suitable for conservation, a special organization would probably be needed, on the lines of the French exercises in conservation. The new system in France, set up by the Law of 4 August 1962, has as its basic intention, formulated by André Malraux, the integration of the past with the future. No better model than this French system could be found, for the underlying legislation and for the general methods employed. It is of such universal application that a brief account must here be given, based on the lecture delivered by M. François Sorlin, Inspector General of Historic Monuments in France, to the York Conference on Historic Towns and Cities in 1968, and afterwards published.

The French system is official and initiated by government. It began with methodical survey of historic centres throughout France, of which an inventory of over a thousand was compiled. The underlying principle qualifying for treatment is homogeneity: the 'historic area must be clearly defined by architectural or topographical landmarks, and it must be complete within itself.' Important factors contributing to homogeneity are not only urban grouping and siting (for example as a hilltop settlement), but the continued existence of old roads, the scale of buildings, and original massing. A crucial outcome of the French survey was that the 'Historical, Archaeological and Architectural Interest . . . lies less in the "monumental" character of particular buildings making up the group than in the overall quality.' This fully confirms what has been said above as to the British experience of a similar national problem since 1947.

A major concession has been made in practice by the French system to the national resistance to over-centralized control. Although the law of 1962 permits the designation of historic conservation centres by

decision of the Conseil d'Etat, the method actually adopted has been
to obtain the support of local authorities and local public opinion. This
leads up to the vitally important financial provisions of the scheme,
which involve a tripartite contribution from the state, local authorities,
and individual private owners of property. Although there are legal
provisions for eviction and compulsory purchase, this is rare. In the
first five years after the law was promulgated the initial nation-wide
survey had been made, and forty centres chosen to be dealt with in the
first instance. Because of the difficulty of finding adequate local finance
in villages, the centres so far chosen have been cities or market towns
of substantial size, or major districts within Lyon, as well as the Marais
district of Paris itself.

The decisions as to the areas chosen and their limits are taken by a
national commission of architects, archaeologists, town planners,
specialists in regional planning, and representatives of local authorities. As soon as a specific area has been named for designation,
negotiations begin with the town and a system of Public Inquiry
operates to obtain the views of the owners and landlords of property.
Definition of the area, jointly determined by the Ministry of Cultural
Affairs and Ministry of Works, is followed by a period of two years
allowed for preparation of the detailed plan for conservation and
enhancement of the area. During these two years there is a moratorium on all work likely to modify the structure or appearance of buildings in the area, except with special permission from the Ministry of
Cultural Affairs. This provision is designed not only to safeguard the
fabrics, but to prohibit any alienation of features and fittings such as
carvings, ironwork, panelling, paintings and the like. Sale of such
fittings to dealers and collectors, formerly common in France, is now
effectively checked.

The plan for conservation comprises two complementary parts, an
architectural directive and a detailed town map. It is prepared by one
or more architect-planners selected jointly by the Ministers of Cultural Affairs and Works, acting in continuous collaboration with
research organizations involving archaeologists, sociologists and
economists. Local demographic, economic and social surveys are
carried out by the research teams, and there is frequent consultation
with the local authority and the residents. At the end of the two years
the plan for a given area is adopted by the two Ministers after con-
sulting with the national commission. The recommendations in the

plan from the date of adoption become obligatory for an unlimited period, and all future growth and development within the defined area are regulated by the provisions of the plan. Enforcement is carried out by the technical departments of the Ministry of Cultural Affairs.

It is unnecessary here to go into the details of the directive issued to implement the technical decisions made. It covers information on every building in the area and all the specific proposals made for demolition, rebuilding, materials to be used, old features to be maintained, and the character of new features introduced such as shopfronts, street signs and lighting. The directive includes a timetable for implementation, based on local knowledge of the possibilities of each case, and the specific uses likely at given dates for each of the restored buildings. The plan and the detailed directive are intimately involved with the uses designated for the area in future. A balance is sought between maintenance of existing uses, which may have reached the point of stagnation and economic decay, and the introduction of fresh uses too revolutionary to be accommodated without inevitable damage to the structures and grouping it is sought to conserve. The particular problems of traffic, access, the parking of cars, vibration and fumes are all dealt with before the plan and directive receive their final shape. The creation of pedestrian streets in the area itself, and the formation of relief roads completely outside it or carried underneath it by tunnels, together with car parks either outside the area or underground, form major provisions in every scheme.

Early in 1968, out of the forty conservation areas already designated, twenty had already reached the stage of approved plans and work started. Actual costs, worked out for what had been done to the full official standards demanded, and compared with demolition and new building of the same standards done elsewhere in the same city, are available and prove that the method of revitalization is in fact definitely cheaper than redevelopment. Translated into sterling, the cost per square metre at Avignon was on the average £114, against £129 for new buildings; in Lyon the contrast was even more substantially in favour of conservation, which cost on the average only £100 against £143 for redevelopment. This provides an unanswerable economic argument in favour of the French system, even apart from the less material aspects of conservation as such.

The residual problem under the French system is, nevertheless, a financial one. Even after the state has given improvement subsidies

1, 2. OXFORD *Sheldonian Theatre* before (*above*) and after rehabilitation. *Architect: Godfrey Allen, with Arthur Llewellyn Smith.*

3

3, 4. OXFORD MASONRY *Christ Church Library*: a detail of the
south side before renewal of facing, and (4) the south side after
completion of work. *Architect: Edward Playne.*

4

5, 6. *Oxford*: the front of Linton House, (St. Peter's College) before treatment (*upper*) and after (*lower*). *University Surveyor*: *J. Lankester*

7

7, 8. OXFORD RENEWED *Divinity Schools*: the Wren doorway
before (7) and after (8) repair.   *Architect: Robert Potter.*

8

9. *Oxford*: three details of the old Ashmolean building showing restoration by E. R. Frith.
Architect: Godfrey Allen

on a slightly higher rate than those offered to landlords of new housing, there remains a gap in outlay which necessitates higher rents being charged for the rehabilitated properties. This to some extent has forced the former tenants to seek permanent accommodation elsewhere, owing to sheer inability to pay increased rentals. This problem has been at its worst in the great city districts of Paris and Lyon, but even then about 80% of the former tenants were able to pay the new rents, leaving only one-fifth of the previous population as permanently displaced. Special measures are taken under the schemes to provide for temporary rehousing during the works. Apart from Paris and Lyon, the proportion ultimately displaced has been relatively low; but in some towns designated, notably Uzès, it has not been possible to begin work on account of the small communal budget and consequent local inability to pay an appropriate share of the costs.

Notwithstanding its financial teething troubles, the new French system is a major breakthrough. It has demonstrated in the course of a few years that large-scale conservation of areas and whole towns is not visionary, but highly practical. The necessary administrative and technical procedures have not only been worked out but have been applied with conspicuous success. Above all, what has happened in France has been a practical demonstration of the right way to set about conserving buildings: not from the individual structure, but from the surviving homogeneous group. Such groups, once identified and clearly defined, are set apart juridically and subjected to a special process of treatment. An integral part of this treatment consists of the moratorium imposed upon change from the moment that an area is defined. In the operation of any effective system there must necessarily be adequate time allowed for planning in every detail and the making of appropriate timetables; but during this time-lag for planning it is essential that the situation should not deteriorate. Any necessary measures of structural first-aid must be taken at once; any other changes are undesirable until the full scheme, as a whole and step by step, is ready to be put into effect. All this has been demonstrated in actual practice by France, and is the correct answer to the objections of many kinds constantly being urged against conservation. What remains is for other countries, Britain among them, to please copy.

⌈2⌉

The Village

Recent French experience has, as we have seen, provided a most practical model for dealing with urban areas, whether complete small cities or large market towns, or complete districts of larger cities like Paris and Lyon. In such cases there is normally an adequate financial background locally for the degree of state assistance available to provide together an economic solution. France has, so far, found it necessary to relegate the problem of villages to a later stage, and in one case of a country town, Uzès, to postpone operations because of local poverty and the need for major expenditure there on a new system of sanitation. Some delay over the smaller towns and villages of the countryside, in France and other countries, can be accepted. The relative urgency of the danger from contemporary redevelopment and new traffic routes presses mainly on the larger and more completely urban units. This must not be allowed to lead to complacency over the future of rural settlements anywhere, and least of all in Britain, where the unspoilt village shows at its best as one of the vital features of the countryside.

Outside the area of Greater London and the Home Counties, the threats to the villages of Britain are mostly of a different character from those of the towns. The village generally does not suffer from the pressures of exorbitant site values which lead to commercial and industrial redevelopment. Except where a village stands in the way of a new motorway or bypass, airport or water reservoir, it is unlikely to suffer from the catastrophic demands of modern transport or the unceasing stresses of increased population. These consolatory remarks refer, of course, only to the true village in the open countryside, and not to peripheral villages in process of being swallowed by some greater neighbour. What then are the major problems of the genuinely rural village, not in any direct way involved in urban sprawl or inter-urban communications?

The greatest change that affects the buildings of the village is the radical alteration in the agricultural background. Until the last generation or so, the village in most parts of England comprised a very few houses of the gentry and the genteel, one parsonage, a number of farmhouses which might be nucleated or scattered according to the historical pattern of the region, and the 'tied' cottages of the labourers who worked the farms. Even the gentry were unlikely to have much spare cash, so that fresh building and alterations were exceptional rather than frequent. It has been precisely this economic pattern of slow change, at times amounting almost to stagnation, that has given our villages much of the charm which they have displayed since the opening of the present century. All this is now changing rapidly under the impact of an entirely new pattern of rural life. The hard facts of economics have forced upon the farmer a high investment in mechanization, allowing reduction in the labour force, with an extensive re-dundancy of cottages as a result. The same economic forces are also, as one generation succeeds another, promoting the steady amalgamation of farms into larger and larger units, and one farmhouse only may be needed in an area where four were used a few years ago. Some of the houses become derelict, but many more are placed on the market, with no more land than a small garden, and command high prices.

The purchasers of such former farmhouses, and also of the super-fluous cottages, are commonly town dwellers prepared to undertake a substantial double journey each weekday in order to escape at home from the noisy stresses of the town where they work. These new residents seldom have roots in the rural community, and what they ask of a home is likely to differ considerably from what was acceptable to the farmer or his labourer. Substantial alterations and improve-ments, or even major structural conversion, have to be undertaken to each house or cottage. It is the changes, more or less drastic, involved in this social transformation of the rural scene that form the principal threat to the buildings of the country village. Subsidiary threats are constituted by the need to build, add or insert garages for the private transport essential for the regular journeys from home to work;* and

* The provision of adequate *public* transport linking the village with urban centres is a vital problem which can only be mentioned here.

the modernization of farm methods which tends towards the demolition of all old barns, cowsheds and other farm buildings, and the erection of new structures of labour-saving character and light construction in modern materials (see also below, p. 57).

In sum all this constitutes a revolution, and very many villages, even when not attacked by urbanization, have been changed within living memory almost beyond recognition. It need hardly be said that a great part of the visual change resides in the use of standardized materials, bearing no relation to the traditional techniques of the region and often presenting a violent and startling clash. The alteration and conversion of the houses themselves, though seldom as unsuitable, often falls far short of adequate treatment. New and old materials seldom harmonize, enlarged windows or increased headroom play havoc with proportions, and incongruous modern fittings substitute a restless uncertainty for the calm repose formerly typical. Finally the profile of the roof against the sky is defaced by the crazy gadget required for receiving television.

Undoubtedly a great many of these changes are inevitable, though not all of them are necessarily permanent – wireless aerials are now in most cases unnecessary, and the television mast may be superseded within a short time. The impact of most of the alterations that are essential can be greatly softened by proper treatment and careful adaptation to the needs of each house, and it is this deft and appropriate handling that constitutes sound conservation. Even more than in towns, the choice of right materials is of vital importance, and all visual changes must be so proportioned to the whole mass and composition of the building that the total impression – even though different from what it was before – may still seem right. An architect with experience in such work ought always to be employed, and in spite of prejudiced rumour, will be more likely to reduce than to increase the cost.

We are not here concerned with such far-reaching changes in the appearance of the landscape as that produced by the grubbing up of hedges and the consequent transformation of enclosure into champion country of vast fields and, it is to be feared, later into a dust-bowl of steppe. What does concern the setting of rural buildings very closely, however, is the analogous removal of live hedges, and in other regions brick or stone walls, in favour of wire fences or other non-traditional forms of demarcation. The front gardens of village houses are highly

characteristic of the scene and provide a perfect setting for the buildings behind them. There is already a substantial measure of legal protection available for the preservation of individual trees, and some
such safeguard should be extended to the types of hedge, fence or wall
traditional in each locality. Changes should not lightly be made, and
the individual house and the group of houses of which it forms part
need always to be considered along with the curtilages in which they
stand.

A particular threat to hedges and gardens comes from highway
authorities, even in rural areas far removed from main roads. This is
the mania for cutting back every angle of every road-junction at an
angle of 45° to provide 'sight-lines'. This is one of the worst possible
defacements of a village, suggesting the planning of a garden suburb
or 'New Town', and should never be used except in those cases where
a 'street' village is strung along an old highway which has become a
route for fast through traffic. Even in such cases the proper remedy is
the building of a bypass, not the hacking of the village plan to conform
to the needs of transport. Here is another instance of the arrogance of
Transport, which badly needs to be put into its proper place as a
servant, not the master, of civilization.

There is another peculiarly intrusive adjunct to the modern road
where it passes through a village: the high concrete kerb used to
demarcate the pavement from the carriageway. In towns a kerb of
some kind is certainly necessary, except in pedestrian or partly
pedestrian streets, though even there the low type of kerb of traditional pattern is preferable on all counts, not least that of danger. A
false step off the edge of a high kerb can result in a sprained ankle, a
broken leg, or even a serious traffic accident. In the country village
kerbs can seldom be justified at all. If, in the interests of tidiness, it is
thought essential to mark the limit between the road surface and a
grass verge, then the appropriate line of markers should be either
flush with the road surface, or form a slightly sunken trough draining
into the storm-water gulleys. Grass verges, kept mown, are traditional in most parts of Britain, and form by far the most harmonious
edging to a road. It is also common in many parts to present a mown
grass bank sloping down from the roots of the adjacent hedges to the
inner margin of the footway. In the North of England this bank, and
occasionally the grass verge beyond the footway also, are planted or
sown with flowers by the frontagers, who thus generously share their

garden with the public passing by. Municipal enterprise has carried this even further, as at York, where, in addition to the famous daffodils planted in the turf ramparts about the city walls, spring bulbs of various kinds are planted in the grass verges beside the main roads leading towards the bars, the gates of the city.

Great caution is needed in planting ornamental trees along roads, anywhere, but more especially in country villages. The typical village green may well have one giant forest tree: an oak, chestnut, elm or sycamore; or a few scattered trees, or a single group. This is the characteristic planting of wayside areas of grass. Trees of any sort are hardly ever seen, in the traditional village, in rows lining the side of the carriageway; ornamental flowering trees were never planted in such a manner. To plant in this way is again to import something which smacks of the garden suburb and takes away from the group value of the houses which, as a whole, it is sought to conserve. Individual planting by householders against their own walls and in their own gardens has always been the rule, and this should be maintained as giving the happiest results (see below, p. 152). Trees planted officially should generally be of long-lived species, few of which are distinguished for their flowers: the horse-chestnut is the main exception and, though an exotic, has become naturalized in Britain. Mere traditionalism should not blind us to the virtues of some innovation, and there might well be rather more experiment with exotic trees of noble aspect. Two species only rarely grown, but perfectly hardy and magnificent in leaf, are the Tulip-tree and the Paulownia; they are both worth growing as specimens in their own right, even though their splendid flowers will not often be seen except in the South of Britain.

To some extent related to the question of planting is that of colour in the village. Largely because of the expanses of grass, the trees and gardens which on the whole distinguish the village from the town, an extensive use of vivid colour on the houses is undesirable. A dark and narrow town street may be very greatly improved by light tones and brightly painted front doors and windowframes. Similar colour-schemes are usually quite out of place in a country setting, and not the least part of the visual result of sound conservation is contributed by well considered use of colourwash and relatively unobtrusive paint-work. The permissible colours will depend largely on the local building materials and upon local tradition in the matter, and it is best on the whole to play for safety in this field. A few suggestions may be offered, chiefly of a negative kind: it is best to avoid pure white, as it looks too cold in winter and glares in summer sunshine; black also is too assertive except for picking out metalwork, gutters and down-pipes. Red paint ought never to be used in the country on houses; purples and bright yellows had perhaps better be avoided everywhere. Red ochre as a colourwash, in a district where it is traditional, is permissible, as are most other earth pigments added to limewash.

Allied to the use of colour is the application of stains to timberwork, especially to timber framing. In the interests of protection from wood-worm and rot, the treatment of timber with chemicals in spray or painted on is unavoidable; but the proprietary liquids obtainable can be supplied in colourless form, and this should *always* be used, not only for external but also for internal woodwork. Creosote and similar crude materials, of aggressive tone, can never be removed and permanently spoil the colour, grain and tonal value of all kinds of timber. By no means all timber framing was meant to show, and this special problem will be dealt with later; but where framing is exposed the original surface of the wood should be left, after cleaning off any remains of mortar or paint. The exquisite silver tone of weathered oak contributes so much to appearance that great trouble should be taken to avoid interference with it. In some parts of the country it is a traditional practice to tar timberwork, either as a contrast to white-washed panels in the 'Magpie' districts of the West Country, or as a protective finish for weatherboarding of softwood. As it is practically impossible to remove tar from timberwork, re-tarring is the only effective treatment in such cases. Black is, however, assertive and dominant, as has been said above, and large expanses of tar are best avoided unless there is no real alternative.

The character of rural buildings is determined even more by the colour and texture of their roof coverings than by those of their walls. In different parts of the country thatch, plain clay tiles, pantiles, various sorts of slates and stone 'tiles', may alone or in combination be the ruling material for roofs of traditional houses and farm build-ings. In conservation it is of outstanding importance to use such roofing materials as conform to the local pattern and harmonize with neighbouring work. There are considerable difficulties in obtaining some materials, notably hand-made clay tiles of the correct local character, and most of the regional types of stone 'tile', which are now seldom quarried. Where the original material is completely unobtainable it may be best to use some other form of roofing which is used in the district.

Although a few villages are entirely or almost entirely composed of houses of a single period, the great majority include buildings of a succession of styles. The ruling materials of these styles may often differ, and the character of the village as a whole will depend upon the largely haphazard juxtaposition of perhaps late mediaeval timbering, Tudor and Jacobean brick of narrow courses, and Georgian brickwork of quite a different type with perhaps a few important houses with fronts or quoins of stone brought from a distance. Where such a mixture of styles and materials already exists, any substantial new work may best be in a normally available material in use now, but of traditional character. It is seldom desirable in rural work to employ, for additions to old buildings, concrete walling or large expanses of glass. Problems of great difficulty have to be faced if such materials are used even for a house of entirely fresh design, if its site forms part of a traditional village group.

A facile objection is commonly made to the use of traditional materials, on the ground that the harmonious mixture of styles found in the typical village itself exemplifies the use of 'contemporary' materials at every period. There are two differences which mark off work of the last century, roughly, from all that went before. The first of these concerns the use of imported standard materials from a distance, instead of using what was to hand near the site. This is exemplified in much building of the late nineteenth century, where harsh and unsuitable brick and machine-made tiles often look grossly out of place in the village scene. To this source of disharmony the twentieth century has added the use of mainly synthetic materials, which contrast sharply in overall character with the surfaces and tones of all earlier work, and of 'modernist' design which is distinguished from all the vernacular tradition, and much of the architectural output, of past periods by its deliberate determination to appear blatantly different. In the traditional scene the employment of such attitudinizing modern design is unseemly and contrary to the basic policy of neighbourliness and restraint which has given to our villages a beauty consonant with the landscape. This is not to say that a house of absolutely contemporary design and materials can never take its place in the village scene: but it needs to be a work of genius.

Many of the villages of England, even in rural districts not yet touched by urbanization, have already lost their real character, and in such cases conservation becomes fragmented. Only single buildings can be dealt with on their own merits, and there is no longer a concordant group. It must be accepted that, even at a future date when more financial help for rural areas may be available, cases of this kind are past saving. What should be done now, preferably by the same hands that compiled the list of towns for the Council for British Archaeology, is to list all those villages which still do possess to a noteworthy degree the value of homogeneity. Some protection, more stringent than that afforded by the general planning law, should be given to such villages listed for their unitary or group value. Some form of major rural conservation area, analogous to a National Park, should be defined to designate a region in which several villages of listed value lie together. Within such areas there should be a close relationship between Conservation of Buildings and Nature Conservancy, in order to build up, over the country as a whole, a series of Reserves of traditional culture, the counterpart of the 'cities of refuge' already proposed.

Undoubtedly the scattered nature of many villages, and their relationship to the transformed modern agriculture carried on in and around them, will make the long-term conservation of villages and zones of village-groups far more difficult than the revitalization of towns already begun in France with such success. There is room for profound study of the possible means for diminishing the worst aspects of modern agriculture, such as the noise and fumes of tractors. It is not suggested that mechanized farming should be banned within the rural Reserves, but steps should be taken to reduce the clash between the traditionalism implied by the conserved buildings, and contemporary methods. This would be, after all, simply an extension of the principle involved in National Parks and Nature Reserves, where interference with many of the general rights conceded elsewhere is accepted as being in the public interest.

The disappearance of traditional farm buildings has already been mentioned (p. 52), and one of the most serious aspects of change in the village is the reduction of building types to the single one represented by the dwelling house. In some cases large barns (not necessarily Tithe Barns, though often so called) have been converted for use as church or village halls, and are admirably suited for adaptation to such new purposes. The massing of the farmyard to which they belonged is not necessarily impaired by this change of function. The position of the barn with regard to public access is, of course, fortuitous, and some buildings which could be re-used as far as their structure goes are rendered unsuitable by the inconvenience of access for the public, or for the occupiers of the farmhouse as a dwelling in continued use. In the case of subordinate farm buildings other than barns, re-use is much more difficult. Occasionally ranges of stables or cow-houses with lofts above them, are capable of conversion into flats or small houses, but such cases are exceptional.

Specialized buildings such as dovecotes, now seldom in use for their original purpose, are disappearing rapidly. The same holds true of horse-mills and cider-presses attached to farms, and still more to brewhouses, hardly any of which now preserve the equipment which was still in regular use until about fifty years ago. It is to be hoped that, if rural Reserves are set up, some encouragement might be given to the active use of a certain number of surviving buildings of this miscellaneous class. The same applies with possibly greater force to corn-mills, whether wind – or water – powered. Stone-ground flour is in demand and is thus a marketable commodity, and there should be room, in the economic administration of the future conservation programme, for actual exploitation of a limited number of traditional mills. The sad experience of the last forty or fifty years has shown that there is no future for the windmill or watermill that is merely preserved; a lot of money has been raised locally for the maintenance and repair of picturesque mills, but within a few years weather and vandalism play havoc with the restored fabric and machinery if there is no continuing use.

This question of buildings which have outlived their utility, and for which no suitable alternative use can be discovered, is one which strikes deep into the general issue of conservation. We shall see it in a particular form when we come to consider the problem of redundant churches (p. 63), but it is here interwoven with the treatment of rural houses and buildings for which uses continue. The removal of most, if not all, subsidiary farm buildings, and of such special building-types as mills of various kinds, village bakehouses and home brewhouses, is manifestly the opposite of preservation; is it equally repugnant to the principles of true conservation? It may perhaps help to solve this problem if we consider some extreme cases. The agricultural revolution now in progress seems, though we cannot yet be certain of the fact, to be one of the cataclysmic upheavals of world history, akin to the impact of metals upon the Stone Age. Even the most ardent exponent of conservation would hesitate to suggest that whole 'villages' of Stone Age huts should be conserved, as inhabited centres, on Dartmoor or elsewhere. Specimens of such huts may be moved to a museum or folk-park, or a group may be preserved *in situ* as an ancient monument in more or less ruinous condition.

It is quite possible that we should regard the traditional farm buildings to which we are so accustomed as outmoded in the same absolute way that we accept as true for Stone Age huts. If so, the same alternatives, namely various kinds of preservation, are all that lie open to us, and conservation is no longer even a possibility. It must be repeated that this would, as yet, be a premature conclusion; but it is all the same advisable to think over the solutions before the problem reaches agonizing proportions. Certainly, at the worst, a few specimens of different regional types of each sort of building ought to be preserved. Should it be (1) *in situ*; (2) by removal to museum or folk-park; or is there any third method? The answer in some cases will undoubtedly be removal, and the important thing in that case, as with all instances of removal of buildings, is that this shall not be accepted as a suitable fate *unless* all possibility of adequate maintenance in its own position has had to be given up. We may enunciate, in advance of more detailed later consideration of removal (below, p. 191), the law that: *Preservation by removal must never be an easy alternative to Conservation.*

In every case of removal, even under the most expert auspices, something is lost. For this reason alone the preservation of buildings by removal and re-erection, whether for use or as museum specimens, should be regarded as a last resort. More thorough consideration of the alternative is therefore necessary. How is it possible to preserve, even if not to conserve, without removal? Obviously it can only be possible in selected cases, that is to say where the preservation of certain disused buildings will be unobjectionable from the point of view of the users of the house to which these buildings belonged. In such cases the idea of preservation *in situ*, in the custody of the occupiers of the house, is the first method, to which preference should be given if it can be achieved. To this there is an alternative, to be regarded as possible only in rare instances: the maintenance of a farm or other group of buildings in order as a 'full scale working model' of a traditional farm of the region. This solution would be outstandingly suitable if it could be carried out in the midst of a village which was altogether designated a Reserve or Conservation Area. One complete farm, with its land as well as its buildings, and a mill in working order and grinding corn, might be kept up as part of the Museums service, in designated villages here and there in different regions.

As has been said above in connection with the fate of restored mills, there is no future for the isolated building which, however well restored, remains abandoned and disused. It seems to be axiomatic that the maintenance of such buildings never continues, however well in theory there may be legal and financial provision. Use, as a living museum specimen, is clearly better than no use at all, and the building will go on functioning as well, or as badly, as the rest of the museum service of which it forms part. The principle of the group, rather than the individual building, is of great importance here, and implies that the fundamental idea of the folk-park should be stood on its head. Instead of saving single buildings and transporting them to become parts of a reconstructed folk-museum, a better way would be to seek for villages which still retained their homogeneity, and set up the counterpart of a folk-museum in the village itself. Although there is no real prototype for such an arrangement in Britain, the United States offers Colonial Williamsburg, where the principle has been carried out and given the fullest expression. It is not necessary to form a number of 'period' imitations of Williamsburg, nor that every house within a designated village should be part of the living museum. So long as the group values of the whole were preserved by sound methods of overall conservation, it would be possible for ordinary dwellings to co-exist with certain farms or groups of buildings that were maintained on museum lines 'in working order'.

It might, while organizing such a village, be desirable for convenience to bring some individual buildings together by removal, but within the limits of the village rather than to some relatively distant spot. So long as small structures were moved to join larger buildings and groups, this would present few difficulties. In the case of timber-framed buildings removal would not even be historically repugnant, for Court Rolls contain many instances of permission being given to tenants to unframe a timbered house or barn from one holding, and erect it on another within the same manor. Occasionally the licence given might be for re-use of the framing of a barn as a house on its new site. Such instances from the past of conservation by means of changed use are valuable reminders of the dynamic quality present in real life, and lost in the mere museum.

As far as is humanly possible, real uses should be found for old buildings, and if this proves impossible, living maintenance in working order should be regarded as the next best thing. In contradistinction to the example quoted of Stone Age huts, it has to be remembered that very nearly all the surviving buildings of England, as far back as the thirteenth century, are quite highly sophisticated. Even the traditional cottage, built it may be in the sixteenth to eighteenth centuries, is far removed from the hut or hovel of the barbarian. There should, therefore, be no hardship involved in continuing to inhabit and use such structures for a very long time to come, provided only that suitable adaptation is made to the requirements of civilized life at the present day. It is largely a matter of fashion whether such converted premises will develop a market value equivalent to that of newly built accommodation on the same scale. There is no doubt that in the case of sound old premises, where serious decay has not been allowed to get a foothold, conversion is cheaper than demolition and rebuilding.

From what has been said it should be evident that the next step as regards conservation in the English countryside is the drawing up of a list – perhaps jointly by the C. B. A. and the C. P. R. E. – of those villages which still retain the homogeneity that was demanded of cities and towns. Within this list, and bearing the same relation to the whole as the 51 towns to the 324 of the total list of urban areas, there should be a smaller list of those villages, county by county throughout England, Scotland and Wales, that reach a level of distinction to be regarded as of national importance. At least six villages, typical of the highland and lowland zones of each of the three countries, should be revitalized on the French model, but with the proviso that they might have to be maintained as working models in perpetuity, if what may be termed natural finance did not operate. These should be pilot schemes to test the viability of such a solution to the problem of constructive preservation.

To enable such a programme, and such schemes, to have a good chance of success, there will have to be enabling legislation. Is it too much to hope that, when this is drafted, it will include adequate safeguards against fresh threats to what has been won? In all contexts of present-day life the fight against pollution has begun. It is not simply a question of oil-slick on beaches, or the fumes from cars and tractors, or factory effluents and detergents running into our streams and rivers. Excessive noise and pollution by vibration as well as by foul odours or poisonous fumes beset us. As has been mentioned, the village as well as the town may be threatened by new transport routes, by airports, by water reservoirs. If there is no other form of interference with healthy and peaceful life, one of the service departments will claim the area as a training ground. If conservation is to become much more than an empty word, protection against all these threats must be awarded, by legislation, as a first priority to the 'city of refuge' and the 'village reserve'. Otherwise the arduous planning, the difficult and costly work, will all be in vain. What is sought is protection for a proportion only of the whole country, a small minority of its area in fact. To give to all of these greater conservation areas, as now envisaged, an adequate umbrella against *all forms* of attack is a modest requirement.

[3]

The Church and Churchyard

Town and country alike are filled with churches of many dates. In the
rural parishes it is normal for the parish church to be very substantially older, in whole or in part, than any other building. Only in
a very small minority of town churches is the church as young or
younger than the houses of the district it serves. This applies mainly
to the Anglican Established Church in England, the disestablished
Church of Wales, and the Presbyterian Church of Scotland. Non-
conformist chapels of various denominations, and Roman Catholic
churches are relatively modern in most cases, though some chapels
and meeting houses are as old as, or rather older than, the dwellings of
their congregations. The architectural quality of most of the older,
and some of the more recent, churches tends to be relatively high, and
this is reinforced by the historical importance of a very large proportion of the fabrics.

The problem of these churches, a great many of which have in quite
recent years become redundant because of movements of population,
is one of the biggest in the whole of current conservation. It must be
said at once that this problem hardly touches any of the 'greater
churches': the cathedrals, collegiate churches and ex-monastic
churches converted to parochial use. Almost all such fabrics are
admitted to be of national importance (though not 'National Monuments' in any legal sense), and even though the sums needed for their
repair are often extremely large, the money needed has so far always
been raised. The special structural problems posed by these large
buildings will be considered later (p. 109 ff.). What will be dealt with
here is the dual question of maintenance of ordinary churches in fitting

63

condition, and the re-use of those church fabrics for which no further ecclesiastical use can be found.

At the start we saw that there is a conflict of ideas on the subject of conservation itself, which some claim to be a merely materialistic worship of the buildings themselves. This argument, though not widely accepted in regard to buildings generally, wins support from a considerable body of 'modern' opinion in religious circles. Money spent on the upkeep of the fabrics of churches is, according to one view, money taken from the legitimate upkeep of the Christian clergy and missionary workers, both at home and abroad. It is suggested that the total number of churches used ought to be greatly reduced and that in general new small churches and dual-purpose buildings, for worship and for social activities, should be preferred to ancient structures often too large for present needs, costly in upkeep (it is said), difficult and expensive to heat, and very frequently on a site inconvenient for the present needs of a population which has moved away from its old parish church. A fair criticism of this viewpoint is that it fails to take account of the fact that outlay on repairs of the new churches will increase sharply when they are more than 25 to 30 years old; whereas the old churches built strongly of good traditional materials can be maintained on a low average of yearly expense, provided only that repair is regular.

A much more radical view is held by extremists: that on purely theological grounds the use and upkeep of church buildings is a grave error, and that all funds raised should be used directly for the relief of poverty and suffering. While it is not the business of the conservationist to enter into theological controversy, it is only reasonable to point out that money spent in this way is being devoted exclusively to the material end of improving the material worldly lot of others. Nothing is left over, in Mrs. Everett's memorable phrase, 'to rejoice the heart and inspire countless numbers' of future generations. It is not clear that the upkeep of church fabrics is more 'material' than the relief of the poor; on the contrary, it is arguable that the numinous and aesthetic qualities of the physical church, its value as an inspiration and as a visible call to worship, render its maintenance a truly spiritual charge upon the charitable instincts of mankind.

It is likely that the main body of churchmen will continue to favour a middle way, in which the support of churches both old and new will rank on the same footing as other acts of charity. So long as this is so, the financial burden of the Christian Churches in regard to upkeep and repair will be eased very greatly by contributions from outside the Church, from those of other faiths, from agnostics and even from professed atheists. For there is a wide spectrum of non-believers, in the dogmatic sense, who cherish the works of art produced by all religions, and are glad to help to conserve the pagan temples of Greece or the East, the mosques of Islam, or the churches of Christendom. There is a great reservoir of good will towards the works of art produced by the ages of faith; but this good will may be dissipated if the Church takes up the attitude of shifting its burden, and *demanding* secular assistance from 'those interested in art and architecture.' It is desirable that the Church (meaning here the Established Church of England) should abandon its objections to churches being included in the legal operation of the law on historic monuments; this would enable state help to be given to fabrics of national or outstanding importance. On the other hand, any tendency to disclaim responsibility for the maintenance *in sound condition* of its heritage of ancient churches can only alienate sympathy.

Though there are many honourable exceptions, there is no doubt that during the last generation it has been the rule to give upkeep and repairs a very low claim upon church funds. This has resulted in a great many buildings, in excellent condition before the outbreak of the war of 1939–45, being now in a state approaching dereliction, or requiring heavy programmes of repair for which public appeals are made. Private donors to the repair of any building, whether ecclesiastical or secular, will always be inclined to give more generously to cases where the owners have in the past done their best, even in the face of shortages and difficulty. This psychological factor must be faced, and there should be a more general determination to carry out those works which are found, by the quinquennial inspection which is now a legal requirement, to be needed to keep the building safe and sound.

It must be repeated that works of maintenance, on churches as on any other building, must be regular if they are to be effective *and economical*. To skimp money on such regular works of necessity as the clearing of gutters and the mending of leaks is to pile up a grossly enlarged charge for serious repairs. As time goes on, what were very small defects turn into grave damage, and a mere 'pinhole' allowing a slight seepage of moisture through a lead roof could well be the root

cause of an outbreak of dry-rot costing thousands of pounds to erad-
icate, or even in practice the demolition of the building as beyond
repair. It is perhaps unfortunate that there is not a statutory proportion of church funds which *must* be spent on the fabric, either year
by year, or set apart in a sinking fund for long-term work such as the
complete stripping and relaying of a lead roof. There is no doubt that
the provision of such a fabric portion is the most economical way of
looking after any building in the long run. The temptation to divert
the money to other more attractive purposes is probably too strong
to overcome, unless there is a legal obligation.

What often bewilders the layman who comes to hear of a church
needing costly works of repair, is to find that, concurrently, a very
large sum of money is being spent on some other purpose, such as the
building of a new organ, or the installation of an improved system of
heating or lighting. In some cases the costs of these works are being
defrayed by generous individual donors; but it seems strange in every
such case that the seriously needed repairs were not given such
prominence in the programme of the church that the money was
offered for this essential need, rather than for optional schemes, however desirable. In some instances the schemes are not even desirable,
and though the Diocesan Advisory Committees in England exercise a
much needed check, they have no power actually to prevent undesirable work from being done, if those concerned are determined to carry
it out. It is to be feared that this is sometimes due to the very great
but improper pressure put upon incumbents and parochial church
councils by donors whose generosity and good will outrun their taste.

Quite apart from the financial question of whether schemes of improvement can be afforded, there is the possibility that they may cause
indirect harm to the fabric to be considered. This has special relevance
to all proposals for increased heating, and in particular when such
work involves the adding of insulating layers outside the main timbers
of a roof. The insulation, desirable on the grounds of economy in fuel,
is a dangerous encouragement to infestation by beetles, notably the
Death Watch, and all the more so if the average temperature of the
building is increased. Nor is this the only damage that may result; a
drier atmosphere may well cause cracking and distortion of organs
and of wooden pipes, leading to expensive repairs and to the need for
further special installations to condition the atmosphere to greater
humidity. In any work which alters either the structure itself, or its

normal conditions – such as temperature – it is vital that every aspect should be thought out adequately by an architect before the job is put in hand.

The importance of employing an architect in all conservation work is very great, but the many complications of church works make it particularly desirable in that case. It is extremely rare for anyone other than a trained architect, and one skilled in dealing with old buildings at that, to be able to carry in mind not only the technical and aesthetic problems, but also the whole array of potential dangers which beset the course even of relatively slight alterations to a struc-ture hitherto left alone over a long period. Any change of conditions represents a threat, and it is normally only an architect who knows the building and other work of the same kind who can weigh up the many factors involved. An architect is also in a position to give guidance in matters of taste, which quite often are also matters of technique. The appearance of a building as well as its structural stability and durability can be affected by the choice of mortar, for example. Types of roofing material and of paint may be of vital importance, yet are sometimes chosen almost at random by laymen, who suppose that there is no real difference between the sorts available except first cost.

Anxiety to save money in outlay on particular repairs is often responsible for very serious extravagance in the long run. In weighing up the claims of different roofing materials, for example, it is not only necessary to know what each will cost to lay, in labour, scaffolding etc., as well as the material; but also to take into account the expected 'life' of each material. When the actual figures are investigated for materials that are extremely cheap in first cost, it is commonly found that their life also is so short that, over the centuries (and the life of a church is usually numbered in centuries), they turn out to be vastly more expensive than the dearer materials. Although some materials (especially the metals lead and copper) fluctuate greatly in value, the expectation of life of most materials is fairly constant, and also the general picture of relative costs of certain categories as against others. Thus it can be said that by far the cheapest forms of roofing are pantiles and, rather dearer, plain clay tiles. These will last for probably 150 years. Materials very cheap in first cost, such as bituminous felt or asbestos sheeting, have lives of only some 20 to 30 years, and so work out as costing in the long run perhaps four times as much as roofs of clay tiles.

The structural safety of the church fabric is the paramount factor in sound conservation, and this in itself involves a great number of technical problems. The nature of these problems, in churches and in other kinds of building, will be described later (Part II, below). Here we must emphasize the importance of a different series of concurrent questions, ranging from aesthetic taste down to common sense and seemliness. The feature which most distinguishes the church from the general run of other buildings is its long life: the local church spans the generations and holds together past, present and future. In a very actual sense it symbolizes the eternal as opposed to the temporary and passing aspects of our world. It should, therefore, be less subjected than other buildings to the vagaries of fashion. Yet the old parish churches of Britain, and more especially those in the hands of the Church of England, have been since the Reformation, and are still, at the mercy of religious fashion, quite apart from changing taste in matters of decoration and movable fittings. Floor levels in particular have been subjected to ruthless changes in the interests of one or another liturgical movement.

Where structural changes have been made to the design of outstanding church architects, or by sound local craftsmen, they may often add to the historical interest of the church as a witness to style and method at different periods. Such works are by no means necessarily a defacement, and the same may be said for a proportion of the changes made in recent years. Changes which destroy or gravely alter older work of high quality are, however, to be deprecated. This applies most in regard to work which has survived from the Middle Ages, the period when the building was at least part of a homogeneous theology and way of life. There is a certain historical distinction to be drawn, in the case of churches which are substantially of mediaeval date, between alterations of work added since the middle of the sixteenth century and changes made to the original Romanesque and Gothic fabric. In the course of the nineteenth century new works or major restorations were the rule at all churches, and fortunate were those that escaped transformation into specimens of Victoriana (see also below, p. 91).

The reader may well ask: what is wrong with Victoriana? In spite of the reaction away from the puerilities and sheer bad taste of much nineteenth-century art, and from the recent exaggerated cult for the period, we must recognize that some Victorian art and architecture were of a high standard in their own right. The unfortunate thing about the impact of the time upon our churches is that the Victorians imagined that they understood the lost secrets of mediaeval art and were in a position to 'revive' a true Gothic. It was their sincere belief that 'the foul torrent of the Renaissance' was a physical enemy that had taken captive the loveliness of a godly and better world; and that they were doughty paladins who must fight to destroy the dragon and set this beauty free. They thoroughly did out a great deal of ham-handed work of three centuries, along with some great masterpieces; they did succeed in rescuing from physical downfall a good number of the greater churches; but at a cost of substituting in many hundreds of cases a painstaking fake for a genuine work of art. Whatever virtues brand-new Victorian churches might have, their spirit was completely different from that of the mediaeval buildings. The deep study of mediaeval details, lacking the actual life of the period which none could recapture, was unable to put new patches into the old garment without inviting ridicule from posterity.

Nor is this merely a question of aesthetic taste or opinion upon architectural values. A great deal of the Victorian patching was constructionally unsound. Because some eminent Victorians were among the greatest of engineers, with a mastery of large-scale structure seldom equalled, it is easy to fall into the trap of supposing that all the building of that time was at least physically sound. Some feats of structural restoration were performed, but a great deal of the work done was highly unsatisfactory. Stone from unsuitable sources and of inferior quality was often used, and sometimes applied as a thin veneer after cutting back the whole of an old weathered surface. A great deal of such work has had to be undone and replaced from sheer physical necessity. Little attention was paid to the physical quality and properties of other materials: Victorian wrought iron is notoriously subject to rust, whereas the mediaeval metal it replaced or imitated was so rust-resistant that it had very nearly the properties of a modern stainless steel. Points such as this, even if they did not pass unnoticed, were neglected in almost the whole of the practical output of two or more generations.

The conservation of our older churches faces, therefore, not only the financial issue of maintenance, but also that derived from earlier restorations and repairs of an unsuitable or even inadequate kind. In all new work, whether of additions or restoration, great care should be taken to see that the mistakes of the past are not repeated, and that what is done shall be both structurally and aesthetically worthy of the ancient building. It is to be hoped that economic circumstances will in general impose a limit on the amount of work done, for cautious conservatism is a safer policy than the ambitious optimism which seizes upon some newly fashionable idea in art or liturgy and finds in it an excuse for the raising and lavish expenditure of funds. It is precisely this enthusiastic but ill-advised type of spending that has led to the very serious state of many churches, which have been starved of the attention needed by their original work in order to provide them with embellishments of doubtful value.

In the conservation of churches the methods advocated for saving towns and villages of outstanding importance are not applicable. It will be largely a matter of chance whether the church or churches included in a conservation area are in their own right of outstanding value. We have seen that, in the case of agglomerations of houses, larger and smaller, it is the group as a whole and its homogeneity that should be conserved. Each church, however, is a single item in its own right, apart from a few rare instances of two or more churches in one churchyard. In attempting to form lists of churches of particular value there is inevitably a return to the method of assessment of individual quality. This can all the same be tempered by regard to siting and to the part played by the church in the landscape, wherever it is associated with buildings of other kinds. The counterpart to the C.B.A. lists of towns, and to the suggested lists of unspoiled villages and groups of villages, should therefore be an inventory of churches dividing them into categories according to their degree of relationship: isolated churches which punctuate the landscape; and at the other extreme, churches which serve as a dominant focus for the views of a whole area. Many villages and small towns are grouped around the church, which thus gains an importance far beyond its own intrinsic merits as a structure.

In larger towns and cities it is the view of individual streets, squares or road-junctions that tends to be dominated by the local churches, as in such cities as Norwich and York; or sometimes the distant view where a hilltop city like Coventry owes its characteristic profile to towers and spires. Even churches of relatively slight intrinsic importance, when graded as architectural and historic fabrics, may assume a considerable significance in townscape. The tower or steeple, as a point of punctuation in the urban composition, is especially important, and this has been recognized, for example, in the preservation of Sir Christopher Wren's steeples in London, even when the body of a church has been demolished. Though the saving of a tower only is an undesirable practice, it may often be the case that half a loaf is better than no bread, and the steeple may, in its own right as an architectonic design, or as a focus of interest in the scene, be well worth the keeping.

On the issue of such preservation much depends upon the question of the surroundings. The body of a church may in some instances be demolished merely to save the cost of maintenance, and its site will be thrown into the churchyard as added open space. In this case the preserved steeple will stand as a monument, and will continue to dominate the scene, even though its architectural value will have been more or less impaired by removal of the church of which it formed part. On the other hand, if the demolition is due to determination to realise the site value, so that new and probably high buildings will go up around the surviving tower, this will lose most of its value. The cost of preservation in such cases is probably unjustified, and any intrinsic importance of the steeple must be used primarily as an argument against redevelopment of the sort proposed.

This brings us to the importance of the churchyard itself. Firstly the churchyard has normally been the burial ground for the local families for many centuries, and thus has both a religious and a sentimental importance. Even when individual families have died out or left the district, the continuity of feeling with past generations is exemplified by the old stones which record former inhabitants of the parish. The open space is of more practical recreational value, and its visual value in the townscape can hardly be overestimated. Regarded as a foil for the church itself, it provides a frame and also space across which the architectural beauties of the fabric can be adequately appreciated. In most cases it affords opportunity for planting trees in a natural way, to give shade and greenery where they are most needed. Even in cases where the church has been pulled down, the graveyard ought to be kept for its own sake.

The churchyard today is threatened by its own high site value in urban areas, and this threat is likely to increase unless all old burying grounds are given general protection by law from the practice of disposal of the remains and redevelopment. Merely as open spaces in areas otherwise built high, churchyards deserve to be kept on grounds of public policy, but resistance to commercial exploitation seems to have dropped to a low ebb, in spite of the extent of lip-service to popular requirements. The great majority of churchyards, however, are likely to survive, but merely as neatly mown areas of turf. In spite of widespread and reasoned protests at high level, a sweeping revolution has gained ground in recent years, removing or destroying all the tombstones and monuments in every part of the country. This is usually justified on grounds of economy in upkeep and of tidiness, to make it easy for a levelled space of grass to be regularly mown by machine. It is not denied that there is a limited validity in this argument, but it undoubtedly is a disguise for the excessive fear of death that has come to play an ever greater part in modern life. The sight of tombstones, as reminders of mortality, has become repugnant to a generation increasingly persuaded that life can be indefinitely prolonged by scientific ingenuity.

In the longer term, common sense will prevail against this futile cult for the things of this world. But in the meantime almost all the memorials of individuals of the last three centuries will have been swept away. The loss is not just of personal sentiment felt by descendants of those local inhabitants recorded by the stones. A very large proportion of the stones themselves are of aesthetic value as works of art and sound craftsmanship, and often of fine lettering of different periods. In their grouping the total aesthetic effect is even greater, and, notably in country churchyards, they contribute immensely to the quality of the scene. In another field of interest they have great importance, as evidence of social history and as an irreplaceable archive of biographical information. It is not adequately realized that, before 1837, when general registration of births, marriages and deaths was made compulsory in England and Wales (in Scotland not until 1855, in Ireland not until 1864), the vital records kept in parish and other registers were so defective as to provide no real basis for family history. In particular, age at death was only sporadically recorded, and the actual date of death (as distinct from that of burial) only rarely. For purposes of serious demographic or genealogical research, and even to establish a probable date of birth as a clue in the search for parentage, the evidence provided by tombstones is unique. This fact has been accorded limited recognition in legislation affecting the removal of tombstones by faculty and otherwise, but in practice the requirement that legible inscriptions be recorded is usually satisfied by a list of bare names and the date of death only in each case. Long inscriptions giving important family information as to descent and marriages are seldom recorded in full, although these are as, if not more, important than many other forms of documentary record scrupulously preserved. It is a final irony that this widespread destruction of inscriptions should be accepted in a society fully awakened to the value of archaeology and in which every fragment of a surviving Roman inscription is preserved and the text permanently recorded in the *Corpus Inscriptionum Latinarum.*

It is to be hoped that public opinion will move away from this form of anti-historical vandalism, and that the Chancellors of Dioceses will become far less ready to grant faculties for the removal of gravestones. A reasonable measure of clearance of broken and illegible stones cannot be objected to, and for the purpose of mowing the grass mounds may be levelled and leaning stones firmly reset. To go beyond this is an inexcusable act of destruction of part of our national heritage, and one which in some way affects all of us. Families migrate from parish to parish, and for a time lose touch with the old burial place of their ancestors; but from time to time individuals seek out and wish to rediscover these memorials. The fact that no member of a family makes an objection to the removal of stones from a given churchyard is no guarantee that the strongest objections would not have come from descendants now living elsewhere, had they been aware of the proposal. It is, however, as works of art and craftsmanship, and as unique archives that all tombstones deserve conservation as a national possession (see also below, p. 144).

Early in this chapter reference was made to the threat of redundancy caused to churches mainly by movements of population. This raises an entirely different aspect of conservation from the threats to the security of used churches and of churchyards in being. Redundancy occurs as a result of the decision taken by the Church that its resources will no longer permit the use of a given fabric for purposes of regular worship. The formal procedure is now regulated by the Pastoral Measure 1968, and need not here be described in detail. Safeguards are provided and financial arrangements have been made for the permanent maintenance of certain selected fabrics by the Redundant Churches Fund. These are welcome moves in the right direction, but they must not be allowed to induce complacency, for it is clear that the available finance will not by any means support all worthy fabrics that become redundant. The conservation of ancient churches by means of alternative use will necessarily play a major part, and demands consideration in some detail.

While the conversion of dwelling houses to the needs of new occupiers demands modernization in various forms, the essentials of living accommodation exist already. The alteration of the fabrics of churches to new purposes is far more radical. In the first place, the church as the House of God has always been set apart from houses of men, even though it was very generally used in the Middle Ages for a wide variety of secular purposes. Leaving for the moment the possibility of religious use by some other denomination, a church is obviously best suited for use as a meeting place, for example a public hall, a concert hall, in some cases a theatre. Suitability differs according to the plan of the individual church, but uses within these and related categories may be compatible with continued unity of the interior as in the famous instance of the Dominican friary church at Norwich, now forming St. Andrew's and Blackfriars' Halls.

The many possible uses to which churches either had been or might be put were described by Mr. Ivor Bulmer-Thomas in 1966 in a memorandum drawn up for the Friends of Friendless Churches and printed in abbreviated form as an appendix to the Report, *New Uses for Old Churches*, published for the York Redundant Churches Commission (the Worsley Commission). After enumerating the different kinds of continuing religious use, as guild churches, university chapels, by other denominations, and as headquarters for religious organizations, this memorandum discusses a series of secular adaptations. Parish halls, institutes, museums, libraries, record offices or stores, concert halls, theatres, columbaria, almshouses, and diocesan stores are all purposes to which former churches have been put or, in a few cases, intended purposes not carried into effect. In almost all these examples it is possible to preserve at least some part of the interior in worthy visual condition.

Should none of these, or analogous, purposes offer for a particular church, there is the possibility of commercial use, and in this case the question of suitability arises. Is a particular commercial use a suitable one? Some churches have been turned into bookshops, and this is obviously unobjectionable; use as storage space, for a furniture showroom in one example at Norwich, or for theatrical scenery in the case of a closed church in York, at least allows the fabric to remain structurally unaltered. The economic pressures likely to be set up by the placing 'on the market' of a considerable number of redundant churches in any one district are, however, almost certain to demand extensive works of structural conversion in many cases. It is here that the crucial problem lies: just how far is it possible to alter the building without losing those qualities, architectural and historic, which it is sought to conserve?

Setting aside churches of outstanding importance, which will probably be maintained by the Redundant Churches Fund, or else by the State, as ancient monuments, the residue can be grouped in several classes. One category comprises town churches of considerable importance to the scene, perhaps forming a focus of interest or, with their churchyards, providing centres about which are grouped other buildings of age and distinction. In a proportion of this class, the interior of the church is of relatively slight interest, and may in many instances have been restored out of recognition. It is in the churches of this type that an opportunity exists for the insertion of floors and partitions to enable the structure to be used to maximum capacity for offices or shops, or for some combination of purposes. So long as the exterior is not altered or not greatly changed for the worse, such conversion should be welcomed. But there is one important condition which should apply in every case except where the interior has already lost all trace of interest: the process of structural alteration should be easily reversible. This means that it would not be satisfactory simply to insert steel joists into the walls to support permanent floors, or to demolish the internal arcades and rebuild them as modern walls.

The principle of reversibility is a most important one, which has hitherto found expression particularly in respect to techniques of conservation of works of art and documents. For example, if sheets of paper in brittle condition are to be preserved by lamination between transparent foils, it is recognized that it is of vital importance that the foils should again be removable without damage to the paper document. A once-for-all process which renders it impossible to retrieve the paper undamaged – for example, if the foils after a long period were to become opaque – would be rejected as inadequate. Now in the case of churches their special original purpose and religious connotation make them specially liable to re-use as churches. Even ruined churches have often been re-roofed and restored to use, and within one generation mosques in Turkey have been secularized, converted into museums, and reverted to use as mosques (e.g. the Iplikçi Çamii in Konya). Attitudes change, movements of population can be reversed; any structural conversion of a former church ought, then, to be done in such a way that, with a minimum of difficulty and expense, the new partitions and floors may be stripped out and the ancient fabric reconditioned.

Hitherto the main losses of old churches have been where they were thickest on the ground: in certain cities such as London and York; or, long ago, in parts of the country such as East Anglia, where many villages went to ruin and disappeared. The main threat of redundancy at present recognized is in towns, and the presence of a number of churches lying close to one another naturally prompts the question: why must all be kept? The answer to this, from the viewpoint of conservation, is that such agglomerations of churches are among the most important features of historic sociology in the places where they occur. London, Bristol, Norwich, Winchester and York are all instances of this multiple founding of relatively small churches serving quite minute parts of a city. Most of these churches were the outcome of the property in the city having belonged to a number of 'lords' each of whom provided for the religious needs of his own tenantry, building them a church and, quite often, seeing that one of his own sons became their priest. During the eleventh and twelfth centuries it was still possible, and normal, for these priests to marry and have legitimate sons who, in turn, succeeded to these family livings. The proprietorial church, or in rural areas the manorial chapel, which later became a distinct parish church, the centre of a district paying tithe to the priest, is an interesting and integral part of historical development. In those towns and cities, generally of early origin, where this phenomenon is frequent, the whole configuration of the scene is affected. It is the many churches which give such towns their special character.

Because urban churches still commonly stand in a churchyard, however small, they are slightly less likely to be overwhelmed by neighbouring development than are dwelling houses. But if they are to retain their visual importance in the townscape it is essential that extremely strict limitations should be placed on the height of new buildings sited close to them. This ought to be part of a general policy affecting the permitted 'ceiling' of development in all historic towns, but the special interest of the profile of a city, punctuated by the towers and spires of its churches rising against the sky, is one of the most vital objects for conservation. Intrusive buildings of modern date should be either demolished or reduced in height when they occur within towns designated for conservation, and as much attention should be given to vertical as to horizontal planning, in regard to permissions for new works of any kind.

Not much has yet been said of churches in country districts. Though many benefices have already been united, it has hitherto been usual for the several churches to be kept up and used for services. This is mainly because of the distance separating one centre of population from another across the countryside. It is evident that in the present context of re-thinking by the Church on its pastoral deployment, many of these village churches will become redundant, and worshippers will have to find transport to services at one of the nearest churches to survive. In these cases, particularly those of the more remote churches, what possible new uses can be found? In general it may be said that no commercial uses will be available to fall back upon, and that there will be no local need for a parish hall, a library, or a theatre. In a very few cases a church might be suitable as an agricultural storehouse, whether for crops or machinery and in rare instances might be turned into a house. Some, those of manifestly outstanding artistic or historical value, will be maintained simply as monuments. The outlook for the rest, as yet a proportion quite unknown, is at present gloomy.

It may be as well, in concluding this chapter on churches, to remind the reader of their number. Twenty years ago the Repair of Churches Commission appointed by the Church Assembly, under the chairmanship of Mr. Bulmer-Thomas, dealt with 15,779 churches in England alone. Of these about 8,300 were reckoned to have been built wholly or mainly before 1537, and presented 'by far the greater part of the financial problem.' On the other hand it was pointed out that 'the period from 1820 onwards was an active period of churchbuilding' and that churches of that time were just beginning to need substantial repairs; furthermore, it was found that 'many of the churches put up between 1790 and 1860 are not well-built.' In short, over half of the total number of churches are mediaeval, and need money spent on them because of their age. A substantial number of others, built between late Georgian and mid-Victorian times, are coming to need costly repairs because money or craftsmanship, or both, were skimped on their original construction. Structures which have already stood for five centuries or more – and more than eight thousand of them have survived out of the total number, some ten thousand to eleven thousand, of ancient parishes – deserve our respect. The best proof of this will be in finding means for their further conservation.

Part two

═══

CRAFTSMANSHIP AND MATERIALS

[4]

Craftsmanship

The excellence of old buildings, the chief quality that makes them worthy of conservation, is due to good craftsmanship. It is true that this is to use the term in a rather wider sense than is usual today, but in earlier times virtually all designers of buildings were themselves thoroughly trained craftsmen. Their hands often wrought the materials, but they had first created its destined form by the use of their brains and imagination. The integration of the craftsman and the architect in a single personality produced a satisfying unity in the product that is now extremely rare. The 'raising' of the architect to professional status in quite modern times has made him ashamed of his origins and in most cases even of the capacity to work with his hands at all. Individual modern architects are not necessarily snobs, but they owe their position and their characteristic form of education to historical snobbery. Essentially it is this factor which causes most difficulty in the practice of conservation, for most of the buildings it is sought to conserve are the products of men trained from childhood to use their hands first and then their brains. The modern architect, like a callow youth showing off on his bicycle, displays his self-satisfaction with the cry of: Look, no hands.

We have to deal with matters as we find them and, as far as concerns tackling jobs at this present time, must get along with the regrettable dichotomy between architect and craftsman. In a later chapter, in considering desirable future changes, we shall have to discuss whether this state of affairs need continue (see Chapter 11). At present effective conservation is hindered by a double problem: that of finding suitable architects to take charge of the work; and that of finding craftsmen able to carry it out. These needs have long been recognized, and efforts have been made to provide specialized courses for post-graduate work by architects already trained, and training schemes in the traditional crafts for men in the building trades. The outcome of more than twenty years of experience since such efforts began on a co-ordinated plan soon after the end of the war of 1939–45 shows, however, that the supply of suitably experienced architects, and of craftsmen skilled in the key crafts, is inadequate to the demands already made. The widening of the scope of conservation, as further classes of building come under threat, and many more churches are declared redundant, will soon make the position untenable.

As long as the generation of architects in independent practice was one trained in the older building materials and methods, there were to be found among them a sufficient number of men who, in the course of their work, had had reasonably adequate experience of repairs and alterations to old buildings. The state of affairs was not ideal, but the position seemed far from hopeless, and a certain number of architects was beginning to specialize, since the early years of this century, in work of conservation rather than a mixed general practice. The youngest of that generation, the last architects to have had a traditional training in building construction and in the history of architecture, are now verging upon the normal age of retirement. A very few of them have been in a position to train, by personal example, a small number of architects of the next generation; but the circumstances have been highly unfavourable to any large intake of junior men into this field of work. The fact must be faced that this is less a career than a vocation. In a highly competitive world seeking adequate material rewards there is little opportunity for the expenditure of time or the painstaking care that are needed, both in training for this work and in putting this education into practical effect later.

It was hoped, some twenty-five years ago now, that the enlarged volume of work on old buildings, foreseeable in the climate of opinion which produced the Town & Country Planning Act of 1947, would automatically lead to an increased supply of men able to undertake the jobs offered. That this did not prove to be the case was due to the counter-attraction of far more lucrative work for architects trained in the latest materials and processes, and concerned with immense schemes of new building and urban redevelopment. In that direction lie the prizes of the profession, and on a merely economic plane, the rewards that go somewhat beyond a bare livelihood. This fact was realized by the post-war generation of architectural students, and it was in response to what amounted to revolutionary agitation that the thorough grounding in traditional methods and in history which had been a feature of the schools of architecture came to be abandoned. There has since developed a sharp cleavage between the architect, as now trained in modern design and methods, and the conservator, acquainted with traditional usage and materials, and with the directing part played by professional architects as they were until recently.

To the awkward division of responsibility between the professional architect and the craftsman there is now added this new fact, the distinction between the majority of architects and the essential training of a conservator. The older system still in part survives, and lives in the memory of the senior generation of building owners and potential clients as well as of the elder architects themselves. Hence the extreme unsuitability of the normal architect of the present day to have charge of repairs and maintenance of old buildings tends to be overlooked. Economic pressures have in any case tended to produce large multiple partnerships in architecture, and this lends an air of specious simplicity to the view that conservation can be safely handled by one partner. It has to be said that this seldom works out well in real life, for the amount of urgent new work taken on by most firms is so large as to preclude the possibility of any one partner being secluded in the ivory tower of conservation. The fact that the relevant partner is trying to deal with an overload, even if exclusively of work of this kind, leads to far too much reliance upon junior assistants whose practical experience is inadequate for the tasks thrust upon them. Thus a vicious circle has begun, and is developing.

While it is certain that only future action of a radical kind can resolve this difficulty, something has to be done at the present time to continue works of conservation already begun and to initiate fresh works of maintenance and repair in the best way. Regardless of whether the men now available are, by training and experience, as well fitted for the task as may be desirable, we have to consider in more precise terms what their task is. In brief and general terms this is to secure sound craftsmanship, which involves the choice of sound materials, in order to prolong the life of buildings which, by hypothesis, were soundly built to start with: that is, had the advantages of being the outcome of a standard of craftsmanship of high quality. The province of the craftsman, as it was before the mid-nineteenth century, has now in fact been split, not just into two, but into four parts; and co-operation and co-ordination between the work of four different categories of technical personality is essential to the production of adequate results. To the resulting complexity of inter-relationships is added, over and above the fundamental requirement of satisfying the client (the building owner), the need to satisfy a far more detailed code of law and regulations than applied at the time these buildings were erected.

The architect, by name the chief or master craftsman, still maintains a notional priority over the other parties involved. It is an architect who is, or should be, first consulted by the client; and it is through the architect that the other parties are approached. Who are these other parties? In the field of conservation in the wider sense, the planner (commonly described as a Town Planner, but nowadays also deeply concerned both in the saving and the spoliation of the country-side) plays an increasingly important part. Men whose professional training has been in planning are employed by local authorities as officials concerned in carrying out the legal regulations now in force, and are also to be found in private practice as expert consultants. No major development, whether of building or of transport, now takes place without the intervention on a large scale of planners. One of the difficulties faced by conservation is that, though individual planners have in certain instances been among the foremost protagonists of sane conservation, all too many planners are thinking only in terms of con-temporary efficiency. Efficiency is not to be sneered at, in its own place; but it is regrettable that all too many plans are prepared with-out any regard to the other values of the existing scene. The existence of buildings listed as of architectural or historic interest is, in such cases, regarded as a deplorable nuisance, standing in the way of – actually 'obstructing' – progress. There is a serious need for more historical training in the curriculum of all planners, leading to a realization that good planning is based on recognition of existing values, not upon a clean sheet.

In the field of structural conservation of buildings themselves, the structural engineer is steadily coming to play an ever more significant part. As the architect has receded further and further from the tech-niques of manual craftsmanship and the full understanding of the theory and practice of construction, he has perforce come to rely more and more upon the professional advice of experts: that is to say, of men who are by profession trained structural engineers. It is obviously no essential part of the engineer's training that he should study ancient structures or the finer points of conservation practice; but, by a strange paradox, it often happens that it is the modern engineer who shows a deeper understanding of what is needed than does the architect. This is undoubtedly because the engineer, concerned with the structural quality of buildings and their capacity to endure, is profoundly impressed by the mastery shown by the builders of past times, notwithstanding the purely empirical nature of their science.

We have now mentioned the architect, who stands at the centre and should comprehend all aspects of the problem within his grasp; the planner, who often determines the environment within which the architect operates; and the engineer, who is to a large extent becoming responsible for the durability of the works in the longer term. The fourth category of persons concerned is that of the builders: the contractors and the skilled craftsmen of the various trades who, by the use of their hands, tools, machinery and plant, actually erect new buildings and additions to old structures, and carry out all forms of maintenance and repair. However well conceived may be the plans, the detailed designs and specifications, and the structural devices, resulting from the conjoined efforts of the consortium of architect, planners and engineers, the actual results depend entirely upon the adequacy of the builders to the task entrusted to them.

As we have seen, this fact has long been realized, and official bodies have concerned themselves with training schemes for craftsmen to enable them, not merely to obtain adequate knowledge of the traditional trades, but also to appreciate the finer points of conservation technique. It was not at all difficult, thirty or forty years ago, to find in any part of Britain local firms of experienced builders with a staff of well-trained craftsmen of the right stamp. As the years pass this becomes more and more difficult, and a time is swiftly approaching when conservation will face an impasse, as the last of the older generation of the operative building trades disappear from the scene. Just as theoretical mastery of the problems of how to maintain and repair old buildings is rising to its apogee, the practical skills needed to put the theory into practice are sinking towards their nadir.

Although this difficulty is felt acutely in Britain, it is by no means peculiar to our country. Even in the traditional Near East, and some fifteen or more years ago, the need for skilled craftsmen to repair the mosques of Istanbul forced the Turkish Government to search the country, finding masons of the right stamp – all of a considerable age – only in the remoter parts of south-eastern Turkey, nearly a thousand miles off. Just in time, a younger generation was trained under these venerable elders of their craft. Similar problems beset other countries, and it must be hoped that speedy steps will be taken to deal with them in every case. It is not merely a question of training men for a series of works now required, but of seeing to it that a continuous supply of craftsmen, generation after generation, can be found and attracted to the needed skills. It is a fundamental fact that has to be faced, that if all new building is shortly to be in 'contemporary' materials, prefabricated or formed out of concrete, glass and various plastics, the building trade will cease to provide services of the sort demanded by all forms of conservation, maintenance and repair.

It is possible that modern materials, being less durable than the traditional ones, will fall out of favour within a comparatively short time. In this case it may be imagined that a state of affairs would develop in which there were two main branches of the building industry: one concerned with the erection of works in the new materials, intended for short-term occupation followed by demolition and replacement; and the other providing for the continuance of work of a more lasting kind. In this case the traditional or long-term builder would also provide the skills needed in conservation. If the course of development takes a different line, however, it will be necessary to maintain a separate body of conservation craftsmen occupied solely in such jobs and altogether separated from the building industry as it is at present constituted. Whether this end could be achieved by normal laws of supply and demand operating, the need producing a number of private commercial firms offering suitable services; or whether it will only be possible as a result of official action, is likely to depend upon the total volume of work of this kind in the country.

Whatever the outcome in the more distant future, it seems certain that there is going to be a period of at least a generation in which some degree of official assistance will be indispensable. So large a proportion of the remaining skilled craftsmen is now employed by the state departments in charge of Ancient Monuments and Historic Buildings, by the Historic Buildings section of the Greater London Council, and by a few other municipalities, that the future of apprenticeship and more specialized training must depend largely on official intervention. This is perhaps not in theory the most desirable solution, but is in practice likely to be the best answer available. It can only be hoped that legitimate criticism of bureaucracy will be held in check by appreciation of the very wonderful work done in the past sixty years by the official experts of what started its effective career as the Ancient Monuments Branch of H.M. Office of Works. At a later stage we shall have to review the paradoxical situation in which a state service which is the admiration of conservators from all parts of the globe has met with a niggling campaign of destructive and unhelpful criticism in its own country (see p. 188).

It is certainly desirable that both official and private architects and planners as well as building craftsmen should as far as possible pursue the same general aims and collaborate with mutual helpfulness. To achieve this in practice it will be necessary to reach a satisfactory consensus of opinion on the aims pursued and on the methods to be adopted. It has to be accepted that no two experts will agree precisely; but there is room for give and take over details so long as there is a general agreement on principle. In spite of lip-service to the ideal of conservation, it is a regrettable fact that, in the past hundred years in this country, almost as much effort has been put into rivalries and mutual disagreements between would-be conservators as into the saving of the buildings themselves. Far too much stress has been laid on theoretical principles, held with dogmatic fanaticism, far too little upon the over-riding need to preserve from atttack, and constructively to conserve, as much as possible of what is left to us.

It must therefore be understood that in what follows the precepts laid down are counsels of perfection, often qualified by a statement of minimum practical targets. There are only two vital provisos: the first is that every worthy old building should be at least *preserved*; if it is lost, it has gone for ever; and the second is that all alterations made to *original* work should, as far as is reasonably practicable, be reversible. The fact that conversion of an old building to some particular new purpose is, at a given moment, the means of saving the building, leads directly to consideration of the likelihood that some different conversion may be required in the future. The more flexible the present scheme and the structural means of carrying it out, the less will the hands of our successors be tied, the more of the old building will survive. Alterations have to be accepted as a part of the price of conservation; but it must never be forgotten that the ideal is to keep as much of the building in its original form as is compatible with living day-to-day use.

It is not within the bounds of practicability that every private dwelling-house should be maintained under the control of an experienced architect. But it is in fact normal for all greater buildings to be regularly inspected and repaired under the direction, either of a local architect or technically skilled clerk-of-works, or of a consultant. The advantages of such regular and continuing responsibility are enormous. The greatest danger of all to old buildings is that of forgetfulness on the part of their owners; the best safeguard is the institution of a positive rota of duty, the purpose of which is to investigate structural needs as they occur, and advise upon necessary action. Provision of this kind is made by many corporate owners of such buildings as colleges and schools and by the individual chapters of cathedrals. Apart from monuments in the charge of the state or of municipalities, the nearest approach to a general arrangement of this sort, applying to a whole class of buildings, is the provision for structural inspection every five years of churches belonging to the established Church of England. This provision, embodied in the Inspection of Churches Measure of 1955, was to become fully effective within three years of that date; at the present time, therefore, most churches have been inspected for the second time at an interval of five years from the first inspection made under diocesan schemes set up under the Measure. In many cases the available funds are inadequate to carry out all the works advised, but the institution of this system of regular professional advice is of the utmost importance. It should never be forgotten how crucial a part was played in formulating this Measure and securing its adoption by Mr. Ivor Bulmer-Thomas, both as Chairman of the Repair of Churches Commission of 1951–52, and as a member of the Church Assembly in piloting it through that body.

It is then the Anglican churches of this country which, juridically, present the nearest approach to the ideal state of affairs presented by the medical system of ancient China: when a patient fell ill, the doctor's fees were stopped. The diocesan architects responsible for quinquennial inspection are not subjected to quite so rigorous a test of capacity; but it would be as well if all architects in similar positions were to bear this principle in mind. A very small degree of inattention or forgetfulness over a period of years can lead to exaggerated expenditure later, or even to structural disaster. The biggest temptation is a mental and psychological one: the thought of getting a given job 'finished'. In fact there is no such thing in the work of conservation as real 'completion'; periods of activity are succeeded by intervals of quiescence, but as long as the building survives, its maintenance has to continue. Many architects suffer from being called in at the last moment, to avert collapse, or the serious consequences of neglect. Instead of their work being preventative (and thus at least relatively cheap), it is commonly in arrears and unduly costly. To the physical problems of the repairs are added the difficulties of raising funds.

When an architect has been engaged, either to take permanent charge of a building or to give advice upon specific repairs needed at a particular time, the first essential is to obtain adequate background information. Unless it is seen, upon immediate inspection, that structural collapse may be imminent, time should be taken to carry out a full survey. If accurate plans do not already exist, the survey will need to include at the least a ground plan, but a conservation survey involves far more than mere planning and survey in the physical sense. At the earliest possible stage a photographic record should be made of the general and particular features of the building, and correlated with plans showing viewpoints. Together with the ground plan surveyed to scale and appropriately marked, the photographic record will enable historical development to be studied, and structural weaknesses (often the result of past alterations) to be suspected. More detailed investigation of the fabric will either confirm or disprove such suspicions and lead to a complete diagnosis of defects, for which the needed remedies are then prescribed.

At quite an early stage it may become obvious that expert assistance of several kinds must be sought. Trial borings into the subsoil and calculations of loading may involve structural engineers; surface decay of materials may indicate the submission of samples to the Building Research Station or, in the case of timberwork, to the Forest Products Research Laboratory; falling plaster may reveal wall-paintings of uncertain age and condition upon which expert advice is desirable. Upon the existence of such paintings, on one face or another of a wall, the choice of a method of stabilization may depend. It cannot be too strongly emphasized that the investigation of any old buildings should be extremely thorough, and that it should include the recording of much detail – for instance, masons' marks and graffiti – which may appear to be only of archaeological or sentimental value. The detailed history of the fabric can only be unravelled with the help of all the scraps of evidence that can be brought together. In the first instance it is the physical evidence of the structure and of all its parts that should be compiled by the architect; in the next stage of the investigation antiquaries, historians and archivists may be asked for their assistance to fill in gaps in the internal, structural evidence with items of external record.

Though not part of the architect's professional duty in the stricter sense, the demands of history and archaeology must not be neglected by him. Even from a severely practical viewpoint it has to be remembered that details of the history and development of a building are often of value in raising funds for its repair, and a favourable current of public opinion may be produced by the incorporation of archaeological excavation or investigations into a programme of structural work. As such ancillary exploration will be bound to affect the timetable of operations it should be given full consideration at the outset. This has the further advantage that consultation with archaeologists and antiquaries concerned with the particular building or site, or with the class of works to which it belongs, will be likely to provide valuable evidence relevant to repair, restoration or conversion. In the case of appeals for financial grants in aid, from official bodies or private trusts, the assistance of the archaeologist and the historian is generally invaluable, for upon their evidence may well depend the precise assessment of the quality and degree of importance of the building.

What has been said in regard to the survey and investigation of a single building applies also to the study of an associated group or of a whole conservation area or city. But whereas the problems of the single building have to be resolved within itself or at any rate within the limits of its curtilage, those of a group demand a great deal more in the way of 'three-dimensional' research. It is for this reason that, while scale models are often desirable in the case of alterations to the visual appearance of a single building, they are practically indispensable when a number of buildings and a multiplicity of viewpoints are being considered. In all such cases the model has to be regarded as an integral part of survey and report, as much as accurate plans and a complete series of general and detail photographs. Models have the special advantage of being far more easily intelligible to the layman than plans and drawings; but they also help the architect himself by bringing together all factors, and throwing into prominence both the advantages and the disadvantages of a scheme or its details.

The thorough study of the building, or of every one of a whole group of buildings as well as of the totality of the group, is a necessary prerequisite of proper conservation. What are the legitimate aims of conservation itself? We have already spoken of the importance of adapting buildings to new circumstances, that they may not cease to possess the dynamic quality of 'life' and become merely static preserved specimens. On the other hand, the adaptation must not be pursued as an end in itself, or the old fabric will suffer from unnecessary changes arbitrarily introduced. It must not be forgotten that in every case the ideal purpose is to keep as much of the old as possible, and to avoid destruction except where partial destruction or alteration is inevitable. The principle of reversibility of work should constantly be kept in mind, considering the repeated changes of fashion and of practical requirements. Another principle of the greatest importance is concerned with the treatment of previous alterations. It may be laid down as a general rule that a historical alteration of a positive and constructive nature (e.g. the substitution in a church of a large traceried window for an original group of lancets) should be respected; but that a negative change such as the blocking of a window or doorway, or the substitution of disharmonious or ugly additions or patches may be remedied by removal. Sometimes historic and aesthetic factors have to be carefully balanced.

Considerations of aesthetic value, especially when taken in conjunction with historic factors, are among the most controversial aspects of the whole subject. Not only are subjective assessments of quality involved, but overtones of an ethical or even sentimental kind. The echoes of nineteenth-century controversies have not died out, and arguments employed by John Ruskin and William Morris in particular are still at times quoted as if they were the outcome of divine inspiration. Reverence for the dicta of certain individual Victorians has played a part also in inspiring the cult of Victoriana for their own sake, tending to a gross over-estimate of the real value of mid- and late-nineteenth century architecture in Britain. For reasons touched upon earlier (p. 68 ff.), a very large proportion of the output of last century was inferior and must take a relatively low position in the scale of works of art worthy of conservation. Much Victorian restoration of older buildings falls into the same category, but there is particular need for caution here. Extraordinary vandalism was committed 'with the best intentions', even by some of the greatest of the Victorian architects. One of the most amazing examples of this was the complete rebuilding of the choir of Christ Church Cathedral, Dublin, in 1871–8 to designs by George Edmund Street, who destroyed the fourteenth-century eastern arm, of great historical interest and considerable beauty, merely to re-erect a pastiche of the original choir. The cost was a quarter of a million pounds sterling, worth quite £2,000,000 in values of today. Yet Street himself, within the ten years before he started his Dublin campaign of destructive restoration, had uttered one of the wisest of warnings against precisely this error.

In his magnificent work of travel and research on *Gothic Architecture in Spain*, Street wrote of Burgos Cathedral that: 'I particularly delighted in the entrance to and *entourage* of the southern transept, presenting as it does all those happy groupings which to the nineteenth-century Rue-de-Rivoli-loving public are of course odious, but to the real lover of art simply most exquisite and quaint.' To this text Street added a footnote after a subsequent visit in 1863, when he 'found the Cathedral undergoing a sort of restoration; masons cleaning up everything inside, and by way of a beginning outside they had widened the passage to the south door . . . the result of doing it being simply that much of the beauty and picturesqueness of the old approach to the church is utterly lost for ever. Of one thing, such an unsuccessful alteration satisfies me – little indeed as I require to be satisfied on the point, – and this is, that in dealing with old buildings it is absolutely impossible to be too conservative in everything that one does. Often what seems . . . the most plain improvement is just . . . a disastrous change for the worse. And when we find old work, the reason for or meaning of which we do not quite perceive, we cannot be wrong in letting well alone.'

Architecturally speaking, this is probably the most appalling divergence between precept and practice that will ever be found; yet it would be wrong to conclude that Street was either a conscious hypocrite or a deliberate vandal. Unquestionably he meant well by the great Transitional church of Dublin and, at the time of decision, sincerely believed that a new choir designed in the most painstaking manner to correspond to the work of the crossing and transepts would be more fitting than the great new choir of the time of Edward III. Posterity, looking at the faded photographs of the remarkable work he destroyed, can see how dreadful was the outcome of disobeying his own true instinct, revealed at Burgos. In a different case, that of Bristol Cathedral, Street was able to design a new nave (to stand where a late mediaeval nave had been begun but never built) which is one of the most conspicuously successful works of the whole Gothic Revival. At Bristol he had a clear site to play with, destroyed nothing of value, and added to the cathedral a worthy nave, inspired by the choir and transepts but not a mere copy of either.

Undoubtedly there must sometimes be some destruction of work interesting in itself but incompatible with changed needs. Yet such occasions are far less frequent than is often supposed. The demolition of substantial parts of an old building is very often the lazy man's solution to a problem which, with more time and hard work put into it, could have been resolved otherwise. Every case has to be judged on its own merits, but it is always best to be guided by the spirit of Street's wise saying that we cannot be wrong in letting well alone. This is notably true, not just of churches and other buildings important in their own right, but in the streets of towns and round village greens. Comparison of photographs, showing the same street in the third or fourth quarters of last century and at dates from 1920 onwards, or with present condition, proves the terrible losses due to a mania for over-neat 'civic tidiness'. In spite of much that was deplorable in mid-nineteenth century taste, and its determination to 'improve' parish churches, English towns managed to survive until well after 1900 in a state that on the whole exemplified Street's dictum. They had been left alone, and to enormous advantage. If general conservation could have taken control at the time that the National Trust was founded in 1895, and had legislation followed the best public opinion at a short interval ever since, there would be little cause for disquiet.

In the wider sense outlined at the beginning of this chapter, crafts-manship of the right kind can only be ensured by strenuous effort. This effort has to be exerted, in the first instance, by the architect as master craftsman and as the leading personality entrusted, by the owners of buildings, with their upkeep. In more detail we shall see, in the course of dealing with the treatment appropriate to different materials, how the effort must be applied, and the particular kinds of skill which must be evoked on the part of the individual building crafts-men. Here there remain to be mentioned or reiterated a few considera-tions of a general kind. As we have just seen, an unduly mechanical tidiness needs to be avoided, and likewise the process commonly known as 'tarting up'. Styles of woodwork, such as mock-mediaeval carved bargeboards; 'clever' details of a supposedly old-world sort, never found in traditional work; eccentric types of lighting fittings; flashy colour-schemes; everything of this kind must be avoided. In a different direction the crude, the coarse and the fiercely 'functional' should not intrude upon the gentle contours and delicate detail of good old work that in every particular displays the loving care of the mason, the joiner or the plasterer.

In designing major alterations or additions it is essential that a unity of feeling with the old work be preserved, and any disproportionate break of scale be avoided. The whole question of proportions deserves deep study when any new work interferes with an old composition. There are times when it is permissible to add a story to the top of an existing house: in the Georgian street fronts of many towns one may discern a slight change, in size or colour of brick, perhaps, between the two lower stories and the third, which was commonly added during the Regency period. But in many instances such care was taken to proportion the new to the old work that the result looks right and the alteration is unperceived. On the contrary, the addition of an upper range of chambers around the quadrangle of New College, Oxford, has been universally and rightly condemned – because it has diminished the scale of the whole and dwarfed the majestic proportions of Chapel, Hall and Muniment Tower. At the sister foundation of Winchester, though at a much worse period, the precious character of Chamber Court was skilfully maintained by inserting dormer windows in the old slope of the roof to light the upper chambers converted into dormitories between 1868 and 1903.

It is absolutely essential that sound materials of suitable colour and texture should be used, and that they should either harmonize with those of the old work, or provide a calculated but not startling contrast. A word must here be said on one of the curiosities of conservation in Britain, considered historically. Ruskin's devotion to what he called The Lamp of Truth produced a theory that the very slightest imitation of old work, which could mistakenly be supposed to be old, must necessarily be wrong on moral grounds. Pursued to its logical conclusion this produces ludicrous results. Suppose that, of the four pinnacles of a church tower, one falls in a gale and is smashed. Is a new one to be made of a different stone, chosen deliberately to look different: and be carved in a distinct way? Or should the old pinnacle be replaced by a mere squared block of reinforced concrete; or built up in brick? Common sense, as well as considerations of general seemliness, indicates that there must inevitably be some degree of replacement of individual stones, of missing members; stained glass must be patched; colour decoration renewed. It is true that this process will, in course of time, reduce the proportion of the building that is authentic work; but it is only by a refinement of casuistry that the imagined end product, a worthless replica, can be used to impugn the legitimacy of cautious and conservative repairs and replacements.

All through their history all buildings, great and small, are undergoing a process of replacement, of fittings, of members, of major parts. This is part of the life of the work, and – though not to be increased beyond the essential – of no more serious moment than periodical redecoration. Major additions should preferably bear their date, but this is even more important when they are not imitative than when they are. In the Gothic Revival a great deal of the best work was imitative in the most exact way: the profiles of mouldings were carefully copied from the best surviving sections of old work; in consequence, we have the best possible copy as a record of the original form. Contrast the purist's more recent reaction to the same problem: given a shattered and weathered window of Perpendicular tracery, he will refuse to replace it with a careful replica, but design a fresh tracery for the window, to be 'in keeping' yet not a pastiche. When this has mellowed it may be indistinguishable in general appearance from the original work, and be seriously misleading in a way that the first-class copy seldom is.

Except in cases where the old material is unobtainable, or so defective as to be out of the question (like the Headington stone used for so many works in Oxford), continued use of the same materials is the best course. The new work should not irritate the eye or the mind but, in the course of a few months or at the most years, should become part of the general scene. The tooling of masonry, the colour and character of joints, the methods of tiling a roof, may all be imitated from the original with gain, not with loss. Such methods have besides the virtue of avoiding altogether the trap of the new and untried material, which may be advertised as an improvement but can prove, after a short interval, to be seriously defective. As a rule of thumb, the experience of twenty-five years of use should be demanded before a new material is employed in work of conservation. It is a matter of sad experience that the tests applied in some laboratories, and regarded as simulating the effect of the passage of years, do not in fact have an equivalent effect.

To sum up: the best craftsmanship in conservation shows respect for all former work, and endeavours to match it or to be in harmony with it. If some former alteration or repair is of poor quality or obtrusive appearance, let it be modified so that its effect is softened. Unsuitable surface treatments, such as varnish on pitch-pine joinery; or ugly machine-made enrichments like many late nineteenth-century ridge-tiles, can be quietly eliminated. Internal walls wrongly stripped to expose the stonework may be lightly rendered with lime plaster or whitewashed. Careful study of the old materials and methods will assist in the attainment of a desirable harmony with them. Patiently controlled experiments by the craftsmen may often be needed, to produce the right effect; but this will appear in the result as time well spent. Supervision by the architect will have to be exercised until full confidence is established with individual craftsmen, and a mutual knowledge of the approved methods and ends. Again, it is as well to stress the importance of doing *the least possible*; but counting no pains too great to ensure that that little is a worthy contribution to the building and to the scene.

10, 11. TEWKESBURY *Merchants' Houses*, an example of successful reinstatement, justified by the aesthetic value of the range of
buildings as a whole. *Architect: J. H. Benson.*

12, 13. *Transformation*: Elm Hill, Norwich, before and after improvement under the auspices of an association of local traders and residents.

14, 15. REBUILDING *Winchester College*: the old Tower in 1861 and (*right*) after its reconstruction by William Butterfield in 1862–3.

16, 17. LEATHERHEAD *Farmhouse and Cottages* (now Sweech House) at the centre of the town, rescued by the Leatherhead and District Countryside Protection Society and adapted to professional use.   *Architect: R. Foster Elliott.*

18, 19. REVELATION *Back Edge, Stroud* (Gloucestershire): the dining room in 1947 and (*below*) after restoration to its original condition. *Architect: Bernard J. Ashwell.*

20, 21. WINCHESTER COLLEGE *Chantry Room*, designed as a library *c.* 1425 and refurnished as such (*below*) in 1951, showing concealment of the poor roof of 1772.

22, 23. *Sickhouse*, built in 1656–57 and enlarged in 1775. During general repairs and cleaning in 1962 the opportunity was taken (*below*) to remove unsightly alterations.

24, 25. *Winchester College*: the original Brewhouse, as abandoned by the last brewer soon after 1900, and (*right*) after conversion to a school library in 1932–4. *Architect: the late Sir Herbert Baker, R.A.*

[5]

Masonry and Brickwork

The care of old buildings calls for special skills of a traditional kind, and these skills are necessarily divided according to the materials used. As in many parts of Europe, buildings in Britain are formed in two main ways: they are made either of blocks of material laid one upon another (masonry); or they are framed of pieces of squared timber, the intervening panels being filled in some way. Leaving timbered buildings for separate discussion, we must deal first with the problems of those of masonry. In common usage masonry means walling of blocks of natural stone quarried out of the ground; but its essential character includes also the use of blocks of artificial material, notably brick (burnt clay). Although much of the fundamental skill of stone masonry and of brickwork is common to the two materials, they are usually distinguished from one another, and the stonemason and the bricklayer are regarded as belonging to different crafts. Whereas the bricklayer is almost exclusively concerned with the setting of ready-made blocks of a standard size, the mason has first to cut his blocks to shape out of the lumps of quarried rock. In the Middle Ages, when large buildings were normally built of stone and many men were employed, it was common for the hewers of stone to be a separate gang of men from the layers or setters; but usually a trained mason was competent in both sides of his trade.

Apart from the division between hewing and laying of stone there was another division in the stonemason's craft according to the type of stone worked. Stones differ in their natural formation, that is geo-logically, and also in quality. Some stones present special problems in cutting because of their extreme hardness, or because they suffer from flaws which, under inexpert handling, spoil the finished block. Specialists in dealing with particular problems arose in areas where there were quarries of unusual sorts of stone (e.g. granite, Purbeck 'marble'), and in some cases were able to found a monopoly on the basis of their skills, deliberately preserved as trade secrets. The Marblers of Purbeck remain to the present day an example of this exclusive handling of the kinds of stone – by no means only the so-called 'marble' – quarried within a small district of Dorset. Because of the quite peculiar methods of handling demanded by these exceptionally hard stones, no normal stonemason is prepared to risk failure by trying his hand on them, and the ancient monopoly is maintained. In the Medway Valley of central Kent there arose in the course of the Gothic period another specialized group of masons, the 'hardhewers' who knew how to cut the hardstone of their local quarries, the toughest quality of what is generically known as Kentish Rag.

It is owing to the fundamental differences between the various kinds of natural stone to be found locally that much of the regional variation of our buildings is due. Districts such as East Anglia, devoid of local stone, developed special techniques by which a small amount of costly imported stone could be used in an economical way to strengthen walls largely built of flints. It is perhaps worth stressing that the prevalence of round church towers in the Eastern Counties is due to the fact that the circular plan offered greater stability and did not need any stone quoins, as did every angle of a square building. Freestones, that is stones which could be cut freely in any direction, lent themselves to fine mouldings and carved details in a way that could not be imitated, or only with simplifications, in very hard materials such as granite. The external surface and appearance of buildings depended not only upon the kind of stone accessible, but also on the quality that the client could afford. A great deal of stone of rather poor quality, and therefore cheap, was used, but its inferiority and impermanence were recognized by covering it with a coating of coarse lime mortar (true roughcast). This historic fact was not appreciated in the nineteenth century when Ruskin's doctrine of honesty, already mentioned, led to the supposition that no builder of the Middle Ages would have 'falsified' masonry by covering it with a plastered overcoat. In very many cases the roughcast was stripped off, to the subsequent detriment of the building's condition as well as its appearance.

The influence of such *a priori* doctrines as those of Ruskin has been very great, and can be extremely dangerous in conservation. Intellectual and verbal ingenuity can and does exercise a fascination over highly literate minds, such as those of a large proportion of the clergy and the civil service who are among the greatest patrons of architecture. The modern 'professional' architect also is too easily persuaded of the truth and utility of what are mere theories, which he rarely has either the technical or the historical knowledge to rebut. The social cleavage which developed in the nineteenth century between the architect and the builder produced a point of etiquette which did not normally permit the professional man to take counsel with his technical brother. It was beneath the dignity of the architect to discuss either points of sound craftsmanship, or matters of appearance, with the stonemasons and other skilled craftsmen who produced the work. A great deal of the disabled state of our architecture, and of the damage done to both fabric and appearance of many of our old churches and houses, are due to this regrettable development of modern times.

One of the main needs of conservation at the present time, at any rate in Britain, is the clearing away of this legacy of false doctrine and, perhaps even more destructive, the stupid and petty controversies to which it has given rise. The objective methods of scientific investigation must be applied without initial bias towards foregone conclusions of any kind. In fortunate compensation for the errors of the nineteenth century, the twentieth has in fact provided us in this country with an unrivalled body of experimental knowledge on building materials and methods, forms of decay and means of preservation. Although there is room for discussion still on many topics, there is now a background of firmly acquired fact upon which the different aspects of structural conservation can be, and should be, based. In the past fifty years the experience of the Building Research Station and related bodies has pointed out the safe course in many details; but it has also had a definite impact upon the thought of conservators in a more general way. Firstly, it has demonstrated that some firmly held convictions have no real basis and must be abandoned; secondly, and still more important, it has shown over a wide field that scientific methods parallel and endorse the judgement of experienced craftsmen.

The practical effect of this on methods of repair of stone masonry has already been considerable, and is likely to become still greater. Since the building of the new Houses of Parliament at Westminster in the middle of the nineteenth century, the question of stone decay has received a great deal of attention. It began to be realised that cathedrals and other great buildings, which had stood for centuries in comparatively sound condition, were suffering from surface weathering at a greatly accelerated rate. An attack of blisters and pustules affected many types of stone, and the raised skins, once removed, exposed a fresh surface to renewed attack. What, it was asked, could be the cause of this sudden onset of a galloping consumption of the stones, when they had seemed almost as eternal as the mountains from which they had been hewn? The mystery grew for nearly a hundred years, but is now a mystery no longer. The new cause, so long sought, turns out to be the chemical pollution of the atmosphere by acid effluents of coal-burning fires. Whereas the main fuel of Britain before the Industrial Revolution had been wood, producing an alkaline smoke, the change-over to burning coal, and the increase in the number of hearths, yielded a poisonous product capable of the continued and unrelenting destruction of stone.

Two points need to be made in regard to the mechanism of decay. The first is that the root cause of the historical change is purely and simply the substitution of coal for wood as fuel; the damage is not done – or not mainly done – by soot and dirt, but by the chemically acid products of combustion and especially by the immense amount of sulphuric acid released. Owing to the poor efficiency of the ordinary domestic grate, it is the home fires of an enormously increased population that are chiefly to blame. The springing up of factories with chimneys belching forth large volumes of visible smoke, though an aggravating cause, was not of itself the reason why masonry surfaces could no longer resist weather conditions as they always had done. Hence the campaign for smokeless fuels and against atmospheric pollution generally, though waged in the interests of human and animal health, is also reducing the dangers to building fabrics from this particular source. It does not follow that the disease will cure itself speedily, or at all, but cleaner air does give a better hope that new masonry and repairs will be able to last longer.

The second point to remember is that the poisonous chemicals are washed into the surface of the stone by the rain, and operate by reaction with constituents of the stone itself. So long as the atmospheric pollution remains it cannot be excluded from the stone except by the interposition of an impervious layer such as paint. According to the type of stone involved, more or less of the harmful chemicals enters through the pores, and is absorbed along with the rainwater which is the carrying medium. Since it is undesirable, both on aesthetic and on historical grounds, to cover masonry surfaces with paint, this can be ruled out as a solution of the problem. Spraying with solutions of wax to form a surface repellent to moisture is a substitute not open to the same objections, and does in practice have a limited usefulness. This is particularly the case where the mechanical penetration of beating rain is itself a major factor of decay, apart from chemical action. In modern types, the wax crystallizes on drying and forms, not an impenetrable smooth coating but one which, under a microscope, can be seen to consist of a thickset body of spikes, repelling the droplets of water. In warm dry weather the moisture already trapped within the stone can breathe outwards, evaporating between the particles of wax, which is thus a one-way seal only. This is essential, for it has been found by repeated experiment that any unbroken sealed surface will be forced off by the explosive violence of continuing chemical reactions, by the pressure of vaporizing moisture, or at times by the expansion of water, as ice, in severe frosts. The main objection to applications of waxes, or to other water-repellent substances such as silicones, is that they require repetition at fairly frequent intervals. Since for a large and high building this involves the erection of costly scaffolding and a good deal of labour, its usefulness is limited.

As an alternative to protection of the surface by wax or water-repellant substances, lime-washing has been proposed and widely adopted. It is vital at the start to make a clear distinction, which has repeatedly gone unobserved, between the use of limewash as a decorative medium internally, and as a protection on exterior surfaces. With internal use we shall deal later when considering forms of decoration for old buildings (below, p. 146). It is the outside lime-washing of masonry that has received wide publicity on the ground that it provides a preventative or a cure for decay. The advocates of this treatment start from the fact that limewashing has for centuries been a traditional surface treatment, not only for plastered cottages, but for great buildings such as the White Tower (so called for this reason) of the Tower of London. In the course of search for a key to the mystery of the aggravated stone decay of the nineteenth century, it was suggested that the reason was the failure to keep buildings protected by repeated coatings with limewash. On this hypothesis, renewed treatment with the traditional limewash would restore the old state of affairs and the serious decay would cease. In its traditional form, mixed with melted tallow or linseed oil, the limewash certainly had some value as a water-repellent overcoat to the masonry. Furthermore, if its application had begun before the onset of modern atmospheric pollution and if it had been renewed sufficiently often, the thin layer of wash would have prevented the entry of a great proportion of the chemical products.

In theory there was, and is, quite a sound case for such limewashing as a form of physically protective coating, not completely impervious, and consonant with traditional practice. In real life, however, there are two difficulties: the first and more serious is that repeated applications have not been kept up, so that deleterious chemicals are already within the stone and the disruptive process is already going on. It used to be held by some architects, as an article of faith rather than as a matter of observed fact, that the limewash arrested this process of decay. Repeated experiments over many years have proved that this is not the case. Limewash certainly has no peculiar power of cure for stone decay. Furthermore, the mystical belief still found in some quarters that it actually becomes absorbed into the stone and forms a fresh outer skin, is quite untrue. So far as any substance may have some such capacity, it is lime-*water*, a very different thing which cannot be discussed in the same breath.* The confusion in the minds of the lay public is understandable, but it is unfortunate that it should have received currency among architects.

The second major problem that besets limewashing is the cost of application at sufficiently frequent intervals. In the case of any building much larger than a cottage it demands the scaffolds and the labour costs which militate so strongly against the general use of waxes and other coatings. Quite apart from all other considerations, the aesthetic factor enters, since a relatively short exposure to urban conditions makes limewash look drab and unsightly. In the case of really large buildings, where a part of the walls only could be limewashed in any single season, the visual impression of sections shading from startling white down to dingy grey is clearly undesirable and an interference with the character of the building hard to justify. The sad fact is that

* Lime-water holds calcium in high concentration but is practically clear; it may have limited value as a hardening bath for detached limestone sculptures which can be immersed in it.

limewash, though a permissible exterior treatment where its use is already traditional, has no special merits as a stone preservative. It has to be repeated that the favourable reputation it has long enjoyed is due to an act of faith, not only not borne out by scientific experiment, but positively discountenanced. For large buildings the cost of application, even if not prohibitive, is excessive, and the sudden change of tonal values disturbing.

Prolonged experiment, both in laboratory conditions and on many actual buildings, has shown that there is a much cheaper process which has considerably greater protective value than that afforded by limewash. This is simply washing, with clean water or, where circumstances make it desirable, with steam. The results of washing are twofold: the obvious visible cleaning of the surface, perhaps startling at first, but rapidly mellowing; and the removal of a substantial part of the harmful chemical salts at and near the surface. Washing, with a fine spray or gentle stream continued over a period of hours,* takes off all but the most ingrained soot and dirt, and reveals the qualities of light and shade intended by the designer. A sufficient number of well known major buildings have now been washed, wholly or in part, to have overcome the first unfavourable reactions, and it is to be expected that the fresh and new appearance with which ancient buildings are endowed will find favour with a younger generation that seeks modernity, and may be prepared to find it even in works of centuries ago, once their original countenance has been restored to them.

There is a special advantage in washing when the process is combined with repairs or patching of any kind. The insertion of clean new stones into old masonry in an uncleaned state is so displeasing visually that many architects and craftsmen have gone to great lengths to tone down the staring pale patches. Various recipes have been given, including strong tea or coffee, and the most notorious consists of the water strained off after standing on a mixture of soot and cowdung. Although such measures may very occasionally be legitimate they are in general a pointless expense. Wherever possible the insertion of new stone should be accompanied by general cleaning of the whole of the wall or front concerned; the work then appears clean, and perhaps

---

* Caution must be exercised if the stone is highly porous, or if the joints are open, to ensure that internal woodwork attached to or embedded in the wall is not soaked. Occasionally, too, problems may arise from the use of iron cramps in the masonry.

startlingly new, just after the work is done, but mellows gradually and all of a piece. It is usually necessary to carry out a thorough re-pointing of the joints at the same time. The combined operation of cleaning, repair and re-pointing of course demands scaffolding, but once this has been done to a building long neglected it can be kept in condition for many years by washing only. In very many cases this repetitive washing of a building already cleaned can be done without any scaffolding by means of perforated pipes slung from parapets or placed in position from ladders.

Repair by patching may be regarded as the normal form of structural maintenance for masonry buildings. Individual stones differ markedly in their resistance to weather and to chemically induced decay. From time to time it will become obvious that a proportion of the stones of a building, or perhaps only of one side exposed to the prevailing wind, needs replacement. All too often this is used as a pretext for the complete refacing of the whole wall: either 'to avoid patchy appearance', or 'to make economical use of the scaffolding while it is up.' This is a fundamentally unsound practice, for it offends against the basic rule of conservation: to keep as much of the original work as possible for as long as possible. As we have just seen, patchy repairs can be disguised by cleaning the whole wall; and in real life the cost of total re-surfacing is so high that the client is prepared to accept some cheap substitute when offered. Formerly this took the course of laying on a thin veneer of real stone; but nowadays the temptation is to use 'plastic' stone, that is to say a mix that is between mortar and concrete, keyed on to the old work which has been hacked away. To employ this method on a large scale is irresponsible vandalism on account of its destruction of the very fabric it is sought to conserve; but it is also aesthetically disastrous. No matter how suitable the mix, artificial stone never acquires the mellow patina which forms on the surface of old masonry, *and which re-forms after cleaning*.

The modern invention of 'plastic' stone is not, however, completely without its use. It can be a justifiable economy when it is used on a small scale to make good details or carving, and in this case there may be the further justification that a much smaller area of the old stone need be disturbed than if the decay is cut out for the insertion of a new block. As a sort of dental filling for local decay of very limited extent this use has a great deal to commend it. It is essential that the mix employed should be carefully adapted to the original stone by means of samples made up with stone dust from the decayed blocks removed. Standard mixes that depend simply on colouring matter to match the old surface must be avoided. Work of the best quality is inset into a cavity formed with undercut (or dovetail) sides, and keyed on to copper wires carefully plugged into the surface hacked back; the production of a mix stiff enough to work to the required surface or detail, and which will not shrink on setting, is work for a mason of high skill.

The correct mixture of mortars is in any case an operation demanding both knowledge and technical skill. In the first place it must be laid down as a general rule that most kinds of modern mortar based on Portland cement are unsuitable for repairs and for the pointing of joints in old masonry. A proportion of cement may be added to lime mortars to give additional strength, but the basic mix for conservation should always be a mortar of lime and sand. Among other objections to cement mortars is the very serious one that they tend to prevent the free movement of moisture from course to course: water collects at the bottom of each block or brick so that the joints do not dry out, and soluble salts become concentrated, giving rise to the familiar cycle of chemical expansion and blistering. Mortars must always be tested, not only as a match for any old pointing alongside which they may be used, but for their staining capacity. The amount of stain is a rough indication of the tendency to efflorescence of salts, commonly seen on the surface of new brickwork. On masonry it may be a symptom of a more serious kind, and it is generally wise to insist on the use of either White Portland cement – particularly useful for making up 'plastic' stone – or tested alkali-free cements.

Before leaving the subject of masonry surfaces, a few special kinds of decay may be mentioned. There is a chemical incompatibility between limestone and sandstone, which should never be used together. Rainwater washes calcium sulphate from the limestone down on to the sandstone – or it may be drawn upwards by capillary attraction – and the sandstone loses its cohesive quality under this chemical attack. It is therefore an important technical rule in repairs that limestone must be patched with limestone, and sandstone with sandstone. Another trouble, common in masonry work from the seventeenth to the nineteenth century, is the lifting or spalling out of corners from blocks, explosively forced apart by the rusting of iron cramps bedded in the joints within. If metal cramps are needed in new work or in repairs they should be either of stainless steel or of a non-ferrous metal. The repair of damage of this kind involves the piecemeal cutting out and rebuilding of the wall, course by course, to remove the rusted cramps and repair the blocks of stone.

Some sorts of stone are far more liable than others to partial and local decay. For instance there are many sandstones which contain soft beds, easily eroded by rain, hail and dust, driven by the wind. Magnesian limestone is especially subject to cavernous decay, where small pits form and are enlarged into deep holes, undercut at the edge. Such pitting is due to inherent defects in the structure of the block, not noticed by the mason at the time of working, and replacement of the whole block is generally necessary. It must be realised that in most examples of local, rather than general, decay of the surface, patching is likely to be unavoidable. Washing, limewash, the application of water-repellents, are all ineffective, and it is usually a waste of time to seek for a panacea. Unlike the chemical forms of decay due to changed atmospheric conditions, these local defects were inherent from the start: the particular blocks of stone ought never to have been chosen.

Turning from faults in the surface to more radical troubles in the thickness of stone walls, these may be roughly divided into three classes. First there is the failure of the wall to cohere within itself: its skins of facing may have parted company from the core, the core itself may have disintegrated, or the wall may be divided into independent sections by serious cracks. Secondly there are defects coming under the heading of subsidence, due to faulty foundations. Finally there is the category of very serious troubles, found mainly in large buildings, due to the active stresses derived from arcades, vaults and domes. All of these forms of decay may be found together, but the remedies are distinct even if they have to be used successively or in complementary fashion.

In designing appropriate repairs it is vital to distinguish between these three fundamentally distinct kinds of defect. If the trouble is essentially a failure of the walling to cohere within itself, no great tensile strength will be needed. The cavities must be filled up, the disjointed fragments made once more to cohere. Several methods are available for doing this, by grouting or by various types of building. Though these are technical problems, something needs to be said of them both to indicate their relative usefulness and to point out their dangers. Grouting offers the advantage that little of the old work is displaced and that the labour involved is low. The difficulty is that it is a method of working 'blind', without sight of what is being done. In principle all grouting consists of opening small holes through one face of a wall at different heights, the lowest close to ground level; washing out all loose material and dust by pouring water in through the next range of holes above; and then pouring grout, that is a liquid mortar, after plugging the lower range of holes. The grout sets in due course and then – and not until then – the process is carried out on the next stage up. In the course of the work all stains and drips of grout must be washed off the face of the stonework at once to avoid disfigurement.

In skilled hands the process just described, known as gravity grouting, can effect great savings of time and money. Its main risk is of adding weight between the two outer skins of the wall without binding them together, in which case there will be the action of a wedge operated by gravity and tending to force the two surfaces apart. This risk is greatly increased when grout is applied under pressure. The purpose of the pressure is to force the grout into cavities which it would not otherwise reach, so as to complete the solidification of the wall; but unless both faces are strutted up (more or less as if shutterings were being formed for pouring concrete) the danger of blocks being forced out is considerable. This relatively elaborate strutting, the labour involved in precautions, and above all the risk of serious damage very greatly reduce the advantages of pressure grouting. In general it cannot be recommended as having anything in its favour when compared to repair by building.

Repair by building, a phrase coined by A. R. Powys, means exactly that: one face of the wall has to be opened up piecemeal, in sections that allow space for working, and necessary strutting and support given to ensure that collapse does not take place. The defective core can then be removed or consolidated, or replaced by fresh work, with full knowledge of all the relevant facts. The cost is likely to be very considerably greater than that of gravity grouting, and there is the added disadvantage that one whole face of the wall is taken down and rebuilt, bit by bit. If this face is to be covered by external rendering or by internal plain plaster, this rebuilding is not in itself a very serious price to pay, so long as it is carefully done. The preservation of an old surface treatment, a good traditional roughcast outside, or wall-paintings within, may automatically determine which face of the

wall will be used for work, and which left intact. Of the various kinds
of rebuilding possible, traditional rubble in lime mortar is the best. If
some additional strength is needed this can be had merely by adding a
small proportion of cement to the mortar. Where any reinforcement
is required it is usually preferable to form the new core in concrete,
the two skins of facework at any given level being used as a shuttering.
A very simple form of reinforcement, adequate where no serious
movement is involved, is provided by unrolling a metallic mesh side-
ways, as the work proceeds at a given level.

Defects due to subsidence generally involve what is termed failure
in shear: unequal loading or the weakening of a part only of the
foundations will cause vertical cracks to appear. On one side the wall
will sink in relation to the more lightly loaded, or more securely
based, walling on the other side. In such cases it is useless to attempt
to patch the crack or hold the wall together until the source of the
trouble has been dealt with. It is common experience that serious
defects in foundations need the services of a structural engineer, at
least in an advisory capacity. The sinking of new piles down to a solid
foundation, or difficult underpinning, may be needed, with special precautions to ensure the safety of the fabric and also of the men at work.
It is worth noting, however, that some degree of unequal settlement
is practically universal in large ancient buildings, and that they have
successfully accommodated themselves to it over centuries. Not every
shear crack requires repair, for it may operate virtually as an expansion joint, the two adjacent surfaces sliding on one another as the more
heavily weighted part slowly sinks.

On the other hand, unequal settlement may produce serious danger
of collapse if a structure such as a tower develops an increasing lean
in one direction. The most famous instance of this is the Tower of
Pisa, which began to lean during construction and was progressively
corrected towards the vertical by its builders. Hitherto it has been
kept up by the ingenuity of several generations of conservators; the
Torre Nueva, the Great Clocktower of Saragossa built in 1504, was
less fortunate, being demolished in 1893 as unsafe in spite of widespread protests. Where a tower attached on one side, as at the west
end of a church, leans away and tears apart from the body of the
building, it is likely that a twofold operation of repair will be necessary. The foundations will have to be renewed or strengthened where
they are defective; and the upper part will require to be anchored back

at as high a level as possible by linking it to a general horizontal band of tensile reinforcement. Before the days of such reinforcements (and, though rare, they were in use as early as the first half of the fourteenth century in England), defects of this kind were usually remedied by building buttresses to support the leaning face. On aesthetic grounds the addition of buttressing masses is now generally opposed as interfering with the appearance of the old building; but they may sometimes cause less interference with the structure than the insertion of a major system of reinforcement.

Reinforcement will almost certainly be inevitable in dealing with the third category of trouble, due to active stresses set up by thrust. Hitherto we have been dealing essentially with matters of statics, or of the simple downward pull of gravity. The matter is far more complicated and serious where an element of movement, continuing even if slow, is introduced. In spite of the conventional application of statical formulae to determine the stresses of a building in a given condition, troubles of this sort have strictly, even though only marginally, crossed over into the province of dynamics. The real or apocryphal eastern proverb: *The arch never sleeps*, expresses a profound truth. Though the rate of movement may have to be measured in fractions of an inch per year, the fact is that an arched construction, with or without superincumbent load, *performs work*. The movement is relentless and, though in one direction only, an abiding cause of change. In statical theory, the thrust of the arch is met by an *equal* reaction of the abutting masses; if the reaction were not equal, there would be a state of disequilibrium and the construction would fall. Now in an underground cistern roofed upon longitudinal arches in series, with solid earth stretching beyond the end walls, the condition of equal reaction is met: each arch in the series provides the equal and opposite reaction to its neighbour, and the outward thrust of the half-arch at each end is completely met by the earth.

This condition of safety does not occur in any ordinary structure above ground: for the steady outward pressure from the arches *takes advantage of* an immense number of minor accidents which befall the buttressing masses. Wind pressure, expansion and contraction due to seasonal temperature changes, earthquake shocks or tremors, and vibration such as that from traffic, all provide occasions when the abutments yield to some degree, however slight. There is no compensation for these movements; the continuing thrust of the arch follows its advantage and wins ground. Each arch acts as an expanding spring, and where there is a series of arches, one after another, as in an arcade wall, the resultant movement at the ends may be substantially more than would occur if only a single arch were involved. This cumulative resultant distortion of the abutments to arcades was observed by my father in his survey of the ruins of Tintern Abbey and described by him as 'drift'. In some degree the results of drift are generally visible in all high arcaded buildings, and the end-product of this slow movement shows itself in striking manner at the central crossings of greater churches. The main arcades abut the crossing piers at a much lower level than the high crossing arches: the piers are visibly deflected inwards (towards the centre of the church) at the level of the arcades; but at clerestory level – opposite the springings of the high arches – the piers have moved apart. A rudimentary S-curve is thus produced instead of a straight vertical line.

The need for tensile members to restrain this tendency of arcades to move outwards towards their ends was already realised by Byzantine architects of the age of Justinian (527–565). It is extremely probable that their technique of longitudinal ties had been produced as an answer to earthquake damage. Observation of buildings after an earthquake would show that, where collapse had not actually taken place, the stones towards the top of the walls would often have been shaken outwards. In the area of Armenia and parts of Anatolia particularly subject to earthquakes, house-walls are traditionally built of courses of stone with occasional longitudinal bond-timbers running from end to end and taking the place of a course. The wider application of this technique to larger and more sophisticated works of architecture would be a natural step. It seems highly significant that in the present church of the Nativity at Bethlehem, a rebuilding under Justinian, the construction of the walls above the colonnades is in fact an arcaded one. In appearance the upper walls are carried upon horizontal beams, but removal of plaster discloses that above every pier is a concealed cubical stone block, from which spring stone segmental arches. The horizontal beams exist, not as carrying trabeations to span the intercolumniations, but as tension-members. The lengths of timber of which the beams are composed are laid in three widths: the central timber abuts against the stone block that carries the springing of the masonry arches; but the two lateral timbers are halved around the blocks to grip them and run on, being scarfed at intervals by semi-dovetail joints to the next lengths. This forms altogether a continuous tensile tie along each side of the whole length of colonnade.

In the visible arcades of vaulted cisterns and of churches of the period, timber ties span the arches at springing level, and similar ties were used in many Islamic buildings rather later. The technique appears to have been brought from the Near East and the Byzantine Empire into western Europe after the First Crusade, and in France (and rather later in England) the wooden beams were replaced by tie-rods of wrought iron. A well known example of their use on an extensive scale is at Westminster Abbey, where all the arcades of the thirteenth-century work are tied in this manner. As a structural expedient the use of such tie-rods is both sound and economical, and the degree of prejudice against them, shown by their uncalled-for (and highly dangerous) removal from many buildings in the course of the last century, is quite unjustified. Even aesthetically they cannot be regarded as a serious disfigurement, so long as they are placed at the logical point, namely at springing level. It should be accepted that original tie-beams and tie-rods were integral parts of the fabric, and as such ought never to be removed. On grounds of safety they should be replaced where they have mistakenly been taken away.

Reinforcement concealed within the thickness of walls plays an important part in curative restoration where structural decay has shown itself in uncontrolled outward movements. Whether due directly to earthquakes or other vibration, or to drift, it is essential that such movement should be halted. As has been said, external buttresses were formerly normal in such cases, but in modern times the desire to maintain the form of the ancient work as unaltered as possible demands the insertion of hidden strength rather than the application of outward props. Where great forces are involved it is usual for reinforcement to consist of metal tensional rods buried in a continuous horizontal slab of concrete. In the case of a large cruciform church such reinforcement might be arranged to run just below the top of the high walls; and this would, at the crossing and perhaps at the main gables, abut on major voids. In such cases the tensional value of the reinforcement would be greatly reduced or nullified, according to the needs of the case, unless the gaps could be bridged in some way. At the springing level of crossing arches, metal tie-rods might well be used in continuation of the line of reinforcement, being firmly connected to it. Such direct linkage has, of course, much greater tensional strength than a connection cranked upwards or downwards, though such less effective methods may have to be adopted where architectural features would otherwise be affected.

On occasion the difficulty of finding an appropriate level where a continuous ring can be formed may be overcome by making this level that of the tops of the aisle walls, and applying some form of struts in compression (in effect buttresses), pressing obliquely from the new ring of reinforcement upwards against the high walls in need of support. The new struts would, in such a case, be concealed wholly or partly by lying beneath the slope of the aisle roofs. A special case of reinforcement is the holding together of the top of a tower by forming a new flat roof in reinforced concrete. This is effective only against outward movements near the top; if there is a 'barrel-shaped' distortion, perhaps due to the ringing of heavy bells at a middle level, such reinforcement far above would be unhelpful. It is an important part of the duties of a conservator to adapt his measures to the individual requirements of each case.

Before leaving the problems of the greater stone building something must be said in regard to crushing strength. Alarm is often expressed at the great weight of towers, spires, or other superincumbent masses, particularly where (as at Salisbury Cathedral) the lower parts of the building were not originally intended for such a load. Such fears, *on this particular ground*, are generally exaggerated. The excessive factor of safety of most mediaeval work generally provides piers of a cross-section far greater than is essential to stability and to weight-bearing; the crushing-strength of most building stones is very great. It is, therefore, not actual crushing that is to be feared, but the fragmentation of supports not adequately bonded within themselves. This question has already been dealt with, and the answers – repair of the corework by grouting or by building – proposed. What is far more damaging than direct vertical weight is the amount of sway that may be imparted to supports, e.g. crossing piers, by the wind-pressure upon a tall exposed steeple. Partially concealed flying-buttresses of stone, and strainer-arches built across the openings, were the devices adopted in the Middle Ages to overcome such risks, as at Gloucester, Salisbury, Wells and Canterbury cathedrals.

By way of transition to the subject of brick buildings, a word may be said about the former popularity of what is called 'tile-stitching'. This is a method of using ordinary clay roofing tiles in thin courses, laid in mortar and bonded, to 'darn' together as it were the two sides of a fracture or to make good other defects. The same form of construction, though not strictly 'stitching' has been used for rebuilding the internal core of walls. Yet again we meet the cult of Ruskinian 'honesty': for tile-stitching was devised as a means of making a patch look unmistakably what it was. The whole purpose is to prevent any possible future mistake in confusing the repair with original work. Although it is certainly desirable that major alterations should bear a date, and that any modern detail carried out in a past style, and therefore liable to deceive the archaeologist of the future, should in some way be clearly marked to distinguish it from genuine work, it is hard to see any virtue in making patches more blatant than they need be. In justification of the tile-stitching method it has sometimes been claimed that it has great strength; but this is by no means the case. It is less resistant to tensional or shear stresses than a normal repair in stone or brick similar to the average old work.

The constructional problems of buildings built of brick are the same in most respects as those of stone masonry. In general brickwork suffers much less from atmospheric pollution, though decay from salt air near the sea or from internal salts (usually from unsuitable cement) trapped inside the brickwork, may cause trouble. The chief difficulty experienced, when it becomes necessary either to repair brickwork, or to add to a brick building, is to find a source of bricks resembling the old ones in size and colour. The texture of modern brick is generally much closer and smoother, the edges straighter and sharper, than in the old material. Nowadays few bricks are handmade, and those are extremely dear; furthermore, whereas old brick was commonly made of local clay there are now only a few brickmaking centres. Mass-production by machine, to a single standard size which is much thicker than that normal in earlier times, yields an intractable result difficult to use in conjunction with old work. None the less, there is some good modern brick, and it is not altogether impossible to harmonize with, rather than to match, the walls being repaired.

A good deal of restoration of brick surfaces consists of making good individual bricks here and there which, being too soft, have weathered away and left small cavities. In such cases the method of 'plastic' stone can be applied, the mix being specially prepared with crushed bricks which, partly decayed, have been removed. A skilful bricklayer can produce a virtually perfect match by this means, and even at the cost of a slight deception this is preferable to a spotty wall. If this method is used, it is essential to make up each brick separately, and to point the joints. Larger patches can be made good with plain tiles laid in mortar, preferably bonded in groups representing single bricks, after the face has been cut back sufficiently. Earlier repairs in hard cement should always be cut out and replaced with a more harmonious surface. It is less easy to restore brick walls that have been completely rendered or roughcast, for the old surface was usually hacked first. A new and improved roughcast in lime may be better than attempting to expose the original surface. Tar is normally impossible to remove, and fresh tarring is the only effective treatment.

Because old brick is much softer than most stone, and more easily penetrated by the weather, it may frequently stand in need of treatment with a water-repellent or waterproofer. A chemically inert wax, such as paraffin wax, may be applied in solution, but this can only be done after a spell of dry, warm weather has dried the wall out adequately. Various proprietary wax solutions are on the market and have given satisfactory results in practice. The length of time between applications depends on aspect and weather conditions; but it has to be remembered that treatments of this kind are likely to be effective only for a few years. In some districts it has always been traditional to give a special treatment to the weather aspect of buildings, commonly the southwest side in Britain. The wall may be hung with tiles or slates, rendered, or tarred. In such cases it may be assumed that the traditional treatment is the best solution for the problem, and should be maintained. Only in the case of unsuitable tiles, or ugly rendering, should substitution be practised.

As will be seen when we deal with timber-framed houses, the panels in some cases have been filled with brick. This was only rarely the original treatment, and is normally a substitute for wattle-and-daub. As brick is a far heavier material it quite frequently causes distortion of the framework through overloading; it moves away from the timbers and becomes cracked. In such cases it is generally better to remove the brick and, after the timber framing has been repaired, to fill the panels with light breeze or other building blocks, rendered over with a lime roughcast and colourwashed. Alternatively the panels can be filled with insulating board, rendered on the outside and plastered inside. Though these are suitable methods of restoration where brick panels are in a bad state, they should never be used for their own sake as long as the brick remains sound, and cracks have not opened due to distortion of the framework.

Between them, stone and brick are the walling materials of most of our buildings. Almost all the greater churches, castles and great mansions are of stone; the majority of smaller houses in most regions of Britain are of brick, dating from the seventeenth to the nineteenth century. The chief problem which faces the conservator is that of supplies of material really suitable for repairs: local and regional stone quarries and brickworks have gone out of business. Much can be done by determined pressure from architects and clients in getting quarries re-opened; occasionally a brickworks can be persuaded to make once more a brick of the old local colour and texture. It is very doubtful whether such private enterprise will solve the problem as a whole, and in the long run intervention on a national scale will probably be required. In the meantime we have to make the best, at times, of a bad job, and accept a compromise which does not seriously damage the aspect of our architecture.

[6]

Timberwork

The use of wooden framing as a form of construction for buildings is found in Northern Europe and elsewhere, but it was in England formerly the main material employed for houses. In Scotland, Wales, and some of the more remote parts of England stone masonry was the traditional usage at all times down to the recent past, and this is one of the features associated with what geographers have termed the Highland Zone. On the other hand, the rich supplies of timber that used to be found over the greater part of the country led to an invasion even of the uplands by this characteristically Lowland method. The rainfall and the winter snows of most of Britain have always demanded high-pitched roofs, so that even churches with stone vaults were built with the prevailing form of tall gabled roof, framed of timbers, protecting the masonry. We shall consider roof constructions and coverings in the next chapter, and are here concerned simply with the remains of the vast number of houses, and a few churches and major buildings, that were built between the thirteenth and the seventeenth centuries.

Since there are hardly any remains of English domestic architecture earlier than 1200, except for a few stone-built houses, our timber tradition starts with buildings of the High and late Gothic periods, and continues through the Renaissance and the Jacobean and Carolean age, when it began to be overtaken by the widespread use of brick. Within the total period of some five centuries there was, naturally, some historic development in style and in details of construction, but tradition was very strong, and there is a family likeness between most English timbered buildings, in spite of the existence of both regional and chronological types. The carpenters of the villages and small towns responsible for the majority of houses were slow to learn new tricks of style, and generally followed at a considerable distance the inventions of the mediaeval architects, most of them master masons. In sharp distinction to this general rule are a few great structural devices of the royal master carpenters, who developed the timber vault (as in the lantern of Ely Cathedral) and the balanced system of the hammer-beam roof, which found its most splendid expression at Westminster Hall.

From the mere fact that most timber buildings were of minor category, while notable monuments were usually of stone, our heritage of wooden framing has been greatly diminished by the normal rebuilding of premises. Easy to put up, the framed structure is also easy to demolish and, as many documents indicate, easy to remove for re-erection somewhere else. This last fact has to be taken into account in any historical analysis of timber structures, in which the re-use of old materials is relatively common. On the whole, it is alteration and demolition in response to changed needs, rather than exceptional liability to decay, that has so greatly diminished our stock of timber buildings, that what once constituted an enormous majority over most of the country is now merely a substantial minority. Two things are crucial in the conservation of timbered work: the fact that it is already getting rare; and its relatively greater age, on the average, than what is built in brick or stone.

Conservation of timberwork, therefore, starts from the premise that it is exceptionally well worth saving, and that a very high proportion of the whole class is, or should be, protected as of architectural and historic interest. Unfortunately this has not yet been achieved within the scope of modern legislative action. The small scale of most individual timbered houses has meant that they have been relegated by most observers to a position of slight relative importance; and legally they can seldom be rated as 'outstanding' in the sense demanded for financial grants in aid. Compared with more recent housing, the timbered cottage tends to have low headroom and has therefore been the target of attack from officials trying to enforce the excessive modern standards which, until a few years ago, were demanded under the Bye-Laws and Building Regulations. Condemnation, without any legal possibility of reprieve, was for long the lot of enormous numbers of fine old houses and cottages at the hands of medical officers of health. It is a great step forward that the survivors may now qualify for adaptation rather than willy-nilly destruction.

Even apart from these major factors, conservation has had to fight against an adverse climate of opinion in several fields. First of all is the belief, or superstition, that wood is a material exceptionally subject to decay. This, an objection which can fairly be made to thatch, for instance, is manifestly untrue of sound timber construction adequately maintained. We have a great deal of mediaeval woodwork still in sound condition, and much that is no longer so has been damaged by improper alterations and bad handling. As a material, wood is inherently long lasting, and is worthy of conservation for an indefinite future. A second justification for destroying timber-framed buildings is a change in aesthetic fashion. Simply because in the nineteenth century country farmhouses and cottages came to be regarded as picturesque, a counter-current of opinion condemns them as lacking in more solid and worthy qualities. To this is sometimes added a rider to the effect that vernacular cottages are material for the archaeologist (who may learn from their demolition) rather than for the antiquary.

There is yet another adverse criticism made in the actual context of conservation, and this is that practically all original timberwork has been restored away already, and that what can now be seen is essentially a fake devoid of historic importance. It is perfectly true that conservation work done in the past has often been far too drastic in its renewal of individual timbers wholesale instead of by conservative splicing in of new patches. Even so, the amount of damage done should not be exaggerated: a vast amount of original work still survives. What is possibly a more justified aesthetic criticism is due to the unwarranted vogue for staining old woodwork with creosote and various proprietary substances used primarily as insecticides. As has already been remarked, only colourless insecticides and fungicides should be applied, and every effort be made to leave the surfaces of old timber untouched (see also below, pp. 123, 143). The grain of oak, in particular, shows at its best in the silvery tone to which this wood fades after long exposure to weather. Almost as harmful as stain is the oil which some misguided preservationists rub into hardwoods, both externally and internally. This not only darkens the tone and takes away from the beauty of the grain, but gathers dirt. If valuable old hardwood seems unduly dry the appropriate treatment is to clean the surface and rub in beeswax dissolved in spirit; but this is usually only desirable for internal woodwork suffering from the rise in average temperature due to modern methods of central heating.

This question of changed temperature has a much wider application to the maintenance of timber, notably in churches. The serious forms of decay which attack wood consist of fungal rots on the one hand, and on the other of boring by the larvae of several species of beetle. Dry and well ventilated woodwork will never suffer from any of the ordinary forms of fungoid disease, for the spores of fungi demand a relatively high humidity before they germinate. On the other hand, the wood-boring beetles love a combination of darkness and warmth, and this is all too often achieved – after centuries of safety – by insulating the roof outside the main timbers and installing a heating system. The trapped warmth, maintained throughout the year, provides an ideal habitat for the Death Watch and the Furniture Beetle. It has always to be kept in mind that relatively slight leakage of rain-water or melting snow may set up conditions of local humidity for long enough to encourage an outbreak of dry-rot or wet-rot. Unless discovered fairly soon, by regular inspection, and adequately treated, such local infections may spread and do considerable damage. What is often worse, the damage done to the timber, perhaps not very serious in some cases, provides conditions quite outstandingly favourable to the beetle. The co-existence of fungal decay and infestation by beetle is extremely common.

Besides the various forms of decay, timber buildings suffer from distortion of the framework due to excessive loading, or to conditions producing drift. It must not be forgotten that the expansive action of a timber truss, if not provided with tie-beams or tie-rods, can be just as disruptive as the pressures from a stone arch. As in masonry buildings, the measures to be taken must consist either of compressive restraints such as external buttresses, or tensile reinforcements, notably metal tie-rods. Old roofs can sometimes be unobtrusively held together by the addition of one or more modern tie-beams, and slender tie-rods are not very noticeable, especially if painted a dark neutral grey. Distortion due to excessive loading is most commonly due to the practice of filling panels with brickwork when the original wattle-and-daub has cracked away. Possible substitutes have already been discussed in dealing with brickwork. It should not be overlooked that wattle-and-daub itself is a sound material, of good insulating capacity, and that it will last indefinitely so long as the outer and inner coats of roughcast and plaster are duly maintained. It should never wantonly be removed merely in order to substitute a modern filling.

As just mentioned, panels filled with the traditional wattle-and-daub require to be protected externally by a coat of roughcast. The picturesque aspect of timber-framed construction led to unnecessary removal of roughcast and plaster surfaces which were carried over the timbers and presented plain wall surfaces, lime- or colour-washed. The appropriate treatment in any given case is still an extremely debatable point. There is no doubt, from the evidence of mediaeval miniatures and later artists' drawings, that a great many framed structures always did display their framing, and that in some regional traditions the framework was given decorative forms. The black-and-white magpie-work of Cheshire and Lancashire is a clear instance of timber intentionally displayed from the start and throughout. On the other hand there are many other parts of England where the usual finish completely conceals the whole of the framework, except sometimes for cornerposts bearing ornamental angle-brackets to support a jettied upper story, and for moulded or battlemented bressumers running along the base of this jetty. In treatment of this kind the coat of roughcast or plaster was finished against the top of the horizontal beam, but did not disclose any of the upper framing. The restful qualities of such smooth surfaces, emphasizing the stages of the building and the form of the frontages in a street, are valuable.

It is, therefore, as well to exercise great caution before deciding to expose to view timber framing which has been covered. In any such case the first thing to establish is whether there is any evidence that the timber was originally exposed and was only later covered, possibly as a means of waterproofing the joints between wood and panels. Even if exposed framing should prove to have been the original treatment, there are two other points to be considered. Firstly, is the surface of the wood so hacked, to give a key for the coating, that its exposure is now impracticable? Second, will the durability of the structure be affected, or its usefulness lessened (e.g. by reducing the insulating capacity of the walls) if the timber frame is once more opened up to view? In many cases the answer must be that it is safer to maintain the plain wall surfaces, leaving the timber concealed.

The conservator's maxim of Care, not Repair, is particularly applicable to timberwork. The oak timbers of large scantling, of which most early houses were built, have very great strength and resistance to forms of decay, but neglect will, as with other materials, rapidly produce a state where major works are unavoidable. Leaking gutters and downpipes, a rise in garden soil level that brings earth into contact with the groundsills and posts, and lack of ventilation in the roof-space, are all potential dangers. In the course of repairs cleanliness is particularly important, and no chips or sawdust should be left about, even in a loft, to encourage vermin, moulds and various forms of decay. They also add to fire risks, though it needs to be emphasized that old seasoned hardwood is not highly combustible. On the contrary, it was observed after incendiary raids on Coventry in the war of 1939–45 that some mediaeval buildings of oak frame, though charred, were still in reparable condition, whereas neighbouring recent structures of steel or reinforced concrete were twisted wrecks.

This excessive factor of safety in the main frames of old buildings is a principal reason why they should not be condemned on a superficial examination which shows some decay to be present. Once infestation by rot or woodworm has been checked (and not seldom it checks itself if conditions improve) there is little likelihood of collapse. There is another particular reason why superficial appearance of timberwork should be discounted: the former prevalence of sapwood on the edges of timbers. This softer sapwood may have been riddled with the flight-holes of the Furniture Beetle, while the tougher heartwood has remained immune from attack, or nearly so. Even total removal of the affected timber will in such cases leave a cross-section still greatly in excess of minimum structural need. In cases where the affected wood forms part of mouldings or enrichment it should be preserved after insecticidal treatment, the wormholes being filled with wax and larger cavities with pieces of new wood or with a 'plastic wood' compound.

From what has been said it will be realised that the greatest danger to timberwork comes from continuous damp. So long as the surface remains open to fresh air and wind currents, dampness will generally dry out of its own accord. It is sources of continuing damp, such as leaking waterpipes, small defects in roofs and gutters, and garden earth in contact with timber, that cause serious trouble. Where wooden beams are built into walls of brick or stone they ought to have a clear space opened around them, for old walls rarely have any effective form of damp-proof course, and rising damp in the wall may affect the bearing ends of the timbers. Timber construction underlying lead or other metallic gutters is best replaced in concrete, but the concrete must be so formed as to leave a clear and ventilated space between it and the timber wall-plates. If the ends of beams are already found to be seriously decayed they must either be repaired with new wood scarfed and bolted through, or else 'sandwiched' between new timbers or metal flitch-plates, bolted through the old timber and projecting beyond it to take up an adequate bearing. It hardly needs saying that the method of repair with solid pieces of new wood is the soundest, but it presents difficulties. It very often means that the whole floor or roof must be taken down and re-erected after the operation has been completed on the affected beams; and in any case it requires a high degree of craftsmanship to make a first-class job.

A word must be said concerning materials. Very little softwood (deal obtained from pines, firs, etc.) was used in English structural carpentry until quite modern times. It should never be substituted for old hardwood which has to be removed. The normal timber for all English construction is oak, preferably English oak, though flooring was commonly of elm and new elm boards are the appropriate material for repairs and replacements. The extremely long life to be expected of sound hardwood makes it an economical material in the long run, even if its initial price is relatively high. Conservation should always seek to put into the building, not merely new material that is consonant with the original, but material likely to last for centuries rather than decades. Strangely enough, and contrary to what is popularly supposed, seasoning is not essential for structural carpentry. In the Middle Ages timber for frames and roofs was commonly worked soon after felling, and resulting twists and 'shakes' (longitudinal cracks) disregarded. This was, of course, possible because of the large factor of safety involved, and smaller scantlings would require full seasoning, as of course does all wood used for panelling and other joinery. Seasoned timber, though not essential, is desirable if it can be obtained, but it is doubtful if the modern speeded-up method of kiln-drying yields a product much, if at all, superior to unseasoned oak.

The identification of the various infestations to which timber is subject is work for experts, and little purpose would be served by a brief enumeration of the chief forms of fungal decay. A little knowledge is a dangerous thing, and there are dangers, not merely in failing to recognize dry-rot in one of its protean forms, but in supposing that every fungus growing on timber is likely to prove a form of dry-rot.

Experience of one identified case of dry-rot will, however, enable most people to recognize other cases by the characteristic odour. Though it is possible for a bad infestation with dry-rot to reach an incurable state very rapidly, it must be remembered that this is exceptional, and that only a small proportion of localized outbreaks ever become general infections. Once the rot has been diagnosed it is essential to dry out the area and keep it ventilated as soon as possible. In dry conditions and with a through draught the fungus cannot live.

Many different species of beetles have been found attacking timber, but only four give serious trouble in this country: the Death Watch (*Xestobium*), the Furniture Beetle (*Anobium*), the Powder-Post (*Lyctus*), and the House Longhorn (*Hylotrupes*). The last is a big beetle, over half-inch long, and as its larvae eat only softwoods, old timber-framed buildings are virtually immune from its ravages. The Powder-Post attacks almost exclusively the sapwood of hardwoods. Though the most serious menace to any hardwood timber containing sapwood, on account of its very rapid working, it does not usually constitute a structural danger. Nor does the Furniture Beetle, though this will attack heartwood if there is no softer wood available locally. The small bore of the holes means that infestation must continue over a very long period to cause serious trouble. This is not the case with the Death Watch, whose larvae are relatively large, and form a very grave menace to structural woodwork if they are numerous. At the same time, it must be recognized that the name causes alarm out of all proportion to the actual risks. Adequate ventilation is useful here too, and for all infestations by beetle insecticidal treatment by spraying into the flight-holes is essential. This may have to be repeated at intervals of a few years in the case of serious outbreaks.

The destruction of timbered buildings in England has already gone so far that the number of towns and villages mainly of this type, among those of a quality ranking for group conservation, is very small. This is particularly true of towns, where modern attempts at conservation have come too late to save the essence of our mediaeval and sub-mediaeval urban scenes. Individual scattered gems remain and should be kept, but the setting as a whole has been torn away. What is left of the villages of chiefly wooden houses should form one of the highest priorities in the listing of special conservation areas as complete groups, and a real effort ought to be made now to obtain full protection – especially by means of a moratorium of several years –

for these precious survivors from one of the great periods of our artistic history.

In not a few of our towns considerable numbers of timber-framed houses survive, but cannot be seen as parts of the townscape. The reason is that they were modernized, generally during the Georgian period, by the provision of false fronts of brick. No doubt the economic level at that time was, in these towns, insufficient for total rebuilding, but the fashion for plain brick fronts was strong enough to insist upon the elimination of jetties by building up flush, and elsewhere by coating the frame with stucco and forming a parapet instead of an eaves along the frontage. Every now and then works of repair bring to light what is left of the older front, and there is a temptation to expose and recondition the timbering. While this may in a few cases be a legitimate procedure, it cannot generally be recommended. Only seldom does the hidden framework survive in sound enough condition to be repaired; what will emerge from the transformation is bound to be an ingenious exercise in faking. The precise design may have been recoverable as a restoration on paper, but the result will be new work. This is rarely if ever justifiable.

There is another reason why alterations of this sort should seldom be countenanced. The rehabilitated timber-framed front, even if genuine, will probably appear out of place in the range of fronts in which it stands. This reinforces the reasons already given for conservation of whole groups, streets or towns rather than building by building. Since alterations to historic houses, like demolitions, are subject to permission, and this restriction is accepted by public opinion, it is reasonable to ask that the harmonious appearance of a group as a whole should be taken into consideration. Thus it is not enough that the alteration – in the case under discussion, back to an earlier genuine form – should be unobjectionable in itself; it should not result in a clash with the general character of the scene.

It must not be supposed that what has been said is in any sense a plea for uniformity. In many towns the charm of streets resides largely in their variations of style and material, and no question of a breach in treatment arises. But just as it would be reasonable to reject a design for an interpolated house of concrete and glass aggressively interrupting a whole street of Georgian terraces, so it would be to prevent a wilful return, in a single house, to its original design of two or three hundred years earlier. Nothing can replace the calm and harmonious quiet of a group of buildings which have, as it were, grown together over the years. Careful attention to maintenance and occasional repair; reasonable alterations for new uses as and when required, but avoiding excessive change in appearance; these will best keep for later generations the charm which resides in our historic scene.

Something needs to be said of the positive advantages of timber-framed buildings. They are put together of organic material, which gives them in some sort a kinship to the living trees which grow near them, and to the rural landscape in which they most commonly survive. Buildings of wood tend to be cool in summer and warm in winter, and they are more easily adaptable to changed requirements than those of stone or brick. Partitions of light construction can be formed within the permanent framing and, if no longer needed at a later date, be as easily removed. Framing is far more elastic than other materials in common use, adapting itself to movements in the foundations, to temperature changes, and to wind pressure. This resilience is part and parcel of the organic nature of the material itself. As dwellings it may be claimed that wooden houses conform quite exceptionally well to the life of their inhabitants.

As we have seen, the removal of timber-framing for re-erection elsewhere was a historical commonplace. Unlike the extremely elaborate procedures needed when a building of masonry is to be moved, preparations for taking apart of a typical frame involve very little in the way of drawings and notes. This is because the framework itself was normally put together in a carpenter's yard remote from the site. The pieces were marked with symbols of numeral type for the express purpose of simple re-assembly after transport. The dimensions of the plan being known, a foundation trench was dug and a dwarf wall built, high enough to raise the level groundsills well above the soil. This wall might be of flints in mortar, squared chalk blocks rendered over, brick, or stone; but whatever its construction it would be finished off to a level surface on which the sills would lie flat. In some instances there seems to have been a levelling course of oyster shells which acted as damp-proofing.

Now all this traditional construction is applicable to modern reconstruction. In case of necessity – and it has already been stressed that conservation by removal must always be a last resort – it is possible to note the series of ancient marks indicating the relationship of members, joints and trusses, take the frame down, carry it to its new site, and re-erect upon a new foundation of the same character as before. The modern rebuilding will incorporate a modern damp-proof course, but in most respects the house after rebuilding will be essentially what it was before. Often it will even be possible to extract and re-use a proportion of the original oak pegs which secure the joints. The filling of the panels, the external rendering, the laths and tiles will be new; but this would generally be the case at periodical repairs. The removal of framed buildings, when they can no longer be maintained *in situ*, or would be seriously damaged by alteration, is an alternative worth considering. In such cases it may well be the right course to restore the building as closely as possible to its original appearance, and this is particularly appropriate when transfer is to an open-air folk museum.

It will have been noticed that no use has hitherto been made of the words 'half-timbering' and 'half-timbered'. They are commonly applied, mistakenly, to buildings of timber-framing, regardless of date or style. So far as they have a legitimate meaning, it is only as a description of the style of timber building that began in England about the last quarter of the fifteenth century. In this style, in contradistinction to the open panelling of earlier and later dates, the walls are formed of a series of vertical posts or studs, separated only by narrow spaces of about the same width as the timber studs themselves. To this style alone, literally half timber and half interstices, is the epithet of half-timbering applicable. It is worth stressing the fact that this is a very late development in the mediaeval period, for a mistaken theory of typology, now exploded, held that the age of wooden construction could be estimated from the amount of timber used: the greater the proportion of timber to the total wall-surface, the older the building. This was supposed to be due to increasing economy as oak timber was more and more reserved for naval vessels.

Although it is true that oak timber was, from about the middle of the sixteenth century, used with increasing economy, and that the scantling of timbers in the latest framed buildings, of the eighteenth century, is relatively slight, this criterion does not apply within the mediaeval period. The phase of half-timbering can be historically associated with the increased splendour of architecture evidenced in all materials from the time that Edward IV returned from his exile in Flanders in 1471. Whether or no there was any direct influence of

Flemish architecture or craftsmen, the onset of this new style in timberwork can be placed with certainty about 1475, and it became typical of domestic work of the early Tudor period in rural England. It is commonly executed in a lavish manner with carved detail of high quality, and represents the impact of deliberate design upon traditional folk-art.

Because of its increasing rarity, timberwork must in future be conserved with especial care. The few remaining villages of framed houses ought to be given special treatment, and attention will have to be paid to training a new generation of highly skilled carpenters and joiners. Though little may be left of the former host of timbered fronts and gables that thronged the streets of our ancient towns and cities, the wooden building is still a significant feature in many parts of the English countryside. It must not be relegated exclusively to folk-museums as a picturesque survival, but brought into first-class condition as a traditional form endowed with new life.

[7]

Roofs

In some respects the roof is the most important part of a building: merely as a protective structure a supported roof, without walls, can be of use, as in the case of a Dutch barn. Regarded as a protection for the substructure, as well as for the inhabitants or contents of a building, the roof plays a vital part. It is the means of excluding the elements, and particularly rainwater, and so preserving the materials of which the lower parts of the structure are composed. In Britain, where the climate necessitates pitched roofs, disposing swiftly of rain and snow, roofs have also a great visual significance, and are a major constituent of aesthetic effect. The profile of the ridge of a roof against the sky is, in particular, one of the most significant features of a building, and one which demands the highest care in works of conservation.

We use the word roof in two different senses: of the actual supporting structure which spans the building and holds up the coating of protective material; and of that material itself, be it tiles, slates, lead, thatch, or some other substance. A number of crucial problems in conservation are concerned with the roof in both senses, and these problems comprise the structural, the aesthetic, the economic, and mere matters of convenience. As has already been mentioned in passing, the wooden roof structure has always been normal in Britain in one form or another. Roof-trusses of different types are used indifferently to span religious and domestic buildings and vary from the simply utilitarian to highly complex structures designed and executed in exquisite style. On the one hand are the traditional forms handed down from one generation of carpenters to another, while on the other are inventions of great architects devised to solve problems of unusual difficulty. Nothing really comparable to the variety and richness of development of the English timber roof occurs elsewhere. It is for this reason one of the special objects of care in conservation, quite apart from its functional importance.

The lavish use of sound material in former times is well exemplified in most roofs, and it is unusual to find that the strength of members is inadequate. Reinforcement is seldom needed, unless the original substance has been very greatly reduced by some form of decay, as was that of the giant timbers of Westminster Hall roof by the ravages of the Death Watch Beetle. In that case modern steel trusses now do the work, but such a transference is rare. Much more common is excessive thrust from early roofs, where the design of the truss did not prevent the feet from spreading apart. Tie-beams or tie-rods may be inserted, though it may be a counsel of perfection to avoid such visible changes in appearance. To restrain thrusts and support walls or frames already pushed out of the vertical, without recourse to ties of some sort, is inevitably a difficult and also a costly problem. The saving effected by the use of ties is on balance usually justified.

Like other timberwork, roof structures require ventilation to prevent the onset of decay, and this must be kept in mind when any form of insulating membrane is inserted. All too often the aim of reducing heating costs by preventing loss of warmth is pursued blindly; the roof structure is overheated and all through ventilation is stopped, with disastrous results. Much of the very great expenditure on repairs to church roofs, in particular, within the past generation has been directly due to this change for the worse in conditions of maintenance. Probably no better example could be given of the ultimate losses caused by supposed economy in carrying out alterations without an architect's advice. There is no reason why the layman – subjected to pressure from advertising in favour of insulation systems – should realise the harmful indirect results of his expenditure. It cannot be too strongly emphasized that every alteration is a potential source of danger to an old building, and that to weigh up the possible advantages and disadvantages of a particular change calls for considerable knowledge and skill.

Another instance of catastrophic losses, both of old work and of money values, is the short-sighted tendency to replace the lead covering of old roofs with some material far cheaper in first cost. It is thought that the balance produced by the sale of the old lead for melting at a high price is clear profit, available to pay for the work done. This is far from being the case, for several reasons, but principally because lead is much the most durable of all roofing materials normally available. As laid on our older buildings it has lasted in sound condition for two, three or more centuries without relaying. When it does have to be taken up it can be melted and re-cast, with the addition of only a small proportion of new lead, to last as long again; and this process can be, and has been, indefinitely repeated. Apart from the percentage loss due to oxidation and re-casting, lead is more or less indestructible, and represents a capital asset of the utmost value in the relative scale of building materials. To dispose of it is to invite bankruptcy at an early date.

While on the subject of the relative economy of roofings, it may be as well to mention the approximate 'life' to be expected of the chief permanent materials. Lead may last for 200 years without relaying, copper for 150; the only other metal of suitable character and quality, pure aluminium, has a much shorter life, of about 50 years. Clay tiles and pantiles will last 150 years, sometimes longer, this depending mainly on the laths and method of nailing; slates, including the various kinds of stone 'tile' will need to be taken up and relaid about once a century. No other materials in general use have long life, and thatch in particular needs to be laid at least once in every generation, and demands fairly frequent repair. For the conservator the choice of material tends to be limited by what exists on the building, but if change is considered for economic or other reasons, it is clearly desirable that it should be limited to one of the substances with high durability, and that cheap but short-lived roofings should be avoided. Relating prime cost to the expectation of life, clay tiles are by far the most economical roof.

Since the roof is the front line of defence of the whole building, preliminary survey should begin with the condition of roofs, outside and inside. Where the slopes of a pitched roof can be seen from the ground or surrounding buildings, or (for example, in the case of a church) from the top of a tower or other vantage point in the building itself, a searching examination from a distance, with the help of binoculars, may save much time. The points where tiles or slates are out of position or missing can easily be noted, together with sags indicating possible weaknesses in the supporting trusses beneath.

Metallic roofs and gutters should be inspected after rain, so that pools of standing water in gutters may draw attention to insufficient falls, or subsidence that has altered the direction of flow. Close-up inspection of a lead roof after rain will show small areas of damp around minute pinhole punctures. These can be marked carefully for reference.

Each material suffers from characteristic defects, and these should be noted methodically during such a survey. The general examination from a distance will indicate areas of damage or suspicion of defects, to be investigated in detail, first from the outside, then by entering the roof-space. Where the roof has already been insulated at some previous restoration, or plastered internally at the underside of the rafters, it may be that no information will be found internally except areas of stain showing where leaks have occurred. The common defects of tiles are crumbling of the surface, cracking across, and the dropping out of the old fashioned wooden tile-pins; slates tend to pull away from their nails as well as to crack. The main trouble with lead is its tendency to 'creep' down the slope of a pitched roof because of its great weight, but it can be eaten away by chemical oxidation if it is laid on oak boards not fully seasoned, or is brought into contact with creosote or certain other products. With all roofing laid on laths or battens the strength of these is one point of risk, but a more serious one is the tendency to 'nail-sickness', when the battens – themselves still sound – draw away from the rusted heads of the nails which secured them, or the rusty nails simply snap.

Upon the results of the survey, as with all conservation works, the repairs of the roof must depend. The structure of the roof trusses, purlins and common rafters will first have to be dealt with if defects are found, before relaying of the outer covering can begin. It is especially when such major constructional work is being done that gutters may well be re-formed in concrete and other improvements made. The special chemical dangers to lead have to be borne in mind when such alterations are carried out, interposing a layer of felt, or painting the under surface of the lead with bituminous paint in order to prevent chemical reaction with the concrete, with creosoted boards (which should preferably be removed altogether) or with oak timber. In the case of any alteration to the total weight of material carried by the roof it is vital to ensure that the factor of safety of the trusses and members is not unduly lessened.

There are many points of continuous maintenance also which need to be remembered when roofs are altered or repaired. There must be reasonably easy access to all flat roofs, and some access to lofts and spaces beneath pitched roofs. As has been said, adequate ventilation of roof timbers is a most important precaution, and it is generally undesirable to place a new insulating layer immediately beneath the outer covering. The best place is above the ceilings of the topmost floor, but beneath the boarding (if any) of the loft. The loft or roof-space is then completely free for ventilation and actually adds to the degree of insulation provided for the lower parts of the building. This practice cannot generally be applied to open roofs such as those of halls and churches, for there is commonly no intervening space except the depth of the common rafters. In such cases the plaster, unless it is of historic importance, should be renewed, introducing a layer of insulating material, or substituting an insulating board for the plaster. Free ventilation between the common rafters is thus left as it was before.

Roofs require inspection more frequently than other parts of build-ings, and ideally there should be a check at least once every year in the autumn, when gutters are cleared of fallen leaves. If great trees stand close above roofing it is commonly necessary to clear the leaves twice: in the first instance removing the heavy weight of the main fall of leaves; and secondly clearing up all that remains at the onset of winter. All forms of gutters and downpipes easily become choked, and it is essential that they should be clear at all times of heavy rain or snowfall. The heads of downpipes and gullies must always be covered with grilles of appropriate type, removable for inspection and clear-ance, but proof against any large leaves or other refuse being swept into the pipes. Blockage in the pipe is likely to freeze in winter, the whole pipe fills up and freezes, and the column of ice by its natural expansion cracks the pipe. The leakage from such cracked downpipes, perhaps slight but continued over a long period, forms a major risk to the building.

Although this book is not a technical manual, it may be useful to insert here a few general comments on what should and should not be done to roofs of different kinds. The roofs of masonry buildings are commonly of slates or stone tiles, or alternatively of lead. Stone tiles are much heavier than slates or clay tiles and the trusses and battens must be of stouter construction to bear them. An important point is to avoid pointing up of stone or slate roofs from outside with mortar;

only the heads of the 'tiles' should be bedded in mortar. Cheap repairs, however temporary, by means of external pointing are a serious source of danger to the roof. The nails or pins used for hanging should always be of non-rusting composition, and softwood employed needs to be treated against the attacks of rot or woodworm. Creosote must not be used where there is any contact with lead. If sections of modern concrete roofing are introduced, they should be covered with asphalte, insulated from the concrete with felt or paper to permit of movement in response to changes of temperature. Asphalte should never be laid on boards.

Lead roofs last for so long that it is worth taking very great pains over every detail of their construction. Certain rules should be adhered to, notably that new lead, or old lead re-used, must always be in cast sheets, not milled, and the weight of lead for roofing should not be reduced below the old average of 8 lb. per square foot on flat roofs that are walked upon; for steeply pitched roofs 7 lb. lead is adequate. Gutters and special works need a heavier weight such as 10 lb. to the square foot. The repair of holes and the jointing of sheets must always be done by 'lead-burning' (i.e. welding), never by the use of solder. Old ornaments in cast lead, names and dates, should always be preserved, if necessary being cut out of old sheets and 'burnt' into the new sheets when relaid. A new date and inscription should always be included.

To minimize the 'creep' of lead on steep pitches the sheets should be laid obliquely instead of straight down the slope; at ridges the sheets should be laid right across the ridge, hanging down each side to be sustained by their own balance. The horizontal joints between adjacent sheets should be staggered in the same way as bond in masonry or brickwork. On flats and slight pitches the head of every sheet should be turned down over the nails to prevent water being drawn upwards by capillary attraction. The downward fall of a lead 'flat' ought never to be less than two inches in ten feet (1 in 60). Where the sheets of lead are joined together, edge to edge, it is common to wrap the lead around wooden cylinders called rolls; these should never be used, as the enclosed wood is highly liable to rot and infestation by beetle. The lead sheets should be rolled upon each other to form 'hollow rolls' on flats and low pitches that may be walked over; on steeper roofs the folds are flat, standing up vertically as 'welts'. In work of the best quality the lead is held by leaden or copper tabs, known as 'tingles', well nailed down or on slopes screwed down. It is important to make sure that no nailheads appear through the boarding on which lead is to be laid, to avoid punctures being formed from below. New boarding should be of the tongued and grooved type, fixed with secret nailing. The nails in old boarding must be well punched down before laying starts.

Roofs of old stone tiles call for highly expert treatment in relaying, especially where dormer windows or other features occur. The treatment around such features, and of ridges, hips and valleys differed markedly according to the traditions of various regions where local stone tiles were quarried and used: for example, the Horsham slabs on the Sussex and Surrey borders, the Stonesfield slates of the Cotswolds, and the Collyweston stone roofs near Stamford. The correct old methods used in the district should be adhered to with care, or the character and feeling of the roofs will be much changed and appear foreign. In general the laying of all the forms of stone tiles starts at the eaves with very large and heavy slabs, while the courses diminish upwards towards the ridge. The stone tiles are trimmed to size to range evenly, course by course, before laying, and every size conforms to a traditional name corresponding to a size in inches marked on the tiler's rule. The names differ, district by district, but commonly include the Cussem or Skussum at the eaves, about 24 inches from the bottom edge to the hole for nailing, Whippets, Muffities or Movedays, Long Cocks, Short Cocks and the All-up or Farewell course, only about six inches deep, beneath the stone ridge-piece.

Over the greater part of England some form of clay tiling is the principal roof covering, and as we have seen it is probably the most economical roof when its lasting qualities have been weighed up with its first cost. For many centuries, certainly from the twelfth to the nineteenth, plain tiles have been made to one standard size with only very slight variations. In this respect they differ from bricks, which have always varied a great deal. It is probable that the uniformity of tiles was due to a sudden nation-wide development of the tiled roof as a replacement for inflammable thatch. From the London Assize of Building of 1189 we know that this great fashion for tile roofs was the direct result of the Great Fire of London in the first year of King Stephen, 1136. Other great fires at York and several other cities took place in 1137 and subsequent years, and it is likely that a relatively small number of tilemakers and tilers moved across the country laying the new fireproof roofs in place of thatch. The tiles, of all dates, are so similar to one another that they provide little or no criterion of date for the archaeologist. In the end the normal size was fixed by Statute of 17 Edward IV, 1477, which laid down a length of $10\frac{1}{2}$ inches, a width of $6\frac{1}{4}$, and a thickness of $\frac{5}{8}$ inch. Since then only one important change has been introduced: the provision of turned-down nibs at the top end of the tile to avoid the necessity for using wooden pins to hang the tiles on the laths. The mediaeval and later tiles of the original pattern had a pair of holes punched in the top edge while the clay was wet; these were seldom clearly punched right through, but when burnt had a crumbling edge or crust into which a square riven pin of wood could be twisted so as to hold by friction. Starting at the verge of the roof, the first tile in each course had to be hung on two pins, but it was a common device to save time and tilepins, to use only a single pin in the angle away from the previous tile. Hence most old tiles depend upon a single pin, and upon the permanence of its frictional hold in the tile. It is an odd commentary upon proverbial usage that 'a square peg in a round hole' should be essential to satisfactory tiling on the old plan.

In any old roof a few tiles, of inferior clay or not well burnt, will have disintegrated or be crumbling away; but the majority are generally perfectly sound and fit for re-use, even after many centuries. The rent oak laths on which they were hung are also quite frequently sound, unless they have been kept damp by mistaken repairs in mortar or by steady leakage from cracks and holes left unrepaired. As has been mentioned, it is the iron nails used to fasten the laths to the slope of the common rafters that are the most frequent source of trouble; and once slip has begun the only course is to strip all the tiles from the roof and re-batten with copper or rustless composition nails. The new battens should preferably be of oak, and rent like the old ones, but if softwood is used it must be treated before use with a suitable preservative. Though most of the old tiles can be re-used, some new ones will be needed to make good breakages, and this is where difficulties begin. It is not nowadays easy to find tiles that really match the colour or texture of the old hand-made tile of local clay. It is a vitally important rule that machine-made tiles must *never* be used in relaying old roofs, or on roofs to new additions which adjoin old roofs of plain tiles. Nor is it advisable to choose tiles of a dark colour in an attempt to match the patina on the old tiles. A sand-faced red or red-brown tile, though it may look too brilliant for a year or two, will weather and collect lichens and patina. If only a small proportion of new tiles is needed, they should be scattered at random through the old tiles. When it is necessary to lay a substantial area with new tiles it is best to choose one of the least conspicuous slopes, keeping all the re-used old tiles together on those parts of the roof that are most seen. The same principle applies with old stone tiles and with slates.

Aesthetic qualities of another kind are a preoccupation of the conservator when roofs have to be completely relaid. Old ridges are seldom level, and may be hog-backed, rising up in the middle, or sometimes cock up towards the gable ends or the peak above a hip. It is advisable to take lateral photographs before the roof is stripped, so that the old profile may be approximately kept. In the course of the work it should be studied to find out exactly what methods contributed to the effect produced. Deliberate tilting of tiles at the eaves and ridge, the sweeping of valleys, and the finish against walls and chimney stacks are all subject to local variations which need careful study to reproduce accurately. In most traditional work oversailing courses were specially built into walls and stacks to prevent rain from driving under the edge of the tiles laid up to the face of the walling. To carry the water away from the wall the surface of the tiles was slightly tilted up as it approached the projection under which it was to be tucked. It has been all too common in modern repairs to cut away the course of brick or stone and to substitute the modern lead flashing, which shows up against the wall or stack. The appropriate protection is given by concealed lead 'soakers' worked into the joints, or a chase purposely cut, beneath the oversailing course.

While it is important to avoid mechanical regularity, freakish picturesqueness must be avoided also, and a great deal of fancy tiling, supposed to be old-world, must be eschewed. Ancient ridge-tiles, with thumb-worked cresting, and commonly glazed, are always to be preserved and re-used, but machine-made or stamped crestings of the nineteenth century should be discarded and plain ridge-tiles used instead. In the case of pantiled roofs, often of hipped form, ridge-tiles have to be used to cover the hips as well as horizontally on the ridge, and the local usage should be carefully studied before work begins. Pantiles, in some districts an important traditional covering, are an excellent roof for rather low pitches, but it is difficult to match the curve of the old tiles. If many have to be replaced it is usually necessary to keep the old and the new to different slopes or sections of roof.

Two more materials used for the covering of traditional buildings remain to be mentioned: shingles, and thatch. The use of wooden shingles, generally of oak, is almost limited to church spires and porches, as well as lich-gates. In both cases replacement involves the finding of one of the few remaining experts, able to produce a sound job in a craft that at present only just survives. Since modern shingles of cedar are used in new work to a slight extent, shingling presents a less difficult problem than thatching. In many parts of the country thatching, which needs to be relaid, or at the least very considerably repaired, at short intervals of from fifteen to thirty years, can only be done by the bringing of an expert thatcher from a distance. This is certainly worth doing in any area where all or most of the houses of a group are thatched; but it is questionable whether isolated examples of thatch ought not now to be converted to plain tiles. It is no longer a cheap, but a disproportionately dear form of roofing, and one suffering from notorious disadvantages. All the same, it has a quiet beauty of its own and it is to be hoped that a few centres of this re-markable anachronism will be maintained.

So far we have been considering the various types of outer covering and the importance of the roof as the building's main protection from the weather. These aspects are very largely constructional, though the visual significance of the roof in profile has also been mentioned. A different series of problems is raised by the repair of open timber roofs in churches, halls and other works of architectural importance. These are complex structures framed out of wood to support the outer cover-ing, but intended to form a major factor in the aesthetic impact of the interior which they cover. Whereas the outer coverings must in-evitably be removed and relaid several, or many, times during the life of the building, these structures – with their enrichments, carvings and paintings – are integral parts of a work of art. Unless in case of absolute necessity they should not be taken down or unjointed; it is a stringent rule that roof trusses and all major structural timberwork should be repaired in position. This is an empirical rule formed as a result of trial-and-error: for it has been found by experience that removal leads in practice to over-restoration. Original work which could be given adequate strength by slight patching is destroyed as unfit to put back, and its place taken by a modern replica.

It is in this field that the more general rule, of doing as little as possible, has special validity. What has to be done must be executed with loving care, and this demands employment of highly experienced craftsmen. Perhaps more than in any other aspect of conservation, the pride in craftsmanship of the well trained man shows in repairs to first-class carpentry and joinery. The matching of suitable pieces of timber, the splicing in of patches with scrupulous accuracy, and the finish harmonizing with the original work, can be brought to a high pitch. Insensitive repair and renewal offend against the sympathetic nature of the material itself. Providing the work is done in the right way it can be displayed by brightening the illumination rather than concealed in a limbo of upper gloom.

The exquisite detail and carving of very many open roofs, with their show of badges and heraldry, indicate that they were meant to be seen. Yet frequently the timber has been stained, or simply left dark and dirty, perhaps as the legacy of a period of lighting by gas. It is particularly necessary that the surface of the wood should be left clean, and not artificially darkened in tone; and the decoration of roofs, as of ceilings, normally should be light enough to reflect the natural or artificial illumination onto the details. The improvement, not merely in the appearance of the roof itself, but of the whole interior, which results from cleaning and redecorating, is remarkable. Instead of considering the view with lowered head, depressed by a weight of gloom above, the visitor's eye is caught up to the glowing roof which shows its beauties of pattern, its structural ingenuity, and the historical allusions of its heraldry or inscriptions.

Although the roof was originally only one of many parts, which included also a brilliant array of stained glass, wall-paintings or panelling, and features such as screens in churches and great fireplaces in domestic halls, it is now commonly the only one to survive in relatively unaltered condition. It is, therefore, very often the roof which alone provides the conservator with an opportunity to give back to an interior at least a part of the aesthetic interest which it has lost. Besides its structural importance the roof is, then, very often the principal display-piece of the interior of a building. In both capacities it deserves special attention. By means of diligence in its conservative restoration and cleaning, and the exercise of taste in its redecoration, it can become the crowning glory of house or church.

[8]

Decorations, Fittings and Furniture

Stress has been laid on the importance of redecoration. While the continued existence of the building, in a physical sense, depends upon structural maintenance and repair, its aesthetic impact is largely conditioned by its surface appearance. This too, so far as such temporary surfaces as coats of paint are concerned, may have great significance in prolonging the life of the house or church. It is not merely that these surfaces are protective, but that when there is any question of deciding the value of a building – for example, weighed against the positive advantages of demolition and redevelopment – the merely surface appearance has a psychological impact for better or worse. Beauty may be in the eye of the beholder, but there are right and wrong ways of catching and holding the eye.

The decorative treatments involved in the upkeep of old buildings are of many kinds, but all can be ranged in one or the other of two classes. Firstly there are the remains of original decorative treatment, or of subsequent treatments that form an acceptable part of the historical development. With these may be included legitimate restoration and renewal of such original forms of decoration, required for the physical preservation of the structure, or for its adequate display as a work of architectural design, or both together. Secondly there are all sorts of modern additions which may necessarily be involved in the process of adapting an old building to fresh uses and in making extensions which themselves require a form of decoration suitable both to their own design and to that of the earlier building they adjoin.

The maintenance of all traces of original works of decoration, so far as is consistent with the care of the structure, is a most vital part of work in this field. The qualification just made is an important one, for it may often be impracticable to retain the fragmentary remains of an external treatment no longer capable of fulfilling its structural purpose, that of protecting the building. Examples of this include not only various forms of pigmentation, but such external coatings as the different sorts of thin rendering and plasterwork which may, at fairly long intervals, have to be renewed. It is poor economy to subject the structure to risk directly occasioned by faulty treatments, and it has to be faced that the surfaces – at any rate the external ones – of all buildings in our climate are inevitably good copies rather than originals, and that exposure is constantly altering the intentions of the original and subsequent designers. Where the actual surfaces of natural materials are seen: the hewn face of stones or timbers, the texture of a hard brick as it came from the kiln, the alteration and renewal of surface may be very slow indeed. On the other hand, paintwork on wooden doors and window frames facing rain and wind ought to be renewed, and not merely touched up, every few years. An interval of five years was commonly regarded as a suitable one, and one building might therefore change its outward appearance ten or a dozen times in one man's life.

The relative frequency of changes of this kind means that the observer of an historical building never does see what was visible when it was first built: the degree of change of course varies. This is not necessarily a bad thing, for some variety lends spice and there is here a valid analogy with nature conservancy. A tree which has significance as a single specimen or as part of an avenue or clump, and which may be the subject of a preservation order, changes its leaves every year. From the time the sapling reached a size where its effect in the landscape could be appreciated, the tree has not been the same identical tree year by year: every leaf of which its total appearance was composed has been different. Yet the overall impression of the tree, throughout the years of its maturity, remains fundamentally the same. So far, then, as the works of man are natural or an extension of man's own nature, they may be expected to partake of this characteristic seasonal and repetitive renewal. The essential thing for our purpose is that the appearance, in spite of minor changes and renewed surfaces, shall not misrepresent the basic qualities of the work as it was meant to be.

In practice there must be caution in introducing changes in treatment, and this applies more particularly when one building is part of a group. External appearance is then largely a problem in good manners, and variations of treatment from the norm of the group have to be kept within limits. This might even preclude, in some cases, a return to an original treatment which had been brought to light in the course of archaeological investigation. An outstanding example of this concerns the painting and gilding of statuary and carving on the outside of ancient buildings. It was long a matter of dispute how far classical and mediaeval sculptors intended their works to appear as pure form, modulated by light and shade, and how far they meant them to be coloured. The intensive studies of antiquaries and archaeologists during the past century, in Britain as well as in the countries of the Mediterranean and Near East (to say nothing of the Orient), have proved beyond any doubt that all works of so-called plastic art from the earliest times down to the Renaissance around 1500 were meant to be given a full and sometimes even brilliant colouring.

Even after the Renaissance, chronologically speaking, a great many works of sculpture, including tombs and monuments in churches, were intended to be fully coloured. In all cases, therefore, except those where there is clear evidence that no pigment was originally laid on, or that colour was contrary to the intention of the sculptor, a polychrome treatment has to be assumed. There is not a scrap of historical justification for most of the long-winded arguments advanced against colouring as such. What may be admitted is that, in certain circumstances, it may be a wise precaution to avoid or to limit colour rather than to go beyond the historical evidence or to clash violently with the surroundings. In other words, such precautions may well be temporary rather than a precedent for all future treatment. In course of time, with further evidence or with a change of fashion towards complete acceptance of polychrome treatment as correct, it may be possible and desirable to return as closely as possible to the colour schemes intended when the building was new.

The psychological resistance of an informed public to the recolouring of old sculpture is mainly based upon a misconception of the historical facts; but this is not its only basis. There is also a perfectly justified objection to a good deal of modern colouring, in that it has been done crudely, with unsuitable pigments, or in ways that have no warrant in the facts produced by observation or research. Where colouring has long ago disappeared completely, or so extensively that no sense of polychromy remains, great caution is called for before fresh pigment is laid on, and in any case the work must be of the very highest quality. This applies both to the physical make-up of the pigments and media employed as well as to the artists, who must have had adequate experience of such work. Paints that are chemically suitable, and compatible with one another; media adequate to give an economically long life, resistant both to weather and to any other adverse conditions; and any necessary preliminaries such as priming or waterproofing, are all essential. Finally there is the problem of aesthetic taste in the choice of the precise hues, for it is rare to find sufficient traces of the original colour to yield more than the outline of a colour-scheme. Generally what is found is faded or stained so that even after careful cleaning it falls short of giving a clear indication which can be directly matched. Some degree of imagination is therefore usually demanded of the conservator or his expert adviser.

Bearing in mind the repetitive character of external colour decoration, a sound policy can be based upon reintroduction of colour by degrees. A light use of points of colour, such as the correct tinctures of heraldry, or the picking out of enrichments with gold leaf, can be a legitimate treatment for the time being, without in any way prejudicing the later reintroduction of a full colour-scheme when, in the course of years, the irrational objection to colouring has subsided. This applies also, though with less force, to internal work, where only the harmony of the building itself and not the outward effect on a group of buildings or on the eye of the public is involved. What has to be studied in every case is the effect upon the building itself, and how far the finer points of its design or qualities of its structure can be emphasized and brought out by colourwork. Not only must the scheme avoid undue assertiveness; it must not, on the other hand, be weak, washy or 'pastel-shady', for there is clear historical evidence that the original intention was always definite and determined, though not stridently assertive.

Passing in review the various forms of surface decoration commonly found, apart from painting, the first in importance consists of rendering and plasterwork. Comments on external roughcast and plaster have already been made (above, p. 120 ff.), but it needs to be stressed that all external work should be based upon lime roughcast or lime-plaster. Internal decorative plasterwork in relief, protected from damp and weather, may be of plaster-of-paris. A helpful factor, which applies to almost all relief decoration, is that it was produced by casting from moulds, the pattern being formed of a number of repeats. So long as one repeat of each part of the original can be saved, it is possible to reconstruct the whole of the decoration of a façade or of a ceiling, for example, by taking moulds from the original sections, and making new repeats. Though this process, and that of refixing the casts in position, calls for highly skilled work, it is just as legitimate in restoration as it was in forming the original.

It has already been said (above, p. 118) that exposed surfaces of timber should be left unstained, and normally untreated. Internally wooden panelling, screenwork and woodcarvings need careful cleaning from time to time, and in modern conditions of heating are likely to require periodical waxing with beeswax to maintain them in sound condition. Oil should never be applied to old woodwork, but oil paint may be used where it is necessary to touch up or renew early colour decoration in that medium. Thorough investigation must first establish the original medium employed, which may often have been tempera rather than oil, though mediaeval documents are explicit that oil was extensively used in painting. Gilding must always be with real gold leaf properly laid on, never with any form of gold paint. Where heraldry calls for silver leaf it is advisable to use either 'white gold', if obtainable, or aluminium leaf, as real silver leaf rapidly turns black, even if varnished or lacquered with supposedly protective coatings.

Walls and ceilings make an obvious impact, and schemes of decoration tend to concentrate upon suitable treatments for them. The floor is quite commonly overlooked, and insufficient care is given to replacement or repair with suitable materials. In this country flooring is commonly of wood, often of elm boarding, but in mediaeval buildings may be of stone flags, or of tiles or brick. Although a change in the kind of flooring may sometimes be an unavoidable part of conversion to new use, it is extremely undesirable, and maintenance of the original floor is strongly to be recommended. This may sometimes mean relaying, for instance with completely new stone flags when the originals have become so worn as to be dangerous, but it is always desirable to keep as much of the old as possible. In stone floors the flags may often be reversed, relaying with the worn side downwards; and it may be possible to relay only those parts which have been seriously worn, while retaining original flooring in those areas little used. If general relaying has to be done in any case, it is usually sound practice to put down a concrete bed and to incorporate damp-proofing. In church floors great care should be taken to make sure that no legible grave-slabs are thrown out; at times a still legible inscription is found underneath an old ledger reversed at some earlier relaying of the floor.

Monumental brasses in church floors present a special problem. They should normally be left flat, and maintained in their old position. As they are easily damaged they need to be protected with suitable carpets of a close weave. Coarse matting is not suitable as it allows grit to pass through and scratch the brass as the matting is walked over. Loose brasses should be refixed at the earliest possible opportunity, but if they prove to be palimpsest – that is, to have remains of an earlier engraving on the under side – steps should be taken to make both faces accessible and to ensure that the face formerly hidden is duly recorded. If brasses are already on walls, fixed vertically, they should not be removed to the floor and, in general, it is unwise to move any form of memorial from its old position, as this often has historical significance. Wills frequently request burial close to some pre-existing grave, and much information, including the former dedications of altars and chapels, may hinge upon correct identification.

While tombs and monuments are under discussion, the problem of churchyards must be mentioned, as in a sense a wider aspect of decorative harmony (see also above, p. 71 ff.). The destruction of old grave-stones in recent years has had a most depressing effect upon many country churchyards, and amounts to a campaign of vandalism under the pretext of economy. It is argued that the high cost of labour does not now permit of proper upkeep unless the whole area is levelled and swept clear of stones, so that it may be mown by machine as a lawn. There is little or no objection to levelling, and kerbs are in any case virtually always work of a bad modern period. To the removal of mounds and kerbs alone it might be the part of an enlightened conservator to agree, in order that the graveyard as a whole might benefit from greater care. Unfortunately, few parishes are content with this, and the setting of very many fine churches has been irreparably ruined, the historic scene being converted into an insipid minor park. Although a proportion of the later nineteenth- and twentieth-century stones and monuments have little aesthetic value, many of the older memorials are themselves works of art of high importance, and a

26. REDECORATION *Winchester College*: the wooden vaulting of the Chapel, designed about 1390 by Hugh Herland, repainted according to the original colour-scheme after repair in 1952.

27, 28. WINCHESTER COLLEGE *Decayed Timber*, removed from the Chapel vaulting, and the new insertion being carved by the late Edwin Laverty in 1952.

29. *Original Oak Doors* in Middle Gate, being cleaned by Reginald Laverty in 1957 preparatory to beeswaxing.

30, 31, 32. RENEWAL OF LEADWORK *London*: St. Paul's
Cathedral. Re-fixing of re-cast lead sheets at the base of the dome and
(*lower*) preparation of sand-bed on casting table.

Messrs. Norman & Underwood.

33. *Elham Church* (*Kent*): the spire, showing herring-bone work carried out in re-cast lead sheets.

RELAYING OF ROOFS
34, 35. *Winchester College:* relaying and (*below*) re-dressing of stone
tiles in Chamber Court in 1957.

36, 37. The reconstruction of roofs and gutters of the Warden's Lodgings in 1954; (*below*) new timber spliced into a hip rafter.

38, 39, 40. REHABILITATION *Winchester College*: School, after complete renewal of rusted 19th-century windows; (*lower, left*) repainting of heraldic plasterwork, and (*right*) a stone swag during cleaning, 1961.

treasury of fine lettering. In particular those earlier than 1840 contain unique information not in the parish registers and not on public record anywhere else. Even after the beginning of civil registration of births, marriages and deaths in 1837, the evidence of descent is often slight without the support given by family inscriptions.

Returning to floors – which for our purpose can be taken to include external pathways – it is important that each material should be repaired with stone, brick or tile of the same kind. Bricks of rather small size, sometimes Dutch clinkers imported as ballast, laid on edge, provide an excellent floor of considerable beauty. It is sometimes possible to obtain small quantities of such bricks from demolished buildings or from floors taken up, and these are generally a better match for old work than any modern bricks obtainable. Floors of mediaeval tiles, both plain and patterned, still exist in considerable numbers, and require great care. Even in fragmentary condition they may display the evidence of original pattern-laying, with strips of tiles contained between borders and parallel bands of narrow tiles which separate the 'carpets' of different patterns. Careful relaying on a bed of lime mortar is the appropriate treatment, after all cracked tiles have been repaired by using cement as an adhesive – all drips and smears of the cement must be cleaned off before drying.

Where the amount of breakage in an old tile floor is such that it cannot be relaid as a whole, it may be pieced out with plain quarry tiles of the same size. An alternative worth considering, if only a few tiles, of outstanding historic value, are left, is to record them fully in position, and then move them to a part of the floor where they will be unlikely to suffer much wear and tear. In this case, of course, the tiles that are left will in effect form simply a museum specimen, as a relic of the old floor. Modern encaustic tiles of the sort widely used in church restorations of the Gothic Revival should never be mixed with genuine ancient tiles, but modern hand-made tiles can be specially produced in the mediaeval manner to match the original patterns. This is, however, now an extremely costly operation.

Upper floors are generally of wooden boards, those of dates earlier than the eighteenth century being commonly of elm or other hardwood. These early floor-boards are wide planks, and cannot be patched with narrow softwood boards without serious incongruity. Like other ancient woodwork, flooring deserves the most cautious and meticulous patching, and should never be replaced as a whole unless it has reached a dangerous state that is beyond repair. Where the supporting construction has allowed the floor to sag or slope up and down, it is often a good plan to bring it up to level in the course of relaying. Where it is not possible to raise the lower ends of sloping joists, they can be made up with tapered firring pieces of the same width and laid on their upper surfaces. These are screwed down to the joists, and the old boards relaid on their upper surface which has been brought into one level plane. Work of this kind should only be undertaken where the inclination is severe and causes inconvenience.

The stripping of internal wall plaster from churches and from major domestic buildings of mediaeval date was formerly common, on the mistaken supposition that plastering was not intended as the original finish. It was in fact normal, and should be put back on all walls improperly stripped in this way. Suitably whitened or colour-washed it will considerably lighten the tone of the walls and thus improve illumination. In churches the plaster should be thin and should follow the irregularities of the walling without any attempt being made to produce a flat surface. It should not, however, be made artificially rough as a measure of picturesque finish. Limewash, bound with linseed oil and with the addition of earth colours such as red ochre, is an appropriate finish for such plastering. It should always be made and applied very thinly: the correct consistency is that of skimmed milk, and this will imply that there should be at least three coats. Where stone quoins are exposed at window and door openings they should always be covered with at least one of the coats of limewash, to prevent a hard edge showing between plaster and masonry. The tone of limewash should never be cold; a warm tone is produced naturally by the use of some kinds of stone lime, but can also be imparted by the addition of an extremely small amount of ochre, umber or Venetian red.

Though there are important fragments of early wall-painting in many churches, and in a few secular buildings, what is left hardly ever constitutes a colour-scheme in itself. It is almost always inevitable that the sections of painting, when restored, should appear rather as stamps on the pages of an album. The page will be represented by the limewashed wall, within which the old painted scenes or figures will be well displayed. The cleaning, fixing and retouching of ancient wall-paintings is work for experts of long experience in appropriate techniques, and there is little point in laying down detailed rules. There is, however, one major point to mention: the serious damage done owing to mistaken advice in the past from chemical experts. Within the last hundred years there have been several successive methods of treatment, each of which has been fashionable for a time, and each later discredited. It must be stressed that the blame, so far as there is blame to be attached to anyone, lies with the scientists who acted as technical advisers, not with the artists who followed their advice. The reason for the ensuing trouble has been fundamentally the same in each case: a process has been invented and subjected to short-term tests; it has appeared to be satisfactory. Only in the course of years has disintegration or blistering of the surface, or fading of the colours, taken place, more or less in the same way as with each earlier and discarded process. As in the case of decay of masonry surfaces, much of the damage is due to sealing the surface of the wall, or the paintwork, so that it cannot 'breathe'. All methods involving a seal proof against damp and evaporation must be considered dangerous and probably disastrous.

From the treatment of walls it is a natural transition to that of windows, the eyes of the building. Externally, fenestration is one of the chief components of architectural design, and the shape of window openings and their proportion to each other and to the whole of a front or side wall are integral parts of the work. Any alteration to windows is liable to cause grave damage to the total effect. This applies not only to the overall window, but to the subdivisions of which it is composed. It has for many years been an object pursued by amenity societies to encourage the restoration of glazing-bars to sash-windows that have been reglazed as single sheets. Rightly so, for it is the subdivision of the sash or casement that relates the scale of the window to that of the individual stones or bricks of which the wall is built, or more particularly to the masonry quoins or brick dressings designed to emphasize the openings. The improvement in appearance produced by the insertion of glazing-bars is out of all proportion to the slight cost.

Windows include shop-windows, and these are too commonly an eyesore. The cutting away of the whole of the walling on ground floor level in order to insert great expanses of plate glass is a procedure which should be absolutely prohibited in conservation areas. Where this has been done it is desirable in the interest of the streetscape that restoration should be set in hand and carried on piecemeal as a condition of every new work of alteration or repair for which permission is granted. This is entirely a matter of aesthetic harmony, and of avoiding crude discordance. Even though the result may to the purist be a fake, it is legitimate as a means of healing the psychological disturbance caused, which may range from disquiet to serious shock. Similarly disproportioned and heavy fascia boards should not be countenanced. It does not follow that shop-windows cannot be allowed: from late Georgian times onwards there have been pleasing street fronts designed to incorporate shop windows, and work of this kind should be restored or reinstated where it is applicable. Modern windows should be of modest size, proportioned to the building, and if fascias are permitted they should be relatively light and their lettering well designed. In many cases it is possible to improve appearance a great deal merely by the removal of existing heavy fascias and the provision of new ones of appropriate design.

In the nature of things the comparatively slight construction of window frames and sashes or casements is likely to demand renewal more than once in the life of a building, and the new insertions have tended to be contemporary in design rather than copies of the original. So long as the proportions are still in keeping with the design of the walls in which they are placed, the new windows form an acceptable part of historical development. It is no longer possible to return to mediaeval openings, defended only by a metal grille or by hardwood mullions, closed by shutters or oiled canvas. The few such original windows which have survived intact through blocking may well be re-opened and glazed with a sheet of glass behind the mullions, but it would invite ridicule in a house still inhabited if all the later windows were removed and 'mediaeval' reconstructions put back in their original positions. Wherever examples of early glazing do survive they should be treasured and most carefully repaired, and where the glass is fixed in lead cames, either in diamond quarries or in rectangles, it may be well to glaze adjacent windows in the same way for the sake of aesthetic unity. In work whose period demands glazing of this sort, but no glass original survives, it is better to avoid the diamond quarry as smacking of old-world picturesqueness. In any case the scale and proportions of good old examples must be followed.

Glass itself, being easily broken, has suffered heavy losses, and this applies to plain window glass as well as to coloured and painted glass. Even single panes of crown glass in Georgian windows deserve care, and the flat appearance of modern sheet glass contrasts most unpleasantly with the brilliance given by the many reflections in old glazing. The preservation of even small fragments of early stained glass is even more important, and it is commonly overlooked that not only churches but civic and domestic buildings have or had windows of stained and coloured glass including designs of heraldry and symbolism. On occasion such glass, removed from the windows for which it was made, may be rediscovered in boxes, and it is then highly desirable that it should be reinstated. Loose fittings of any kind are liable to breakage and loss, and the choice is between reinstatement and gift or loan to a museum. Disposal, to a museum or otherwise, is to be considered a last resort, when neither reinstatement in an original position nor equivalent re-use is possible.

This is not the place to deal with the highly technical problems of cleaning and repair of ancient stained glass, but a few general principles or rules of thumb may be stated. So far as concerns church windows, wire guards should be avoided except in districts where vandalism is a serious risk; the guards quite seriously impede the passage of light, and disfigure the exterior. If guards are essential they must be of copper or other non-ferrous metal. Alloy bronzes such as delta-metal are also particularly to be recommended for all new fittings such as saddle-bars, though stainless steel is permissible and may be needed at times when exceptional strength is required. In making up windows where there are only fragmentary remains of the original glass, it is better not to incorporate new coloured glass except for simple borders or patterned quarries. The fragments may be well displayed in a background of clear glass of the type called 'antique'; the tinted glass known as 'cathedral' glass ought never to be used. Although small pieces of an early scheme of glazing, found in inaccessible and often invisible spandrels, may sometimes with advantage be brought down to form a patchwork centre of interest for a window, such pooling of fragments from more than one source is generally undesirable. If such mixing of glass from different sources is carried out it should be only after a very thorough record of the original positions has been made and, preferably, published in a relevant journal.

Architects and conservators are frequently placed in the position of advising on the retention or disposal of stained glass windows, and on the insertion of new fillings of coloured or painted glass. Great caution is required in both cases. It is true that much stained glass of crude colour and poor design was put into church windows during the Gothic Revival, between about 1845 and 1905, or some two generations in all. At times the glass, besides other dubious qualities, was extremely dark, so that the real qualities of the interior were obscured. In such instances there is often a strong case for removal, and the substitution of either clear glazing or new painted glass of better design and lighter tone. An outstanding example of such substitution is Glasgow Cathedral, where dark and inferior German glass of the nineteenth century has been extensively replaced by new stained glass within the past generation. In a few English churches foreign glass of mediaeval date, generally acquired as a result of the French Revolution, has been inserted, as in the Lady Chapel of Lichfield Cathedral. Such collecting, and the opportunities for it, are now mercifully rare, but the conservator should firmly discourage his client from acquiring glass for insertion from other, particularly foreign, sources, as it imparts a flavour of the museum. An exception may be made in favour of glass from neighbouring churches demolished or converted to secular uses, where glass and other fittings may well be kept in the church to which their former parishes have been joined.

There is an important matter of principle involved in this transfer of fittings, in any class of building, but particularly from one church to another. In all buildings the original fabric and fittings form together a single aesthetic whole; in buildings where there has been long historical development and renewal and substitution of fittings, these provide essential links in the story, and should not be dispersed. To this general position added force is given in the case of churches by the specifically religious or charitable intentions of individual donors. Without invoking rarefied ethical judgments, it is a sound principle of law on charitable trusts that there is a right of visitation inherent in the founder and his heirs or, in their default, the Crown, to prevent perverting of the charity; and the modern Charity Commissioners act on the principle that, where an original object has become obsolete, the charity should be applied to some purpose as closely as possible in accordance with the founder's intention. These principles have, in recent years, been flouted by many church authorities who have decided, *in anticipation of* the closure or ultimate redundancy of a church, to remove fittings such as pulpit, font, screens, bells, pews, and stained glass windows, to other churches. The practical effect of such action has been seriously to prejudice the actual future of the church involved. Very often churches of great historic value, with fittings of outstanding importance, would as complete entities be regarded as far too valuable to demolish. Once stripped of its fittings, the mere shell of the fabric may well be regarded as of relatively little importance.

It is true that the Church of England has its own system of Faculty Jurisdiction, under which all fittings brought into or taken out of a church are subject to strict regulation. In modern times this system has been improved by the setting up of the Diocesan Advisory Committees with legal status; but it must be remembered that their capacity is advisory only, and that they have no power actually to impose any given work or to prevent it. It appears to be a serious anachronism that the ancient parish churches, commonly the most important historic buildings in the parishes of the country, should be exempt from the general law on structures of architectural and historic importance. It may well be that there were legitimate fears, early in the present century, that Anglican churches might become unduly subject to the decrees of a lay bureaucracy. On the other hand, two generations have passed, during which the Established Church of Scotland has had the advantage of state maintenance and control of a number of its ancient fabrics, including Glasgow Cathedral and Dunfermline Abbey, and has had in practice no cause for complaint but much for thankfulness. It is to be hoped that something based upon the Scottish system may be applied to England and that Anglican ecclesiastical buildings in use will be subject to the same control, and the same financial and other benefits, as all others.

The conservation of old fittings, and the design of any new fittings that have to be introduced, call for the greatest care. This is true anywhere, but particularly of old churches, where new lamps, heating apparatus, loudspeakers and the like may introduce elements of incongruity or sheer ugliness. The mannered designs of eccentric artists and the mass-produced banality of firms of furnishers are alike unsuitable. But in seeking to limit the possibilities that arise for spoiling the appearance of a fine old building we have to beware of merely negative advice. This is the weakness, both of church advisory committees and of advisory panels appointed to consider the designs of new buildings submitted for planning permission. Simply to reject work that is aggressively bad sets no premium upon production of design of a better standard. In the last resort there is no substitute for the positive good taste of a patron – be he the owner of a private house or the parson of a church – who will choose his artist with discernment and make upon him such demands as are likely to bring out the best of which he is capable. The conservator's business is to make sure that all factors involved in the old building itself and in its existing fittings and furniture, shall be clearly recorded and presented.

In making a full survey of any building, there should be a complete schedule of all fittings of historic significance, and this should include also movable furniture in churches, civic buildings, or greater homes. It is highly desirable that the schedule should be fully illustrated with photographs, for piecemeal loss goes on continuously, and examination of quite recent photographs will often reveal damage to items which remain. The record should also be incorporated in some form of log-book, kept by the responsible owner or occupier, showing what works of repair and maintenance are done, with their dates. Not only major fittings, such as the Altar, Font and Pulpit in a church, or items of furniture like chests and panelling, but also all the lesser items should be noted. These include original hinges of different forms, latches, locks and keys, handles, knockers and other metalwork. There are also several kinds of highly specialized church fitting, notably Bells, Clocks, Organs, and Plate. It is an essential part of the conservator's work to do all he can to see that these valuable contents are not merely there, but are kept in working order: the bells rung, the clock keeping time, the organ tuned and playable, the plate used and, when not in use, in proper safe keeping.

In discussing memorials, mention has already been made of the special problem of churchyards, laying stress on their great importance as a decorative frame for the church. This principle applies also to gardens, which too are closely related to what has been said of tree planting in villages (above, p. 54). Both in town and country there is an appropriate relationship between house and garden, and while it is not the business of architect or conservator to dictate landscaping or horticultural method to his client, there are several ways in which his advice can be of direct value, both structurally and aesthetically. On the practical side advice can be given on plants which may damage the building (such as ivy) or which may unduly conceal its architectural features (Virginia creeper); or which when fully grown will darken its rooms (as cypress and many other conifers). Positively, certain other plants of light habit, fragrant foliage or sweetly perfumed blossom (rosemary, jasmine, roses) may be recommended as being outstandingly suitable for cultivation near to or against the walls or in other close relation to the building.

Turning to less ponderable factors, the whole relationship of the house to its immediate surroundings has to be considered. As an aesthetic problem this is no new thing, for it was recorded of a bishop of Le Mans in the middle of the twelfth century that he laid out a manor-house with a hall whose windows were of great beauty, and looked out upon a garden below, planted with many sorts of fruit trees, so that those leaning out of the hall windows might admire the beauty of the trees, and those in the garden could equally delight in the fair show of the windows above. In the fourteenth century many kinds of trees were well known to Chaucer, and the rosemary was introduced from the Continent to the royal gardens, later to become the favourite English evergreen trained on walls, until more exotic introductions took its place. Such interrelationships between the home, and for that matter the church, and its garden or yard, demand time to grow, like the turf of English lawns. In the first place they have to be laid out as a result of careful and devoted thought, based upon knowledge and experience. When this work has been well done, and fate has favoured growth, the result is to give to the building, with all its fittings and its decorative elements, the finest possible setting.

Part three

===

CONTINUING
CONSERVATION

[9]

The Past

It was observed in the introduction to this book that in Britain the movement of public opinion towards conservation had been slow, in spite of early activity by antiquaries and collectors. As was remarked, the development of modern care for ancient monuments and old buildings has come from the nations of the continent of Europe. This development has been in two main phases: the first, aiming at protection of prehistoric antiquities and other material of very early date, was pioneered by Gustavus Adolphus of Sweden in the first half of the seventeenth century; the second, concerned with buildings of mediaeval date and, as time went on, more modern structures that had become old enough to be 'historic', almost exclusively depended upon the enterprise of German princes. It is striking that, although the rise of German nationalism provoked by the Napoleonic invasions was largely responsible for forming a wide public opinion on the subject, this had been anticipated by the rulers of individual states in the pre-nationalistic period. Though it may well have been Schinkel's appeal of 1815 that was the pull on the trigger, the well-aimed shot that has re-echoed ever since was really fired by the Grand-Duke of Hesse. Active conservation promoted by governments and applying to the whole field of buildings and associated works of art, along with field-antiquities, began on 22 January 1818.

The recognized subject of Conservation is then quite a new one; but the actual fact is obviously very much older. So far as this country is concerned, the British attitude stems far more from an earlier insular tradition of empirical approach than from adoption of formalized continental attitudes during the last hundred years. The practical and firmly realistic approach was forced upon this country in earlier times because of its relative poverty. Mediaeval England (and mediaeval Scotland, Wales and Ireland were still worse off) was a poor country by European standards, in spite of the overwhelming commercial importance of London. Even a metropolitan position in northern trade did not provide enough surplus wealth for sweeping destruction and rebuilding on the scale practised in Italy or France. Most of the great English churches took several centuries to reach approximate completion, and even single phases of the work might be interrupted by shortage of funds. The strategic aims of Edward I did, it is true, involve the construction of a chain of great castles, but even these were not fully completed. The England of his grandson, Edward III, even before it was struck by the catastrophe of the Black Death, was under-capitalized. The king's difficulties with foreign bankers, and his reluctant rejection of the Imperial Crown, indicate the cramping effect of inadequate finances. It was quite largely similar difficulties over money that led Richard II, by inclination a great spender upon architecture and art, into a conflict with the mercantile interest of London that lost him vital support in the revolution of 1399.

It was not until the concentration of a great mass of monastic wealth by Henry VIII after the Dissolution, that even the Crown was able to build lavishly, and the English age of large-scale domestic construction did not set in until the second half of the sixteenth century. For some three centuries, from about 1600 to 1900, there was indeed a great surplus spent by the monied classes of England upon great mansions and their surrounding grounds. In many cases these mansions involved the destruction of some older house and the period may be regarded as led by anti-conservationists, keen to leave their new mintmark on the country. Yet there was always an undercurrent of protest against the abandonment of the past, even when there were the strongest reasons for a policy of the clean sheet. While short-term economic reasons account for the fact that little of the new town-plans for London took effect after the Fire of 1666, it was a strong sentiment for conservation that forced Wren to restore the Gothic tower of St Mary Aldermary and to design in Gothic style at St Dunstan in the East. There were protests raised at the destruction of mediaeval Woodstock to provide a site for Blenheim.

At all times there was at least a minority that expressed its attachment to the old and its doubt of the need, let alone the desirability, for such radical renewal involving rejection of all past tradition. Although the Gothic style had gone out of Court favour by 1550, the steady persistence of the Gothic Survival for more than two hundred years proves the point. The last significant work in English Gothic was the rebuilt nave of St Margaret's, King's Lynn, begun in 1742; but by 1735 the Scottish poet Samuel Boyse had put in a serious plea for conservation of ancient buildings for the benefit of posterity. Thus there co-existed, even in the heyday of the early Georgian period, an awakened concern for memorials of the past and the importance of continuity of tradition; and the concept of consonance in architectural design, rather than the crashing discord of mediaeval and revived classical in juxtaposition.

These two factors in opinion can be traced back to a very much earlier date, both on the Continent and in Britain. We know that the monks of St Denis resisted Suger's projected rebuilding in the twelfth century, just as those of Canterbury were to protest their attachment to their old choir against the complete rebuilding insisted upon by William of Sens. There are many survivals of early work in our cathedrals and churches, sufficient to show that even uniformity might be upset in order to preserve something of a more ancient fabric. The substantial sections of the twelfth-century aisleless nave of Ripon Minster, enough to show the design, and standing alongside the new arcades of the early 1500s, are a notable demonstration of this. The other factor of Consonance with ancient work of a superseded style is also shown by the instances of a Gothic use of semicircular arches alongside those of Norman work. An outstanding example is the outer arch of the fourteenth-century porch at Malmesbury, echoing the great inner portal of Romanesque carved orders, deliberately preserved as an historic monument of two centuries before. The whole of the Norman south porch was in fact enclosed within an outer cloak of Decorated Gothic, brilliantly associating the Romanesque main entrance with the new south aisle and clerestory economically based on the older structure.

The principle of consonance with an earlier Gothic design was also applied at a number of great churches where progress was very slow. As is well known, the naves of Beverley Minster and of Westminster Abbey are noteworthy instances of this usage. At Beverley the outlines of the internal design are carefully maintained but externally the change of date is made clear by the insertion of traceried windows instead of the lancets of the earlier work at the east end. The effect of the whole is extremely harmonious, and it is evident that this was no accident. Similarly at Westminster, though a very long interval separated the interruption of works under Henry III from their continuation in the time of Richard II by the royal architect Henry Yeveley, there is no break in the composition in spite of completely changed detail. These instances are sufficiently striking to disprove the theory that in former times artists were concerned exclusively with the contemporary and paid no respect whatever to antiquity or to earlier design. In the ancient usage of the German masons there was even an explicit injunction demanding respect for the design and work of the dead: 'When a Master dies and another comes, he shall not remove the first master's masonry already set, nor throw away the unset but hewn stones, that the Master whose work has been interrupted by death may not be put to shame.'

As a mere matter of practical maintenance a great deal of minor repair was done during the Middle Ages, as surviving account rolls and books bear witness. It is likely that the relatively low cost of labour in that period even encouraged the carrying out of steady repairs and that at any rate the greater buildings were then better looked after than they have been since. In some cases permanent appointments were made of master masons to have general charge of upkeep, as John de Weldon had in 1308, over the whole fabric of Old St Paul's. Weldon was already architect in charge of the New Work – the eastern Lady Chapel – and was in addition to take full responsibility for maintenance, reporting defects to the Keeper of the Fabric and, in case of neglect, direct to the Bishop of London or in his absence to the Chapter. It is worth noticing, in passing, that St Paul's, London, was unusual among mediaeval cathedrals in that primary charge of the fabric lay with the bishop, and not with the chapter in the manner usual at most English cathedrals, both secular and monastic. Weldon was to put aside all work except his charge of the Lady Chapel in order to watch for defects in the church and tower. In addition to yearly allowances he was to be paid 6*d*. a day when at work on the church or absent on the church's business, but 8*d*. a day if working on the tower, presumably by way of danger money. These sums have to be multiplied by something like 200 to give a rough idea of present-day value – thus £5 a day normally, and one-third more for dangerous and arduous work.

Among the jobs regularly done, as shown by mediaeval accounts, were periodical recasting and relaying of lead on the roofs, at the greater churches involving the appointment of a permanent plumber to maintain a rota of repairs; and the whitewashing, or 'redding' with red ochre, of internal walls. In 1440–42 there was such a general lime-washing of the whole of the inside of Norwich Cathedral. Not only white- or colour-washing, but simple cleaning was done, as in 1432–3 when a man was paid by the bursars of Winchester College for 13 days spent on cleaning the windows and buttresses on the north side of the Chapel. The replacing of pinnacles blown down in storms, and regular patching of walls were more or less regular occupations. Quite apart from the abundant documentary evidence, close examination of a mediaeval wall, stone by stone, will produce evidence of patching with stone from various sources over the centuries. There was, however, comparatively little done between the reign of Henry VIII and the later seventeenth century. The Dissolutions of the monasteries and of chantries, colleges and hospitals, with their background of theological fanaticism directed against superstitious uses, undoubtedly did much to discourage the continuous maintenance which had been normal. It was only after more than a hundred years of religious and civil strife, in the course of the repairs done to the churches damaged in the Civil War, that works of conservation began again in a notable way.

The outlook of the Middle Ages had been well-informed and thoroughly practical. In the light of modern diatribes against the policy of H.M. Office of Works in removing ivy from ruins, it is curious to find that the removal of ivy was one of the recurrent works on which money was spent by the Crown and other building owners. In 1407 two iron hammers, evidently special claw-hammers, were made for pulling out ivy from the walls of Launceston Castle in Cornwall; and in 1471 the bishop of Winchester paid labourers for several weeks' work in plucking, drawing out and destroying ivies, bushes and harmful herbs growing in great quantity on the walls of Wolvesey Palace. The bishop's architectural advisers of five centuries ago had no doubt that the growth of herbs was harmful to the masonry of the walls, and their findings are supported not only by common sense but by modern scientific investigation. Elsewhere the building masters had to devise means to deal with serious structural defects and deformation. The story of the tornado of 1091 in Flanders, which dislodged a timber belfry from its seating on the top of a tower at Oudenbourg, is well known. The townsmen summoned craftsmen and promised rewards for the replacement of the leaning steeple, but by the time they had by the end of a week erected their cranes and slung ropes, a stroke of lightning miraculously restored the belfry to its original position.

There is a record in the accounts of works done for Henry III at Windsor Castle of timber props supplied to Simon, the master carpenter, for restoring to the vertical the side of the king's wardrobe which was leaning outwards. This is a remarkable coincidence, for at exactly this time Villard de Honnecourt set down in his famous album a diagram showing how, by means of jointed props and levers, a timber-framed house might be pushed back plumb 'however heavy it may be.' In course of time the same principle emerged once more and was applied on a vastly larger scale to the north transept gable of Beverley Minster by the carpenter William Thornton in 1716–20. This is not merely of interest as showing the continuous development of building and conservation techniques, but as a demonstration of the advanced state of methods of construction and repair as far back as the first half of the thirteenth century. 'There is nothing new under the sun' and it is as well to beware of looking back with any condescension at either the eighteenth or the thirteenth century.

A highly sophisticated skill was shown in several major works of structural conservation carried out in the Middle Ages. One of the most important was the reconstruction of the circular chapter-house at Worcester Cathedral. Originally built in Norman style quite early in the twelfth century, without adequate buttresses, the wall was pushed outwards by the vault until, at the end of the fourteenth century, it was almost in a state of collapse. A major work of consolidation and repair was undertaken in 1386 under the master mason John Clyve, and stone was quarried. In the next year scaffolds were erected and actual work begun; by 1392 the leaded glazing of the windows was being fixed and the job must have been complete. Willis, who made a detailed examination of the chapter-house, in 1863 published an account expressing his admiration for the mediaeval restoration. 'The whole principle of the repair (i.e. that of 1386–92) consisted in remedying the defective mechanical construction of the Norman masons . . . Nothing more was done than was absolutely necessary to introduce their improved constructive system, and thus to ensure the stability of the edifice. The Norman work was in the interior respected as far as possible, the central pillar and the semicircular ribs, with all the central portion of the vault, was carefully retained.'

It is possibly significant that John Clyve, before becoming master mason at Worcester, had worked for the Crown at Windsor Castle. He would thus have had the chance to learn the special techniques which the architects of the king's works had developed in the course of the two hundred and fifty years since the opening of the Gothic period. In England this central tradition of architectural and building skills held sway over a great part of the country, in the same way that throughout the German-speaking territories of the Holy Roman Empire there was an acceptance of the leadership of the master of the Strasbourg Cathedral lodge. It is, incidentally, a curious sidelight on the internationalism of mediaeval art that it was 'after the English fashion' of free jurisdiction that the Strasbourg lodge was formally acknowledged in 1275. Hitherto the earliest evidence in England for this exemption of the masons from the ordinary courts comes from a generation later, when Master Walter of Hereford was allowed his claim to hold a free court over his subordinates on the works of Caernarvon Castle. The extent to which building craftsmen had to move from place to place necessarily freed them from the usual mediaeval rule of regular attendance at local courts, and there is thus nothing surprising in their independence. What was also implied was an opportunity for rapid spread of special skills across the country. These skills included methods of repair and conservation, as well as of design and construction, and we can regard Simon the carpenter and John Clyve as in the direct line of ancestry behind the experts of the modern Office of Works.

Another outstanding example of conservation was the work done at Fountains Abbey in 1483 for Abbot John Darnton. The east wall of the eastern Chapel of the Nine Altars, though a Gothic work, had buttresses insufficient for the thrust of the vault. Darnton had the vaults removed and substituted wooden roofs, but also added to the depth of the two central buttresses to support the lean that had already developed, and repaired gaps and fissures in the masonry. A carved angel, carrying a scroll bearing the date, and another carving with a rebus representing the abbot's name, provide satisfactory evidence for the chronology and the responsibility. That methods of repair occupied a place in formal technical education, though not directly evidenced in this country, is proved by the German records. In 1514 there were six masterworks which had to be successfully undertaken by a journeyman mason who wished to pass as master. The fifth of these was the repair of walls at an angle, where the foundations had become damaged. Where an actual example of such damage was not available for repair, the candidate was to carry out his proposals by means of a model. This tells us something of the experimental use of models before the end of the Middle Ages, a subject of which only a little is known from other sources.

Closely related to the structural problems of conservation were those which arose when major additions were made to mediaeval buildings, such as the tall central towers or spires at Canterbury, Gloucester and Salisbury. Contrary to general supposition, it was not normally the great additional tonnage of materials that constituted the main danger in such cases. As has been mentioned, the factor of safety in Gothic buildings was usually enormous as regarded crushing strength. The new risks came largely from lateral sway under wind-pressure and greater thrusts which added to the possibility of deflection or side-slip in one or more of the crossing piers. It is probable that structural models were used to some extent, at any rate from the fourteenth century on, to find solutions by experiment to these problems. Certainly the outstanding architects from the early fourteenth to the mid-sixteenth century were well aware of the nature of the problem and discovered highly sophisticated solutions. These were of three main kinds, of which the first consisted of inserted buttressing masses, largely concealed by 'stitching' into the existing fabric. Flying buttresses in appearance or in character were in this way used at Salisbury by Richard Farleigh and at Gloucester. Secondly there was inserted metallic reinforcement, imbedded as a tension-ring in the original masonry of the Salisbury tower and rediscovered by the late W. A. Forsyth in 1945. Thirdly there were inserted screens of pierced masonry, appearing as decorative grilles, but in fact stiffeners or distance-pieces preventing deflection of the main piers. It is an odd commentary on 'progress' that, while the architects in charge of cathedrals from the fourteenth to the sixteenth century were well aware of the structural effect of such strainer-arches and screens, it was the arbitrary and ignorant removal of the Arundel screen at Chichester in 1859 that led directly to the collapse of the spire a year later.

Another aspect of modern conservation practice was fore-shadowed after the Dissolution of the monasteries in the structural conversions effected in a number of them. Among the most remarkable of these conversions was that done at Titchfield Abbey in Hampshire. The aisleless nave of the Premonstratensian church survives because it was converted into a front range with a main gatehouse inserted centrally. The conversion was designed by Thomas Berty, already architect to Winchester Cathedral, in 1538, for the grantee Thomas Wriothesley, afterwards Earl of Southampton. Surviving letters show, however, that Berty recommended the demolition of the tower on the ground 'that smoke shall not be avoyded by the chymneys of your chieffe lodgings if the steple stand.' This probably implies that there had been a desire to keep the steeple as a landmark or as a thing of beauty, incorporated in the new Place House.

There was undoubtedly a substantial amount of public opinion in favour of conservation at that time. There were divided views on the religious and political issues involved in the Dissolution, but it is evident that there was a decided anxiety to preserve the great monastic churches as far as possible. Henry VIII himself drew up an elaborate plan for converting a large number into new secular cathedrals. Financial stringency caused this plan to be whittled down to six, of which five survive today: Bristol, Chester, Gloucester, Peterborough and Westminster Abbey. Oseney Abbey by Oxford, the sixth, was soon superseded and the see transferred to the former monastic church of St Frideswide's, already accidentally saved from demolition by the downfall of Wolsey. This may not seem a large total, though in quality it includes some of the finest church art of the whole mediaeval period. Several other great churches of overwhelming aesthetic importance were saved by the readiness of the local townsfolk to raise funds for their purchase from the Crown as parish churches. Thus the spirit of conservation succeeded in keeping for us St Albans, Southwark (both now cathedrals), Christchurch, Hexham, Malvern, Romsey, Selby, Sherborne and Tewkesbury, as well as substantial parts of a good many more, both great and small.

The monastic dissolution of 1536–40 under Henry VIII tends to overshadow the subsequent abolition of chantries, many colleges, a great number of hospitals, and a sprinkling of parish churches. The buildings affected were usually on a smaller scale than those of the abbeys converted, or considered for conversion, to cathedrals. In many cases their quality as works of art is very high, and this was certainly a main reason for the efforts, successful in many instances, to preserve them. By one means or another, complete or almost complete churches in this category survived at Arundel, Chester St John, Darlington, Howden, Manchester (now a cathedral), Ottery St Mary, St Cross by Winchester, Warwick St Mary and Wimborne. Among parish churches there were saved in the city of York alone by private or parochial activity, four out of nineteen condemned as redundant in the years 1548–1586. Three of these four churches: St Cuthbert, St Helen Stonegate and St Martin Micklegate, were of a higher rank of architectural importance than the rest, so far as can be deduced from documentary and archaeological evidence. The fourth to survive, St Andrew, did not return to use as a parish church, and its small-scale shell is mainly of interest as a sample of the type of church then lost.

It is evident that during the Middle Ages, and also during the turmoil of change which succeeded, there were powerful instincts in favour of conservation at work. Even after making allowances for the restraining effects of thrift in a relatively poor country, a good deal more than a line of least resistance was involved. This becomes still more marked if we turn to consider another aspect of conservation, once more in our own times an acute question of the moment. This is the maintenance of civic amenity in the streetscape. Inured as we are now to the long period that may, and often does, elapse between demolition of old housing and the completion of new development, with the resultant gap-toothed impression, it comes as a surprise that both royal and municipal authority was active in earlier times to prevent this state of affairs. The documents on the subject in York are particularly numerous: as early as 1298 Edward I gave order that ruinous houses in Bootham – the main road towards Scotland – were to be repaired. This was at the time that the king had moved his whole court to York, which became a base for his Scottish campaign. The context is thus obviously that such unsightly dereliction could not be endured close to a royal residence. But when the subject recurs, after the depression of the fifteenth century, it was the corporation of the city itself that began to take strong measures. From 1524 onwards there were repeated proclamations that 'no man shall take downe no houses that stands towards the common strete withoute lycence of the Maier', and it was expressly stated that the reason for the orders was that the appearance created by open sites 'defaseth the Citie.' On not less than fourteen occasions in just over sixty years such proclamations were made or other action taken, fines sometimes being imposed. In 1555 the city instructed its Members of Parliament to take action on the subject, and in 1562 an order was made for dilapidated houses to be sold to those who would maintain them adequately, the occupiers to have the first option. One William Gylmyn was imprisoned in 1568 for refusing to restore his house, which he had unroofed. On 28 July 1587 the Lord Mayor gave order in the Queen's name that rebuilding must take place on decayed sites, of which a blacklist of twenty-seven was annexed.

What is of particular interest in this long record of York's concern for amenity in the sixteenth century is that it began well before the period of the Dissolution and Reformation, and continued through four reigns until the country had become resettled in peace and prosperity after a whole generation spent under Elizabeth. This was neither a flash-in-the-pan, nor the sudden response to an exceptional state of emergency. It was recognized that there was a recurrent threat to the appearance and dignity of the city's streets and that, like any other breach of law and order, this must be set to rights. It is of interest to consider this attitude as a study in the psychology of leading citizens: they were not primarily concerned with pure aesthetic values, but felt that such defacement of their city derogated from its dignity. Even if York was not prosperous, it must at least put on a good face to the world. Outward show and seemliness were felt to be positive assets and the appearance of dereliction likely to lead to the reality. There is a telling lesson in this for the twentieth century, in spite of much lip-service to the same ideals.

The leadership in sixteenth-century conservation certainly came from above. Even though Henry VIII's great plan for new cathedrals was thwarted, it was his own and it did have some effect. His daughter Elizabeth in 1560 issued a proclamation against 'defacing monuments of antiquity set up in the Churches' and ordered that offenders were to set up again what they had broken since the first year of her reign (1558). This order specifically refers to the breaking of images in windows, and thus went beyond the preservation of the evidence of inscriptions as family memorials. Religious fanaticism was still active, and a fresh proclamation on the subject had to be made ten years later, and was apparently effective. From the sovereign an attitude of respect for antiquity sent its ray downwards to a circle of highly literate antiquaries who, later in the century and the reign, actually formed a Society holding regular meetings. Though the aims of such men were more concerned with the study of ancient relics than with conservation as we understand it, their writings leave no doubt that they did appreciate the wealth of historic buildings in town and countryside. William Camden in his great descriptive book *Britannia*, published in Latin in 1586, shows a positive sympathy for outstanding works of architecture, including those of the Gothic period. Seeing that he was a noted classical scholar and, at the relevant period of his career second master (later headmaster) of Westminster School, this attitude goes a long way to refute the legend of universal contempt for mediaeval art from the Renaissance to the Gothic Revival. Such contempt there was, but it was far from general.

With the seventeenth century conservation reached a low ebb, and the physical maintenance of St Paul's Cathedral, for example, took the form of massive cloaking with classical details by Inigo Jones, completely out of keeping with the magnificent design of the old work. The Fire of 1666 brought old and new together to an irreparable state, and so to a clean sweep and Wren's new St Paul's, crowning the city's forest of new steeples. Not a great deal of London was left to conserve, and as matters fell out there is room for congratulation on two facts: that the ancient street-plan was preserved; and that Wren was so far influenced by Gothic precedent as to design a great array of towers, spires and steeples, piercing the skies in most unclassical verticality. In the country at large there was a continuing trickle of Gothic survival, marked by such distinguished churches as Groombridge (1623), St John's at Leeds (1632), Staunton Harold (1653), Compton Wynyates (1663), and at Oxford the whole of Wadham College, built in 1610–13. To these must be added the very fine Chapel of Lincoln's Inn, designed in 1618 by – of all people – Inigo Jones himself.

If we put the end of Gothic, as a ruling style, at 1540, it nevertheless remains true that it was not dislodged from the minds and affections of many patrons of art for well over a century. Even designers of the first rank had to maintain their ability to satisfy a demand for several generations. The same phenomenon occurred elsewhere, notably in Germany, where it could be said that genuine Gothic never did become altogether extinguished. There can be no accident in this:

Germany's leading position in modern conservation from the later eighteenth century onwards was directly due to its attachment to a living style and deprecation of the merely imitative psychology of the Renaissance. Although Germany was, in the end, infected by the similar imitative qualities of the Gothic Revival, it was by no means to the same degree as in this country. We have suffered, from Jacobean times onwards, to an increasing extent from coming to our traditional buildings as it were *from outside*. The viewpoint of the Renaissance, exalting the Vitruvian and Palladian Orders as the sole criteria of taste, made the bitter conflict symbolized by the Gothic Revival inevitable. For a long time the fact that the battle of the styles in Victorian England was only a mask drawn over the real problem passed unnoticed. The true crisis was the disappearance of the craftsman-architect with technical training and the installation of the genteel professional man at the drawing board.

The whole of the embittered discussion over the applicability of the term 'architect' to the designers of the Middle Ages was a phenomenon possible only in Britain, where the lines of hard-and-fast class distinctions, not between nobility and commoners, but between the genteel professions on the one hand and mere manual operatives and retail tradesmen on the other, formed an impassable frontier. The practice of architecture became progressively divorced from real life, with disastrous results. Effective progress in constructive matters passed, during the Victorian age, almost entirely into the hands of the engineers. Engineering, because it was essential to the forward march of industry, on which the profits of the period were based, enjoyed a happy exemption from the general rule. It was possible for an engineer both to have his cake and eat it, to train in the shops, mix with riveters and boilermakers, and yet sit above the salt and take a truly honoured place in society. In this respect it was the engineer who became the inheritor of the great tradition of development in inventive construction which had been handed down by the mediaeval masters. In Germany a fundamentally different outlook was shown by the survival of the word *Baumeister*, literally 'building-master', as the normal equivalent for our term Architect to the present day.

Before England slipped into this regrettable dichotomy, from which we are now only slowly and fitfully emerging, there had been a remarkable episode: the career of Sir Christopher Wren. Wren was not in any ordinary sense of the word either a building-master or an architect, but a gentleman of enquiring mind who was one of the greatest scientists of his time. Much to our purpose, he was not simply a theoretician, but an intensely practical man and a first-class observer. Coming of a clerical and episcopal family, Wren was called in to exercise his universal knowledge on old churches manifestly reaching a dangerous condition. To a series of happy accidents we owe the beginnings of Conservation as a subject adequately considered and approached. For it is Wren's three reports on great mediaeval structures: Old St Paul's before the Fire, 1666; Salisbury Cathedral, 1668; and Westminster Abbey, 1713, that inaugurate a new epoch with a flourish as of trumpets. Nor did Wren confine himself to sound and clearly expressed reports based on first-hand observation. The Fire made it necessary to clear the site and rebuild St Paul's to a fresh design; but it is to Wren's enlightened works of physical conservation, well designed and well applied under his direction, that we owe the survival of two of our greatest mediaeval monuments. Furthermore, there can be no doubt that repair and maintenance of old buildings benefited indirectly over a wide field from the example of Wren's reports and the work he had done.

The link between antiquarian studies and conservation of the fabrics themselves remained informal, but played a highly significant part in developments during the eighteenth century. Out of the Elizabethan, Jacobean and Carolean cultivation of antiquities there arose a more firmly co-ordinated outlook on old buildings. To the mainly documentary and historical *Monasticon* of Roger Dodsworth and Sir William Dugdale, published in 1655–73, there succeeded in 1727–30 *A Survey of the Cathedrals* by Browne Willis. Serious monographs on individual cathedrals and other great buildings, descriptive as well as historical, led up to another landmark, a very detailed account of Salisbury Cathedral published in 1753 by the Surveyor to the fabric, Francis Price. The study of both design and construction of Gothic buildings had begun in earnest, and before the close of the eighteenth century had led up to the publication of the first series of large-scale details, plans and drawings. It was recognized that thorough record of the work that existed was a necessary companion to architectural study and to maintenance and repair of the works themselves. In this field of early, and irreplaceable, record honourable mention must be made of Joseph Halfpenny (1748–1811), the York housepainter, clerk of works, draughtsman and engraver, whose *Gothic Ornaments in the*

Cathedral Church of York (1795) inaugurated a new era of accurate representation.

Meanwhile the Society of Antiquaries of London, which had obtained its Royal Charter in 1751, took the initiative in making and publishing adequate records of English monuments fit to take their place beside those of Classical antiquities abroad that had already been published by British travellers and artists. John Carter, draughtsman to the Society (of exhibited antiquities) since 1784, was in 1790 set to survey the ancient Palace of Westminster, and later a number of the cathedrals. Carter also published in his own name a large folio of details as *Ancient Architecture of England* (1795), forerunner of the many collections of engravings of Norman and Gothic buildings which were to herald the Gothic Revival in architectural design of new works. A generation or more was to elapse, however, before the collections of details became in any sense didactic exemplars or copy-books for designers. Carter and his successors, who worked very largely under the aegis of the indefatigable John Britton, were concerned to make simply a clear and precise record of the old work that existed, to preserve its form from destruction in the spirit of archaeological scholarship. It is interesting to speculate on the possible debt owed in this field by modern antiquarian studies to the continuous tradition of English common law, conveyed through cross-fertilization by the many legal antiquaries. The preservation of legal records, from the thirteenth century, had taken a leading position in work on Archives, the documentary counterpart to structural conservation. As far back as 1292 a dictum which had far wider application had been expressed in the words: 'You can do nothing beyond the record which is your warranty', and it was at the same period that Edward I had appointed the first Master of the Rolls, responsible for the permanent custody of all the records of the royal chancery.

Alongside its work on behalf of adequate recording of architecture, the Society of Antiquaries had begun to take a stand for the proper conservation of ancient buildings. Serious and constructive criticism of unsuitable restoration was voiced at meetings of the Society, with special reference to the drastic methods employed by James Wyatt at Salisbury from 1780 and at Durham in 1795. Wyatt had influential supporters, and though blackballed when first proposed for the fellowship of the Society in 1797, he was subsequently elected. The objection to his candidature was firmly based upon the principles of true conservation and, even though defeated in this campaign reflected honour on John Carter, who had raised the question of the vandalism committed at Durham, upon Richard Gough, Director of the Society, who resigned his office and his Fellowship in protest, and upon Sir Henry Englefield, who in 1811 was to become President. The whole question of Conservation had been placed on the map for the first time in this country, never again to be overlooked.

After the opening of the nineteenth century it became clear that the study of ancient buildings, along with that of almost every other subject conceivable, was to become popular. The wide sale of works such as those edited by Britton on topography and on architecture prepared the way for the foundation of open societies devoted to objects of every kind. The earlier societies, such as the Royal Society and the Society of Antiquaries, were 'closed', in the sense that their membership was conferred only upon those in some way distinguished. This distinction in fact had a largely social basis, but did represent a theoretical ideal of academic scholarship actually represented in practice. The closed bodies were, as they still are, essentially meant for specialists. There was also a need for organizations to which anybody of general education and with interest in or devotion towards some particular subject or cause, might belong. A considerable element of this kind of appeal to the general public had been present in earlier bodies such as the Dublin Society, founded in 1731 and the Society of Arts, founded in London in 1754. These early and general societies existed primarily for the encouragement of the useful arts and sciences, but these could be made to cover almost any subject. It was not, of course, possible to devote much time to the less obviously useful subjects, and though these and other bodies of wide scope performed, and still perform, a valuable service in many fields, they left an opening for the formation of more specialized associations.

The period during which most of the relevant bodies were formed covered the half-century from 1820 to 1870, from the death of George III to the Elementary Education Act. Some of the earliest were local, as the Leeds Philosophical and Literary Society founded in 1820, or regional, as the Yorkshire Philosophical Society of 1822. The arts, sciences, history and antiquities all tended to be catered for, by specialized sections of the membership. Such diverse interests commonly found themselves uneasy bedfellows, and antiquarian studies called forth a whole range of societies, both national and regional, the latter usually on a county basis. In some cases the connection with science remained, and in 1836 the Warwickshire Archaeological and Natural History Society set a pattern followed by several which have survived to the present day. It was in that same year that the Royal Institute of British Architects was founded as a professional body, though for many years it devoted much energy to the history of architecture. The first of the local Architectural societies, non-professional but open to the general public, were formed within the next few years, starting with the Oxford Architectural Society in 1839 and by 1850 comprising a dozen scattered over most of the country.

During the same period the Archaeological Societies were being launched, county by county. In a few cases (e.g. Somerset, Wiltshire, Hampshire) the link with Natural History was maintained; several were joint Architectural and Archaeological Societies (Buckinghamshire, Chester, Leicestershire, Liverpool, St Albans and Sheffield). On the whole the two subjects remained distinct, but it was unusual for the same county to have both an Architectural and an Archaeological Society. Though with varying emphasis, societies of both types concerned themselves with conservation. The rules of an Architectural society commonly described its objects as 'the study of ecclesiastical architecture, antiquities and design, the restoration of mutilated architectural remains, and to improve, as far as may be, the character of ecclesiastical edifices to be erected in future.' Besides the study of all subjects comprehended as Archaeology, and the encouragement of excavations and recording of antiquities, it was common for Archaeological societies to 'oppose and prevent, as far as may be practicable, any injuries with which Monuments of every description may, from time to time, be threatened; and to collect accurate drawings, plans and descriptions thereof.'

By about 1870 virtually every part of the country had been covered by one or more societies, and it might have been expected that the extensive and enlightened memberships would have made it practically impossible for widespread vandalism to occur. Perhaps an even stronger potential guarantee might have been seen in the foundation, in 1843, of a national body open to all interested persons, the British Archaeological Association. This was intended to provide, under the leadership of experts, a rallying-point for all who were seriously concerned about the past in any of its aspects. Not merely concern for monuments, but active protest against demolitions, formed a noteworthy part of the association's work from the start. Regrettably, personal quarrels tore the organization apart within its first year, and the dissident party formed the Archaeological Institute of Great Britain and Ireland in 1844. What for very many years amounted to civil war between antiquaries ensued. The rights and wrongs of the case are not now relevant, but the sad results of this unfortunate precedent for dissension are still with us. At the same time bitter controversy accompanied by theological fanaticism bedevilled the liturgical aspects of the Anglican church and its fittings. The quiet and even quietistic laissez-faire of England's long pudding-time was over : churches which, even if inadequately maintained, were still unspoiled gems of ancient art, became the objects of lavish expenditure. The aim, laudable enough, was the beautification of the House of God; the result was all too often the terse entry, in guide-books of a later day, 'over-restored.'

As seldom before or since, zeal outran discretion. The passionate addiction to the 'restoration' of churches, as a moral and religious duty, almost became an article of faith. The Gothic style, as reconstructed on paper by patient research, uninformed by any proper technical understanding, became a shibboleth and was itself maintained by a series of heresy-hunts. In the end a surface imitation of the Decorated Style was canonized orthodoxy. Late Gothic, the Perpendicular and Tudor styles were decried as debased and degenerate; magnificent windows of the fourteenth, fifteenth and sixteenth centuries were torn out, and imaginary reconstructions of earlier and 'purer' style put in their places. Scores, possibly hundreds, of parish churches were so altered as to be to all intents and purposes unrecognizable, even when the 'before' and 'after' photographs are set side by side. When E. S. Prior in 1899 was writing the preface for his great book, *A History of Gothic Art in England*, he had to state that his survey had 'brought him face to face with the obliterations of this national and local history in our art that have come from the methods of the Gothic Revival during the last sixty years.' It had become necessary in almost every case to search for records made before restoration in order to discover evidence of true forms.

The indictment is a terrible one, and even allowing for some exaggeration the fact remains that the pretence of reviving Gothic and restoring churches as living places of worship was actually more destructive of genuine mediaeval art than Reformation, Renaissance

and Civil Wars put together. With few exceptions, the ruins that
either Thomas or Oliver Cromwell knocked about remain valid as
evidence, so far as they survive in fragmentary condition. The dreadful aspect of what happened to most of the cathedrals and to many
hundreds of the parish churches – as well as to many of the surviving
domestic buildings – was that the wells of truth were poisoned. In all
too many cases it is now impossible to be sure of the original details;
even the general composition, when checked against old photographs,
prints and drawings, has been falsified, sometimes grossly. We may
well ask: how was it possible that this should happen in a civilized
country, already alerted to the dangers of demolition and over-
restoration, and abounding in well-informed societies both nationally
and locally. This is indeed a hard question to answer.

Undoubtedly the greatest blame falls upon those who pressed for
lavish expenditure on churches as a visible sign of repentance for past
neglect of religion. The climate of opinion and the earnest frenzy of
the apostles of Faith got completely out of hand for a whole generation: the thirty years from 1847 when George Gilbert Scott was given
charge of the restoration of Ely Cathedral, until 1877 when he completed that of Exeter. The architectural blame was not, of course,
entirely Scott's. As we have seen, even G. E. Street, well aware of the
right course, could fall into the same trap. Yet it was Scott who, filled
with daemonic energy, got the lion's share of the restoring business.
The now stale little joke, that on reaching a remote railway station he
telegraphed to his office: Why am I here? tells a tragic tale of overwork. It was a sheer impossibility that one man, however gifted – and
Scott was not only a gifted but a great man – could fittingly control the
hundreds of separate jobs that made up his working career. Though
we must not accept the exaggerated view of the opposition: that
mediaeval architects were in charge of only one job at a time, it remains true that the highly specialized demands of conservation work
are incompatible with the hurly-burly of a giant architectural practice.
All but the smallest works require a very great deal of personal care
and attention from the man in charge. Such care was evidently impossible for Scott, who averaged about 25 different jobs every year for the
last thirty years of his career.

A great deal can be said in Scott's defence, and most of it was said
at length by Scott himself in his *Recollections*, published soon after his
death. An extremely fair and balanced summary has been given by

Mr Martin Shaw Briggs in *Goths and Vandals* and it is unneccesary to repeat the facts here. What must be said is that Scott did on many occasions resist vandalistic proposals, sometimes successfully; that he saved the wonderful chapter-house at Westminster; and that his restoration at St Albans was infinitely better than the horrors later perpetrated by Lord Grimthorpe when left to himself. In the last months of Scott's life he was not only being attacked as a vandal by William Morris and W. J. Loftie, but in the opposite direction by Grimthorpe for being too conservative in his work at St Albans. Already ill with chronic overwork, Scott was hounded to death by the opposing extremists of both parties, and it is impossible not to feel sympathy for the giant of almost superhuman energy thus brought low.

So far as there was a lead given to the forces against over-restoration, it came from the Society of Antiquaries. The days of Wyatt were long past, and the views of Carter, Gough and Englefield vindicated. In 1854 John Ruskin asked the Society to 'undertake the management and disposal of a Fund to be subscribed for the preservation of Medieval Buildings', and offered to give £25 a year. The Conservation Fund was duly set up and was able to help several deserving cases, but never attracted adequate funds. Its launching was, however, the occasion of an admirable manifesto on restoration circulated to all Fellows in the spring of 1855 (see Appendix II). In spite of the relative failure of the Fund, the Society was active in other ways and succeeded in preventing several vandalistic demolitions, notably that of the Guildhall at Worcester in 1876. As the building is of 1721–4, in classical style, this was a remarkable and far-sighted act of conservation for the time. The Antiquaries also took the field against the devastation of St Albans Abbey.

Although Grimthorpe's onslaught upon St Albans was not finished until 1885, the tide of restoration was slackening by the time of Scott's death. It is an irony of history that the worst was already over when Morris launched the Society for the Protection of Ancient Buildings in 1877. Stranger still, Morris's vituperative attack was occasioned by Scott's comparatively mild and unobjectionable work on Tewkesbury Abbey. Commonsense was already overcoming the earlier perfervid Revivalism in architectural circles, and the last of the noted designers in Gothic style did much good work and relatively little damage. It is now impossible to take very seriously the unmeasured invective and abuse heaped by Morris upon John Loughborough Pearson and Sir Thomas Graham Jackson. Such an unbalanced attack was contra-productive, for against it most of the architectural profession tended to close its ranks and assert its freedom of professional action. We may regret the constitution and educational methods of architecture in modern times, and yet see that no professional man, bound in law and in etiquette to serve his client, can be at the beck and call of critics, whether individual or associated. Unless and until there is far-reaching reform in the training of architects, or alternatively the setting up of a separate profession of conservators devoted to all work on existing buildings, architects as we know them will continue to have control of conservation work. The remedy for defects of every kind, those of the fabric which it is sought to repair, and those of wrong method and faulty design, lies mainly in the architect's hands.

[10]

The Present

In a necessarily superficial way the historical background of conservation in this country has been sketched, down to the point where the destructive excesses of 'Restoration' called forth the equal and opposite excesses of William Morris's famous Manifesto of 1877 (see Appendix III). Like it or not, it is now a matter of historical fact that the opening of the modern period was marked by the founding of the Society for the Protection of Ancient Buildings, with this Manifesto as its foundation. The general climate of opinion on related subjects today has been formed very largely by the impact of that confession of faith, not only upon its disciples, but upon those stirred by it into violent opposition. In doing honour to the sincerity of Morris and his immediate followers, and justice to the excellent work carried out by many of those who have subsequently espoused his principles, we must also remember that there is another side to the medal. Much of the disrepute in which 'Preservationists' are held in some official quarters and by large bodies of the general public is directly due to the extreme form in which Morris's protest was cast.

In a longer perspective it is now possible to see that what Morris wrote in the heat of the moment was a perfectly permissible piece of pamphleteering. It was called for by much, though not all, that had been done by Scott and the other church-restorers, and had immediate relevance in face of a threat not yet removed. Morris was not to know that the restorers themselves had been learning by experience and were steadily moving towards the more moderate position that had been counselled years before by Scott and by Morris's own old master, Street. Morris's career was, as has been said, based upon passionate enthusiasm for an inaccessible artistic ideal, but most of the phases of his enthusiasm passed away as he fell under the influence of each new phase. It was a misfortune that his ephemeral attack upon the Restorers (who indeed deserved attack at that moment) should, by becoming in effect the Rules of a society and thus fossilized in the hands of a perpetual trusteeship, have been elevated into an Infallible Dogma.

Before considering the effects of this dogmatic and proselytizing acceptance of the Manifesto, we should look at the text. The first thing to notice is that it was in no sense original: though stated at considerable length, it enunciates no principle not contained in the succinct paper (Appendix II) circulated to the Society of Antiquaries in 1855 at the instigation of John Ruskin. In 1855 Morris was only 21, but another 22 years went by, during which the greater part of the vandalistic restorations were committed. Throughout these years Ruskin had continued to oppose 'restoration' and to make his opposition known. Furthermore, as Briggs pointed out, in the years immediately preceding the Morris outburst, the lead had been taken first by F. G. Stephens (1828–1907), the art-critic, and then by the Revd. W. J. Loftie (1839–1911). It was Loftie who was regarded by Scott as the leader of the party that found fault with him 'for doing anything at all.' What then did Morris contribute that was new? First and foremost, the idea of starting a society specifically devoted to the fight against the restorers. Secondly, as a left-wing democrat moving rapidly towards socialism, Morris represented the protest against the success-story careers of men like Scott. He canalized two great forces: the universal envy of the have-nots for the wealth and power on top; and the peculiarly British delight in uniting to prevent someone else from doing whatever it is.

There is little fault to find with Morris's main premises, that the previous fifty years had been the period most destructive of our ancient art; and that the nineteenth century (in what was then accounted Architecture) had no real style of its own. But he did less than justice to the fact that a great many buildings were almost ready to fall down, and had been physically saved from total disappearance by a part of the works done; and he could not see that, with all its imitative character and weakness, Victorian style did in fact exist. The qualities of the new designs of the time were not, as their authors imagined, those of genuine Gothic work; but we can now see from the distance of a century that real qualities were there. Morris could not admit this, and arbitrarily denied that the works of 'restoration' were themselves part of the history of the buildings for which he fought. In fact, to use his own phrase, the restorations were alive with the spirit of the deeds done in their fashioning. Besides, he lumped together under the same head for detestation two very different methods of repair. He drew no distinction between the results of imagining 'what the earlier builders should or might have done', and the restoration to completeness of features fully evidenced by parts actually surviving. Though there was force in his contention that much restoration tampered with the whole surface of the building, he made no allowance for the mellowing effects of weather after a few years, nor for the inescapable necessity *at all periods* of some degree of patchwork repair. The reason for the far greater amount of surface patching and refacing needed in the nineteenth century, unknown to Morris and his contemporaries, was as we have seen the pollution of the atmosphere by chemical effluent from coal fires.

The crux of the matter lies in Morris's final programme, the only part of the Manifesto which urged a specific and positive course of action. Morris, who had spent a single year as articled pupil to Street, does not seem to have acquired much understanding of the common-sense needs of buildings. He asks that those who have to deal with old buildings should 'prop a perilous wall or mend a leaky roof' by means 'obviously meant for support or covering, and show no pretence of other art.' If this clause has a meaning in practical terms, it calls for support by crude buttressing masses or pillars, deliberately deprived of all stylistic detail; and for drill-hall roofs asserting plainly that they are not forgeries made to harmonize with the ancient building. In the light of nearly a hundred years of subsequent practice, not least by the architect members of Morris's own society, we may safely say that this was rhetorical nonsense. It was not a feasible suggestion, in that hardly any building owner could be expected to consent to repairs of a permanent nature being done in such a way.

Finally, Morris put forward another positive plea: that if a building were no longer suitable for its purpose, it should not be altered or enlarged, but preserved as a monument of bygone art, while a completely new building was erected to serve the changed purpose. Theoretically desirable as is an untouched array of old buildings in exquisite and unspoiled condition, we now know from bitter experience that the disused becomes the derelict and soon the irretrievably lost. A majority

of the ancient buildings that Morris so loved were the product of
more or less continuous adaptation to circumstances: any building
that is artificially deprived of a reasonable degree of adaptation becomes a fossil or a preserved specimen. The Committee of the
S.P.A.B. in April 1924 found it necessary to add a gloss to this section of Morris's Manifesto in its annual reprint. The Committee
noted that the point had been 'frequently misinterpreted' and stated
that: 'Where there is good reason for adding to an ancient building a
modest addition is not opposed to the principles of the Society, provided (1) that the new work is in the natural manner of to-day, subordinate to the old, and not a reproduction of any past style; (2) that
the addition is permanently required and will not in any sense be a
building which future events will render inadequate or super-
fluous. . . .'

Thus, nearly half a century from its foundation, and more than
twenty-five years after Morris's death, the Society bowed to the inevitable and made public admission that in at least one major particular it was not feasible to adhere to the letter of what the founder had
written. In fact a really strict adherence to precept would have rendered most of the serious structural problems of conservation insoluble
in practical and economic terms. As the years passed the body of
experience in much actual work carried out by architect members of
the S.P.A.B. diverged further and further from the original letter of
the law. Though the pressure of Morrisian orthodoxy – and behind
that, the possibly stronger psychological effect of Ruskin's Lamps –
insisted upon a good deal of nonsense in the form of tiles-and-
rendering rather than renewed stones, the actual body of expert tradition which evolved came to deserve high praise and produced immense
good. When a large part of that tradition was codified and published
by A. R. Powys in 1929 as the book *Repair of Ancient Buildings*, the
preface contained some highly significant remarks.

Powys, who was Secretary of the S.P.A.B. for twenty-five years
until his death in 1936, was himself a practising architect and a man of
great common sense. As re-defined in his terms, the object of repair
'is to preserve and give renewed life to fine and old buildings that
have been neglected or are decaying, and in so doing to avoid making
reproductions to take the place of damaged features or missing parts
when this involves the destruction and not the protection of what remains of the original work.' The final qualification is all important,

and explicitly supplies the point that Morris had failed to make: that the real objection to much Victorian restoration was that *it involved destruction of the old*. Powys went on to quote a warning given by Lethaby some years earlier against making it a principle that 'no work *which has to be renewed* should ever be put back in the form it had or in the material it was.' Powys accepted Lethaby's caution, and added 'that it is not wise to lay down dogmatic rules, for when they are made one is apt to be confronted with a case where they do not work.' Because Powys was both a great and a modest man, undogmatic and ready to learn, and because he was a man of surpassing energy, the S.P.A.B. became transformed from a negative and preventative body into a positive force for good.

Yet the inherent danger of a written creed that did not in fact correspond to the living principles of the Society, but was none the less integrally reprinted every year, remained and remains today. The Morris Manifesto has always been used as a quasi-sacramental test, intending members being asked to sign a form saying that they are in agreement with its principles. Doubtless a great many members join because of general sympathy, and are not really concerned with the precise definition of principles. But there has always been a substantial body, deeply concerned for the fate of old buildings and anxious to take part in the campaign for conservation, who have felt unable to accept this credo. For them it is a matter of conscience not to make formal acceptance of something which they do not believe, or which they feel is impracticable and, as an expression of conservation doctrine, far from complete. The curious position has arisen that, whereas the need in Victorian times had been for an open society of conservers, what arrived was a closed society of anti-restorers. The original need had not been fulfilled.

The fact that the S.P.A.B., as founded by Morris, was not a complete union of those linked by a definite and positive aim was always implicitly recognized by the older societies in the field. The Society of Antiquaries in particular redoubled its efforts in the last years of the nineteenth century, and has remained in the forefront of the battle, and particularly concerned with all relevant legislation, ever since. Both the British Archaeological Association and the (now Royal) Archaeological Institute have played their part, as have the county and local societies. The old Architectural societies, before they died out around the period of the Second World War, or became transformed in character, were especially active within their own areas. Gradually taking over their role since about 1930 have been the local Amenity societies and Civic Trusts, founded in towns, rural districts and cities as a positive spur to improved appearance of buildings and landscape – conservation in the widest and most positive sense. This twentieth-century movement really took its rise from the founding of the National Trust in 1895, but more specifically from the Council for the Preservation of Rural England and from the Design and Industries Association which was formed in 1915. The ancient (now Royal) Society of Arts also came to the fore in the campaign to save old cottages in the 1920's and in 1929 saved the whole village of West Wycombe, one of the best instances of group preservation. Though many different bodies and individuals were concerned with the inter-wars movement, one person deserves special mention for the outstanding part he played: Mr Clough Williams-Ellis.

While the main threat to old buildings in the nineteenth century had come from well-intentioned but over-zealous restorers, recognized and combated by Ruskin, Morris and many others; and from an atmosphere chemically polluted in a way unknown before, but not yet scientifically recognized, the twentieth century faces dangers of a different kind as well. Until the outbreak of the First World War in 1914 Britain was a relatively affluent country. There was not only money to maintain old buildings, but such a surplus of ready cash as to constitute a threat in itself by encouraging undue 'improvement' and wholesale rebuilding. The Great War in the course of five years changed both the economic and the social background. An impoverished country emerged, suffering from inflation, succeeded by industrial depression, and both the time and the particular circumstances fostered a gigantic social revolution, enormously accelerated by the Second World War and its aftermath. The nineteenth century had seen a religious revival prepared to spend great sums on the building of new churches and on the restoration of old ones, but a high proportion of the people remained content with the houses, large and small, in which they had been brought up. In less than fifty years the picture was to change completely. A wave of scepticism has shaken organized 'church' religion to its foundations, and insists on spending money on people – mostly abroad – rather than on things at home. Inland building is largely for state charity in the form of schools, universities and hospitals (for the diseased not, as formerly, largely for the aged). On the other hand the standards of much older housing have been officially condemned, and a rapidly increasing population, dislodged from its roots in the country at large and pressing into a few giant conurbations, is demanding space on which to build new dwellings, often blocks of flats rather than separate houses.

The increased population and new methods in industry and commerce are also asking for an extensive network of motorways and widened roads for motorized transport. The new housing, the new schools and institutions, and the new communications are in all making extremely serious inroads upon the available land, and the rising values of space near the centres of all urban areas with increasing population place a premium upon demolition and redevelopment. Along with all this, taxation has reached a level so high that the private funds which can be tapped for purposes of conservation are relatively slight, and tend to be pre-empted for a very few giant schemes, very greatly to the detriment of the general background of parish churches and private houses and cottages. All this is happening in other countries as well as in Britain, but it is not happening in so aggravated a form, nor all at once. What has befallen this country in the twenty-five years since the end of the Second World War has occurred with a terrifying acceleration that leaves no room for calm thought or clear planning.

Taking all these factors into account, it is evident that the basic needs of conservation now differ radically from those of Morris's time and earlier. In a world now dominated by public agencies – the state and local authorities of various kinds – a much bigger part is played by legislation and by official intervention. The proportionate scope for private enterprise is less than it was, and has changed almost completely in character. Whereas the main body of interest in conservation came from a small but cultured minority, it now – and this is a potentially hopeful factor – has an immensely widened appeal to large numbers of people. The need for leadership from informed specialists is as great or even greater than before, but given the leadership, there are far more available recruits than ever there were. The popularity of historical and social studies, and of archaeology including industrial archaeology, shows that there is a widespread interest on the part of many in the younger generation in subjects favourable to conservation.

So far little has been said of the great positive contribution made by official sources to conservation. This is the greatest factor to offset the

unfavourable trends of our time. To all intents and purposes this is
something that did not exist at all until after the twentieth century had
dawned. It is true that the building of the new Houses of Parliament
in the middle of the last century had called forth detailed studies of
supplies of building stone, and further studies of durability and some
aspects of repair. There were works carried out under government
departments at a few Crown buildings actually in occupation. But
there was virtually no official participation in conservation as a science
until the passing of the Ancient Monuments Consolidation and Amendment Act of 1913. The first British Ancient Monuments Protection
Act, the outcome of background work by the archaeological societies,
was first brought before Parliament in 1873 – four years before
Morris's campaign against the restorers – but took nine years to reach
the Statute Book, having had a first reading on nine occasions and a
second reading on six. The main reason for its slow passage was the
intense opposition from those who regarded official protection of
monuments as an unwarranted interference with the rights of property.
All that was achieved by this first Act was protection of sixty-eight
monuments (several of which were extensive groups, however),
mostly prehistoric. A considerably wider scope was given by the
second enactment of 1900, which followed the enlightened lead given
to the country by the London County Council in its General Powers
Act of 1898. The L.C.C. then obtained power to purchase by agreement buildings and places of historical or architectural interest, and in
April 1900 made use of these powers for the first time.

The L.C.C. had already taken the important step of starting to
prepare a list of historic buildings in London on an official basis, and
called a conference which took place on 4 December 1896. The conference was attended by representatives of fifteen societies whose names
deserve wide publicity: Architectural Association; British Archaeological Association; City Church Preservation Society; Committee for
the Survey of the Memorials of Greater London; Kent Archaeological
Society; Kyrle Society; London and Middlesex Archaeological
Society; London Topographical Society; National Trust; Royal
Archaeological Institute; Royal Institute of British Architects; Society of Antiquaries; Society of Arts; Society for the Protection of
Ancient Buildings; and the Surveyors' Institution. It transpired that a
list had already been begun by the Committee for the Survey of
London; this Committee was prepared to hand over its work; and the

conference urged continuance. The upshot was that the L.C.C. accepted the offer and resolved to print the resulting register of buildings. This decision, with the voting of finance for the purpose, took place on 27 July 1897 and marks the beginning of the fruitful co-operation of the London Survey Committee and London County Council in one of the finest inventories of buildings ever compiled. An ancillary work, hitherto carried out by the Society of Arts, but also taken over by the L.C.C., was the indication by inscribed tablets of houses associated with historical events or distinguished individuals.

What has become the Historic Buildings Section of the Greater London Council therefore had a start of the nation of some fifteen years in the three important fields of (1) listing, (2) marking, and (3) acquisition and maintenance, of buildings of architectural and historic interest. It had been preceded in each of these fields by private enterprise on the part of societies, and as a public authority by the City of Chester, which had acquired some protective powers over the city walls in the Chester Improvement Act of 1884. None the less, London must be given the credit of pioneering the main line of future advance in conservation. Its lead was followed by the country at large,* but unfortunately piecemeal and without any form of unified control. On the administrative level the achievements of Britain in the past seventy years compare most unfavourably with the beautifully precise and complete procedure envisaged by the Grand-Duke of Hesse in 1818, and actually achieved in several continental countries before 1900. What has been done in the way of legislation is comprised in fifteen different, overlapping and sometimes conflicting, Acts of Parliament, and in various complementary orders and circulars. Even the summary in *A Guide to Historic Buildings Law*, produced as a work of necessity by the Cambridgeshire and Isle of Ely County Council, extends to 54 large pages. Although at last, in 1970, a measure of co-ordination between the ministries concerned was imposed by the creation of an over-ruling Department of the Environment, this still has no official control over or liaison with the Royal Commissions on Historical or Ancient Monuments (for England, Wales, and Scotland) or the National Monuments Record, responsible for the production of inventories and for most official recording.

Against this picture of slow and largely self-defeating official

---

* The pioneering work done by the Ancient Monuments Committee of the Surrey County Council, from 1912 onwards, deserves special mention.

activity spread over the last two generations there are two immense positive gains to be appreciated. The later of these in date is the completion, after more than twenty years of work by the former Ministry of Housing and Local Government, of lists for the whole country of all buildings regarded as of special architectural or historic interest. Although these lists are naturally subject to some amendment, they may be regarded as providing the necessary key to the problem as a whole and in all its details. The other great gain is the formation of the 'Ancient Monuments Branch' of the former Ministry of Works, started under the 1913 Act in the then H.M. Office of Works. This consists of an Inspectorate of historical experts, linked with a section of the Architects' Division exclusively concerned with the specialized treatment of monuments and old buildings. Under the directions of the Branch there is also a large force of skilled craftsmen working by direct labour and controlled by regional superintendents of works, themselves mostly skilled craftsmen of distinction who have won their experience on the monuments in their charge. In spite of its late start, when compared to what was done in other countries, this organization as a whole has won deserved renown for its complete mastery of technical resources and the fine results achieved. It should also be mentioned that the Inspectorate controls a large programme of archaeological excavation, directed by its own staff and by outside archaeologists.

The technical mastery achieved by the Ancient Monuments Branch over the physical problems of conservation has been due to a large extent to close liaison with other government agencies including particularly the former Department of Scientific and Industrial Research. That Department's Building Research Station and Forest Products Research Laboratory have published reports on every aspect of the use and maintenance of building materials, decay, and the means of treatment and repair. In this field the British contribution to the literature of conservation is accepted as in advance of what has been done in most other countries. A most important aspect of this wide range of official publications is that they are mostly published at very low prices; and in general the methods of treatment advocated, as a result of prolonged experiment, are simple and not unduly costly. A much wider use of this valuable literature should be made by architects and everyone else concerned with the actual work of conservation.

At an early stage mention was made of the inadequate appreciation shown in this country for the work of the 'official school' of conservators represented mainly by the Ancient Monuments Branch (above, p. 87). This has amounted to something a good deal worse than mere neglect, for at times it has constituted a veritable campaign of denigration. Several different viewpoints, each deeply embedded in the history of the subject in this country, have made an unholy alliance for the purpose of negative and destructive criticism. Probably the most influential of these, at any rate in the early years of work on monuments placed in official guardianship, was the sense of affront and grievance felt against bureaucratic interference by the owners of property. This feeling had delayed the first Ancient Monuments Act for nine years, and was again expressed in the debates on the Bill which was passed in 1913. The determination of the Church of England to obtain exemption for its churches in use from any form of state intervention, however helpful financially, was closely linked to the attitude of the landed proprietors. The general trend of political life in Britain towards the 'Left' and socialistic measures also contributed to this resentment. From quite a different direction came unexpected reinforcements. It might have been supposed that the socialistic outlook of William Morris would have left in his spiritual descendants some sympathy for state control over the buildings and monuments belonging to the propertied classes; but this was not the case. The modern bureaucracy of 1913, and still more that conditioned by the First World War, with controls and the atmosphere of D.O.R.A., was regarded as completely inimical to mediaevalism, to cottage industry, and to the aesthetic judgments of the individual.

By a freak of fate, the revolutionary enthusiasm and the resentment against the propertied wealth that financed church restorations, canalized by Morris in the foundation of S.P.A.B., now found themselves allied with the same propertied stratum as a movement of protest 'agin the Government.' Actual power had passed very largely out of the hands of the men of property into those of the professional politicians: hence not merely anything done by the new party of power, but anything effected under their aegis, was felt to be a legitimate target for attack and even for abuse. For many years the Ancient Monuments Branch, like poor Scott in his day, found themselves under heavy fire 'for doing anything at all.' The holy ruins of England, ivy and all, should have been left to crumble gradually away, haunted by their ghosts and visited at rare intervals (by gracious permission of the noble proprietor) by poets of sensibility. The late

William Woodward was for many years the apostle of this school of thought, and found expression for it, frequently and at length, in the columns of the national press.

There were, as was only natural, things to criticize in the early work on ancient monuments taken into guardianship. There was certainly a tendency to fly from ivy-clad neglect to an extreme of neatly regimented care. The fact that most monuments were no longer 'living', that they were subjects merely for preservation, inevitably tended towards presentation as museum specimens. The point should be made that, so long as it is an enlightened and well run museum, this is a treatment appropriate to a great many such monuments. They lose a little in the process, but they gain far more, as intelligible specimens of the castle, the monastery, or the prehistoric complex. Now that the work done has mellowed, the turf is mature, and minor vegetation flourishing (a good deal of wild wallflower seed is scattered about the walls by custodians), the official monuments of Britain can stand comparison with anything of the same sort done in other countries. The chief justified criticism, in certain cases, is the unfortunate juxtaposition of a car-park; this necessarily has to be on part of the land that can be acquired with the monument itself, and forms no part of a Philistine policy.

One of the main sources of criticism in the early years was the extremity of purism which forbade the re-erection of even a single fallen stone let alone the reconstruction of features found as dismembered fragments. It need hardly be said that this purism was itself founded upon the disrepute of 'restoration' in the post-Morris period. As time has mellowed the legacy of Morrisian orthodoxy, so it has become possible for the policy of successive Chief Inspectors of Ancient Monuments to relax in this respect. Though with suitable warning tablets recording the fact of reconstruction, there are now, for example, sections of cloister colonnades re-erected on ruined sites, greatly to the illumination of the visiting public. Let it be said firmly that, in the interests of both aesthetics and intelligibility, fragments which can be re-erected *without any doubt* of reproducing their correct effect, ought to be put back. This has been acknowledged by Italy, in the justified rebuilding of the Campanile at Venice after its downfall; by the conservative replacements at the Parthenon in Greece; and – outside the state service – in the late Walter Godfrey's splendid reconstruction of the Temple Church in London.

Adverse critics of the work of the Ancient Monuments Branch tend to overlook the real issues of today. Unless the whole of the available resources for conservation are used to best advantage, much that might be saved will inevitably be lost. This is outstandingly true in regard to technical resources and expert knowledge. If the worthy buildings of Britain are to be saved for future generations, and put into a condition of sound general maintenance, every scrap of available knowledge and manpower must be brought into play. The tradition of care built up by the Ancient Monuments service, not only in regard to ruins, but also in the constructive conservation of such historic buildings as Hampton Court Palace, Windsor Castle and the Tower of London, is absolutely vital, and cannot be sacrificed by hair-splitting over matters of transient fashion or personal opinion. Not only the destruction caused by sheer vandalism or by so-called 'progress' has to be fought; the effects of weather and of atmospheric pollution by themselves are providing more than enough work for the skilled forces of experienced directors and artisans.

This situation calls for a massive and united front of opinion favourable to conservation, enlightened as to method and attitude, and determined to defeat 'the Beast' represented by the sum total of destructive forces. It is essential that it should reject outmoded sectarian attitudes and particularly the continued vendettas against the work of the official Ancient Monuments Branch and against architects whose methods of conservation offend in some marginal way against strict canons of orthodoxy. What has to be faced is that the country as a whole is losing not merely enormous numbers of individual buildings, but, what is far more important, the whole feeling and character of what is spared. There must be a far wider application of the important proviso made in regard to additions to buildings by the S.P.A.B. in its gloss on Morris in 1924: that what is done is permanently required and will not be rendered inadequate or super-fluous by future events. Nobody can be certain of the future, of course, but we should already have learnt from the past how closely this applies to the building of new roads and the widening of existing ones. The appetite of modern transport grows by what it feeds on, and one of the most vital aspects of the fight is uncompromising opposition to further surrenders, however marginal, to an *alleged* need for communications.

The same principle still applies with great force to additions and major alterations to buildings, and any assessment of a house for conversion or a redundant church for new use should always look for the minimum of alteration which can make the alterations effective. Where there is any real likelihood of further change being needed, or of reversion to former status, every precaution must be taken to provide for easy removal of, for example, inserted partitions or additional floors. This applies with particular force to churches, where the experience of the last century and a half shows that liturgical fashion and what are regarded as necessities of worship vary greatly from one generation to the next or even more frequently. In the case of churches still in active use a very great menace is represented by the tendency to revert to early liturgy with a central altar. It ought to be recognized that major alterations to the structure and choir fittings of old churches planned for an eastern high altar, separated by a screen from the congregational nave, are in most cases aesthetically as well as historically deplorable. Here the possibility of a change in churchmanship should rule out all but the most easily reversible changes in arrangement.

This is a convenient point at which to discuss another grave threat, mainly to churches, but also to buildings of other types: the principle of preservation by removal (see above, p. 59). As has been said already this does have some historical justification in the case of timber-framed buildings. It may also, though only as a last resort, be an acceptable way of saving, for re-use elsewhere, a church or house designed in classical or other precise style and built in sound ashlar masonry. The physical dismemberment, after a drawn survey has been made and every stone numbered to correspond to a set of drawings, can be carried out in an orderly way, and all the parts be re-assembled on the new site. Technically this is quite feasible, even if costly; but the possibility of such preservation should never be allowed to weigh in the struggle to keep an ancient structure in its original position. This applies, of course, whether the removal is for active re-use or merely for re-erection in a folk museum. A very few instances of successful removal of large old buildings in other categories could be mentioned, of which the most important in Britain is probably Walter Godfrey's re-erection of Crosby Hall at Chelsea. Against these few successes there is a melancholy tale of attempts to move mediaeval churches, usually doomed to failure because of the character of the design and materials and the condition of most of the stones. In general removal should be discouraged.

Removal of old buildings is one particular instance of a kind of problem in conservation where a clear ranking of priorities has to be established. As Powys wrote of methods, it is not wise to lay down dogmatic rules, but common sense does indicate the more desirable of choices in certain instances. Seeing that in all conservation it is desired to keep as much as possible of original work for as long as possible, several consequences logically follow. As has just been said, the building ought to be kept on its old site rather than removing it to another; it should continue to be used for its intended purpose rather than for a different one. If this is clearly impossible, then the new purpose should, where a choice exists, be the closest possible to what it was before. Thus a large family mansion is better maintained in living condition as a boarding school or an Old People's Home than by being turned into a museum or art gallery. On the other hand, the museum or gallery will be preferable to such a utilitarian purpose as a warehouse or store. An Anglican church of mediaeval foundation would be more appropriately used by one of the ancient Christian denominations than by a business firm for shops or offices. The less favoured uses are not excluded, but should not be preferred.

There are instances where the chequered history of a particular group of buildings raises more complex issues. This is notably true of the considerable number of cases where the claustral ranges of monasteries were, after the Dissolution, turned into private residences for the nobility or merchants who had acquired the property from the Crown. Each instance is unique, and no rule can be laid down, but much would depend in such cases on the amount of the building that survived from the monastic period. So long as the user continues to be as a private dwelling, no problem arises, for dispossession of the new owners was not generally possible even under the Marian Reaction of 1553–58. The law and public opinion in the sixteenth century healed any moral doubts as to soundness of title. But if a fresh social revolution has depressed the families which that of the sixteenth century threw up, so that they can no longer maintain these buildings as their homes, an entirely new situation arises. Proposals for reconversion of such buildings for use by religious orders would command a high degree of sympathy, provided that re-conversion could be carried out with a minimum of destruction or alteration to genuine ancient work – not only the mediaeval parts, but sound and worthy additions of any period.

41. REPOINTING *Winchester College*: Outer Gate after cleaning and complete repointing of the flintwork with lime mortar, 1956. The previous (modern) pointing had been artificially darkened to match the dirt, as can be seen in the walling on the right.

PROTECTION OF SCULPTURE

42, 43. *Winchester College*: the Statue of the Virgin and Child over
Outer Gate before treatment. Traces of a colour-scheme of 1466 showed
how the carving had formerly been protected.

43

In 1956–57 the fragile surface required a new coating (*above*) with a
fine slurry of lime and sifted sand, a cosmetic application which impedes
weathering.   *Adviser: Mr. E. Clive Rouse.*

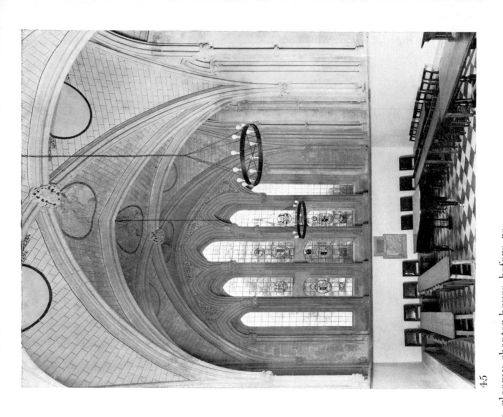

44, 45. *Oxford, Christ Church*: the gloomy chapter-house before re-decoration and (*right*) after cleaning, limewashing, preservative work on vault-paintings, and re-glazing.
Consultants: paintings, Mr. E. Clive Rouse; glazing, Mr. Dennis King.

46, 47. WOODCARVING *Winchester College*: Altar rails of 1680–3 by Edward Pierce, replaced in the Chapel in 1952. Changes of temperature required expert re-glueing of fragments (*below*), the last work of the late Edwin Laverty in 1955.

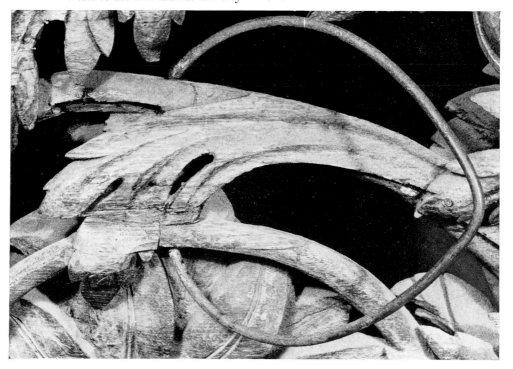

48

FITTINGS AND FURNISHING

48, 49, 50. *Winchester College*: removal of a Victorian fireplace revealed that the floor level of the Warden's Study, formed only in 1597, had been lowered in 1615 to allow of the insertion of an elaborate over-mantel. Incorporated in the removed work was the moulded surround of the Warden's Drawing Room fireplace of *c.* 1690 (49). This was put back (50) where it belonged in 1963, four years after the panelling had been cleaned and waxed.

51. IRONWORK *Winchester College*: the east window of Fromond's Chantry, with the wrought-iron grille or *ferramentum* which protects the window and gives aesthetic scale. Damage by rust has been repaired and the grille supported on new non-rusting ends to the stanchions.

In every individual problem a sense of proportion is requisite; there should, as far as possible, be no panaceas and no fixed ideas. Lack of proportion can lead to seriously damaging results and bring discredit upon the cause of conservation. Within the last few years this was regrettably exemplified in the storm-in-a-teacup controversy over the ruins of Bury St Edmunds Abbey. There the vast precinct of the greatest British monastery lies almost wholly in ruins, the exceptions consisting of two gatehouses, preserved as monuments, and two parish churches, one now the cathedral. There are also, formed out of the massive structure of the western front of the great abbey church, several modest dwelling houses of virtually no architectural interest beyond the curiosity of their contrivance. They do not represent the normal type of post-Dissolution conversion of lodgings; that did happen to the Abbot's Palace, which survived as a house until demolished in 1720. The unique archaeological and architectural importance of this great mediaeval front, which these houses obscure, has long been recognized, and in most continental countries there is little doubt that the occupiers of the intrusive houses would have been expropriated in order that full investigations might be carried out and the mediaeval work exposed and consolidated. Yet when it was announced that, *when the relevant leases fell in*, the Ancient Monuments Branch would, at last, be able to proceed with this outstandingly important project, a violent campaign was opened in the press to prevent it. The false analogy to monastic buildings converted to private use and continuously inhabited was used to oppose the scheme on the ground that it destroyed the history of the building; and, far worse, the occasion was taken to heap obloquy upon the state service for its methods in the care of monuments. No incident for many years has done so much damage to the cause, and with such complete lack of justification.

If success is to crown the efforts of all those who, for the past two centuries, have actively striven and are striving to maintain our heritage, it is vital that sane and balanced leadership should prevent incidents such as this. There is need for calm discussion, *in private*, of all possibly contentious issues, and a firm outward front towards the overwhelming dangers which threaten the very existence of a large proportion of our monuments. For too long the subject has been bedevilled by divided counsels and infirmity of purpose, by petty squabbles and by failure to discriminate between the essential and the insignificant. As has been said, the fundamental mistake has been to attempt to save ancient work negatively, by preserving it as a fossil – the inevitable outcome of Morris's arbitrary conclusion to history at *c.* 1800 – and not to produce, as a result of positive thinking, the means to incorporate all that can be kept as integrated contributions towards a living continuum. There is room for preserved ruins, for archaeological investigation, and for the formation of regional folk-museums. All these play an important part in our cultural outlook on the past and its relation to the present. What is of even greater importance is that the best of our ancient art, not as isolated specimens but as intelligible entities, should survive.

That there is, *in fact*, a clear division between '*dead monuments*, i.e. those belonging to a past civilization or serving obsolete purposes, and *living monuments*, i.e. those which continue to serve the purposes for which they were originally intended' was laid down by a resolution passed at the Sixth International Congress of Architects held at Madrid as long ago as 1904: the authority of the Congress stands behind the decision that restoration, i.e. constructive repair and alteration for changing purpose, is permissible in the case of the living monument. The dead monument, which includes a large proportion of Ancient Monuments under official guardianship in this country, is simply to be carefully preserved. While methods of *preservation*, suitable for the dead monument, have been brought to a high pitch, there has been a terribly long and indeed inexcusable time-lag in reaching general agreement on right principles of conservation for the living monument. Yet this is the most vital problem of all those with which we are faced, apart from preventing the wholesale destruction of our monumental riches. We are then looking into a future where the guarding of our older buildings from destruction is the first necessity, and the proper means to maintain them the next.

[11]

Looking Forward

In the early chapters of this book consideration was given to the question of what it is, among our old buildings, that is most worth saving, and to means by which they might best be saved. It became evident that an exercise of power is required to prevent wholesale and indiscriminate destruction, and that this in turn implies fresh legislation as well as a stricter employment of existing powers. In looking towards a future in which conservation will follow a constructive policy and be a main aspect of the human environment, we must assume a sufficient growth of public opinion to ensure the passage of any necessary legislation, and to insist upon the right policy not merely being laid down on paper, but implemented to the full. What follows here is intended as a general picture of the action needed: much of it is explicit or implied in present legislation or procedure.

We saw that the first step towards a satisfactory policy is the setting apart of whole areas, both in towns and countryside, where future development must be strictly controlled in order that the city, the town or the village – or group of adjacent villages with the intervening landscape – may survive complete. These areas will be sanctuaries, cities of refuge, zoned for a completely different kind of development from that permitted elsewhere. The structure of local government and local planning must be adapted to this end. The national government must likewise see to it that, rare exceptions apart, there are no over-riding requirements slashing across the demands of conservation in the area or region. Maintenance of conservation must be given primacy over, for example, through communications and the demands of the services departments. Once these districts have been set apart they must be sacrosanct, and not subject to whittling away at the whim of administrators. Thus it would be essential that, within the places set apart but not elsewhere, there should be no right of appeal from decisions affecting conservation. Furthermore, in certain fields there would have to be a strict limit placed upon the right even to apply for permission to develop or re-develop. Change there would be, to adapt to new conditions, but the type of alteration permitted would have strict limits set upon it, and these would not be extended. Except for an initial period, when un-worthy parts of a conservation area would have to be demolished and redeveloped in harmony with the local atmosphere, comprehensive redevelopment would be outlawed.

One of the main attractions, in practice, of living in such an area would be the relative freedom from adverse changes. The occupier of a house would have the certainty that his surroundings could not be sacrificed to blocks of overscale flats or offices, to road-widening or to the construction of new routes. These benefits would tend, in the open market, to offset any drop in values which might be due to the ban on major developments. A requirement to maintain properties in sound condition should be coupled with a system of adequate grants in aid. While interference with normal redecoration and minor running repairs should be minimized, there would here and there have to be comprehensive schemes for the uniform external decoration of terraces, groups or neighbourhoods. Similarly, methods of reducing the number of visual excrescences such as television aerials would have to be found. The related question of the multiplicity of road signs, parking notices and the like should be solved by having a different and much more restricted system of signs within a conserva-tion district. For example, the disfiguring yellow lines would not be painted on the road surface, and parking meters and other types of obstruction would be abolished.

It is certain that, within conservation districts, traffic flow would have to be strictly controlled. The method of marginal parking at the perimeter, immediately linked to public transport – preferably free – should be adopted, but the needs of different places might require special arrangements on individual rather than uniform lines. It should be axiomatic that both major bypasses and relief roads should be kept outside the perimeter of the group to be conserved. Air flight paths, except those at great altitudes, should be moved so as not to overfly conservation areas. The existing control of advertising would have to be very greatly strengthened within conservation areas, and in particular certain kinds of shop window display would be banned altogether, along with the use for publicity of luminous and radiant paints and printing inks. Local and neighbourhood amenity societies, including associations of those living or working within a single street (as with the existing Elm Hill Association in Norwich, or the Goodramgate Traders Association at York) should be warmly encouraged, to promote individuality.

The principle of pedestrian precincts and foot streets must be greatly extended in the centres of ancient cities and towns, and this again would demand full co-ordination of public transport services with parking for out-of-town shoppers. While provision for servicing of the shops at certain hours, or by service roads where feasible, would have to be made, a long-term aim would be the removal out of all conservation districts of heavy industry involving the use of outsize vans and lorries. Quite apart from the construction of bypasses well outside the limits of the old built-up area, there should be a total ban on vehicles beyond a limited size passing through the area. Railway facilities should be improved as an alternative form of transport where necessary. It is obvious that the reduction in traffic due to bypasses and to limitation on heavy freight vehicles would greatly assist in freeing the air from polluting fumes, and in reducing noise. It would further this aim if the internal public transport provided were powered by electric battery, a system suitable for relatively low speeds and short distances.

Something must be said of the position of historic buildings not within one of the privileged areas. They would, of course, be unprotected so far as noise or traffic pollution is concerned, and would enjoy only a relative, not an absolute, immunity from the threat of redevelopment. But it is essential that they should enjoy not merely the degree of protection already accorded to statutorily listed buildings, but more precise safeguards. At present buildings are in danger both from acts of the public authorities and from either the vandalism or the sloth of their owners. Dealing first with the public sector, it is ridiculous that legal protection should be given with one hand and taken away with the other. Once a building has been awarded statutory protection it should be exempt from all external threats unless they are certified as in the *national* interest: it being presumed that such certification would not lightly be granted. While existing law offers substantial protection against positive vandalism extending to demolition, it is far less effective against the owner (including some local authorities) simply letting the building decay through lack of maintenance. Here again there should be intervention on the national level, on information received through one of the recognized societies concerned with conservation. The procedure must be prompt, so as to make it impossible for a building to be subjected to another season of decay after action has once been initiated.

The provision of checks at the national level should be instead of, not in addition to, the present wasteful system of public enquiries. The public enquiry causes inordinate expense both in time and money, to say nothing of the burden of worry and uncertainty placed upon owners and occupiers in many cases. It has been said already, and must be repeated here, that statutory protection, once imposed, should normally be irreversible. In any case it should not in any circumstances be possible for a private developer to apply for permission to demolish a listed building. So long as any legal possibility of obtaining such permission is available, so long will valuable buildings be improperly subjected to threat. Another gross abuse would be halted by this same provision, namely repeated applications for demolition, or disastrous alteration, differing only in minor detail from a previous application that has been rejected. It is essential that the public should have complete confidence in the impartiality of the decisions reached, and this demands that the power to alter the state of absolute protection should rest with the central authority alone.

If the protection demanded for fine and old buildings be regarded as excessive, the question must be asked: is conservation a policy seriously relevant to modern life, or is it to be reduced to farcical lip-service and mockery? The statistics of crime in recent years show plainly that this country has become far more lawless than it was within living memory. Similarly the statistics of traffic accidents indicate the increasing danger to life, even where no actual crime is involved. There are no adequate statistics for the losses sustained through pollution, vibration and noise, but it is beyond doubt that all these form very serious threats to life, to health, and to the condition of buildings and the landscape. In a certain sense this change for the worse in our environment is comparable to the change from Roman civilization to the Dark Ages. During the Dark Age and the mediaeval period that followed it was found necessary to provide strong backing for the sanctity of the Church. Churches and monasteries, as far as law had the power to maintain them, gave a higher degree of protection from the threats of an adverse environment, and were supported for centuries by public opinion. The need for cities of refuge has always existed, and has seldom been felt more sharply than in the mid-twentieth century. Just as adequate holidays from work are agreed to be necessary and are given legal sanction, so must the equivalent in escape from the worst features of modern life be provided by means of the setting aside of conserved regions and their protection by adequate laws.

One of the most crucial problems arising from large-scale conservation is the provision of funds. There are already state and local grants available covering some part of the range of expenditure on conserving buildings; but so far these grants do not go far enough to bridge the gap left unfilled by private resources. This can be seen in several parts of the whole field. In the case of listed buildings used as dwellings the possible sources of grants include the Historic Buildings Councils; but such funds are limited and are given only to buildings officially regarded as 'outstanding'. Several town schemes exist also, where funds are provided half by the state, half by the local authority; but the amounts given to the general run of old buildings – i.e. those which are clearly not 'outstanding' – are usually very small. A great many buildings which undoubtedly were deserving cases have been lost in the last quarter-century solely because the available funds and obtainable grants were not enough. Another aspect of finance is seen in the public appeals for immense sums for such famous buildings as Westminster Abbey, York Minster, and St Paul's Cathedral. A very few such giant funds exhaust the greater part of the public money that can be subscribed for purposes of conservation. For this reason they have a disastrous effect upon conservation of almost all other buildings. There is here a very strong argument for making all major public buildings in a certain high category, reparable at the charge of the state. This should apply to the greater cathedrals as much as to public offices and buildings in Crown occupation.

If the disproportionately costly cases could thus be removed from competition with the main body of buildings, it would go a long way towards solving the problem. The remaining gap could be filled by adopting the American taxation plan, by which donations to such a purpose as conservation would become deductible. It has always been objected by a vociferous minority that anything that aids the private individual to look after his own, e.g. his dwelling, is an improper and unjust privilege. The answer to this is that the owner who maintains a building within the protected category is not just adding to his own assets or his own comfort. He is making it possible for future genera-tions to enjoy what they would otherwise lose. It must be recognized, legally and by the public generally, that the person who acquires an historic building is taking on great liabilities, and that he deserves consideration in return for a duty which he shoulders. It is the nation as a whole that derives benefit from his maintenance of the building, as well as the owner himself. Since both derive advantage, it must be for both: the nation as well as the individual, to contribute.

Before leaving the subject of finance it is as well to reiterate a warn-ing against over-spending on vast schemes. This is generally done on the plea of making a building permanently safe. It cannot be too widely known that this is *impossible*: all buildings need continuous main-tenance from year to year, not immense lump-sum payments at intervals. It is quite true that, in the nineteenth century, many old buildings had reached a stage of dereliction where extensive collapse was a real possibility, and in a few cases actually occurred (e.g. the tower of St John's, Chester). The church restorers were partially justified in their labours, in that a good deal had to be done if the cathedrals and other great churches were to stand at all. Yet there is no doubt that, considering the national heritage of buildings as a whole, far more was done than was strictly necessary. Financial re-sources were then abundant, and were extravagantly spent. At the present day, costs of work are relatively much higher (even in pro-portion to the general inflation), and there is therefore a stronger reason for strict economy. In fact there can never before, or elsewhere, have been a period when so many inflated estimates have been made. Conservation, along with everything else, is suffering from the worst vice of our materialistic age: the desire to make the biggest possible job out of every opportunity.

The scale of twentieth-century voracity has increased, but we must not fall into the error of supposing that the same outlook has not been with us for a long time. John Ruskin in 1874, in refusing the Gold Medal of the R.I.B.A., told the official body of architects in Britain such home truths about their profession that they kept his letter confidential for more than a quarter-century, until after his death. Ruskin wrote, of the R.I.B.A. and of all such professional bodies of artists: 'The primary object of all such Associations is to exalt the power of their own profession over the mind of the public, power being in the present [nineteenth] century synonymous with wealth. And the root of all the evil . . . is summed up in four words, "Commission on the Cost".' The letter was intended for publication, and to suppress it was an act of almost incredible meanness and spite towards a critic of such standing. All the same, suppression was only voted in the council of the Institute by a majority of one – 15 votes to 14 – something far more creditable to the world of 1874 than might have been thought. *Even* in the council, the 'Establishment' of the world of architects in Britain, over 48% of Victorians sufficiently believed in fair play to give their opponent a hearing.

It is tempting to wonder whether the fourteen just men were not honestly attracted by the alternative that Ruskin had put before them. His letter continued: 'from any body of architects, however small, who will bind themselves henceforward to accept a given salary (whatever amount, according to their standing, they may choose to name) for their daily work, and to work with their men (or at least with their own hands on the sculpture of the building) while they take such a salary – from such a body I will take a medal tomorrow.' Ruskin's outlook, and even his words, seem to echo that French Dominican, Nicholas de Biard, who in 1261 preached against wealthy bishops by likening them to the masters of the masons (i.e. architects) who say to others 'Cut it for me this way', doing no (manual) work; for 'in those great buildings there is wont to be one chief master who ordains by word alone, rarely or never setting hand to the work, and yet gets higher pay.' The cathedrals Ruskin so admired had themselves been designed by architects; but there was this great justification for his reproach (though not for the implied one in de Biard's sermons), that the mediaeval architect had first been trained to use his hands.

There is a lot of fundamental truth behind Ruskin's bitter outburst and in spite of the considerable seasoning of nonsensical overstatement in his views on truth in art. The labourer is worthy of his hire; but not of an excessive rate. The fourteenth century had had plenty of experience of 'alliances and covines between masons and carpenters' to raise pay, on modern trades union principles, and Wycliffe had condemned this action on theological grounds. Ruskin and Morris were in turn mistaken, perhaps misled by the theory of the noble savage popularized by Rousseau, when they quite unhistorically imagined that the motives of mediaeval artists were altruistic. The difference was not one of kind, but only of degree; yet that difference of degree was substantial. It amounted, in the famous phrase put by Kipling into the mouth of Henry VII: Steal in measure. What was wrong with the nineteenth century was that its acquisitive attitudes were beyond measure – even so, they were extremely modest by the standards to which we have now become inured. There are both honest and dishonest men at all periods, and a middle third, possibly even a majority of the total, who pursue a cautiously neutral line and take on colour from the governing trend in their time.

Even though Ruskin's call to duty was based on premises largely false, it was timely. There were great abuses which he rightly sought to check. At the present day we are still faced with the profoundly unsatisfactory division between the professional architect and the skilled artisan. Psychologically there is everything to be said in favour of a general not requiring his men to perform actions he is himself unable to do – not by accident or injury, but through fault of basic training. This is a valid criticism of the modern profession of architecture even if the other bases of Ruskin's complaint were completely reformed. The natural law of self-preservation can be urged in defence of trade and professional organizations intent on raising wages and fees in a highly competitive society; but no natural law defends the inefficient from the penalty of their own inadequacy. What the modern professional architect faces now is extinction, or fragmentation into a group of minor and parasitic quasi-professions. The role of chief-constructor is now firmly in the hands of the engineer; that of social co-ordinator rests with the town-planner; the interior decorator and the church furnisher between them have taken over large territories as designers of enrichments to be superimposed on or fitted into the fabrics of buildings. There is still room for the traditional architect, but the space is now decreasing, and no sign of a return to the methods of fifty or one hundred years ago can be discerned.

For reasons given earlier (p. 81 ff.), it is at least arguable that the architect should be replaced, so far as work on existing buildings is concerned, by the conservator. The conservator would share a part of the basic training required by architects at all periods, but a sub-

stantial part of his skill would have to come from manual apprenticeship to a craft, followed by studies of the history of architecture at all
periods, and practical work on old buildings. For nearly two centuries
it has been unthinkable that an architect should, by practical demonstration, show a building craftsman how to mix mortar, how to hew stones
or timber, how to lay bricks. The professional has, throughout this
period, relied upon the builder's technical skill to interpret his drawings and written specifications. Right up to the present time he has
been and is incapable of performing the job himself. A rude awakening
is at hand, for the last generation of building craftsmen fully trained
in the use of the old materials is steadily approaching retirement. Not
many years will pass before the architect in general practice finds that
there are no longer any firms possessing competent craftsmen for the
purposes of conservation. All that will remain will be the body of men
officially trained and maintained by the state for direct labour work on
national monuments. Either the architect-conservator will have to
become a civil servant, or see the whole of his professional work taken
over by the official departments of the state and local authorities; or
else he must equip himself with the requisite knowledge and train his
own body of men, able to work competently under his own direction
and personal leadership.

To a limited extent professional conservators already exist, but
their training has been far removed from that of the architect. They
are, generally speaking, trained scientists with specialized knowledge
of chemistry and of techniques relevant to the safe-keeping and repair
of works of art: of painting, sculpture, fittings and furniture. With a
staff of laboratory assistants whom they are capable of instructing
personally, they both experiment in fresh methods and carry out the
skills already existing and approved. Though not yet architect-
conservators, their approach to many of the problems common to all
kinds of restoration shows that another alternative to the present
system exists. It may be asked whether there is really justification for
calling into being an entirely new profession. The answer lies in the
actual need, and there is a close analogy to the emergence, within the
last generation, of the parallel profession of archivist. Historic buildings, no less than historic documents, demand special knowledge and
special skills. The fact that buildings are themselves historical evidence, on a par with that of written records, is highly relevant; it is far
from being the only reason why old buildings are conserved, but it is

a reason that has played an important part in creating a public opinion favourable to conservation.

In the last resort everything that has been under discussion in regard to future policy and activities will depend on public opinion. The enunciation of proposals for legislation and for treatment, however excellent in theory, will remain utopian unless backed by the conscience of a majority of the adult thinking population. It is this public conscience which has to be, not merely aroused, but kept alert, in order that 'fear of public ignominy' as Moller put it one-hundred-and-fifty years ago, may restrain not only 'ignorant officials of low rank' but also the large and highly influential vested interests in destruction. It is not only the weather and various kinds of decay that are continuously on the attack, seeking out every weakness in the building. Far more to be feared than these blind forces are the malicious intelligences of men who, under one pretext or another, deliberately seek for means to derive private benefit from destruction, and who in the course of this pursuit sneer at 'Preservationism' as obscurantist. 'Progress' is a machine with a reverse gear, and there are times when 'flying in the face of progress' is a necessary operation and a title of honour.

In the course of our historical summary we have seen that in Britain the course of attempts to produce the necessary body of public opinion has not been smooth. When, some two centuries ago, John Carter secured influential backing within the Society of Antiquaries for his valiant defence of Durham Cathedral against vandalism, stronger influence was brought to bear to instal the arch-vandal Wyatt, and Richard Gough resigned. Fifty years later the first great open society devoted to antiquity, the British Archaeological Association, was rent apart into two more or less evenly balanced rival bodies, filled with animosity against each other. The early Architectural societies, imbued with most of the essential principles of conservation, suffered from becoming associated with the controversial theology of the Cambridge Camden (Ecclesiological) Society founded in 1839. The need for a national body positively devoted to the subject of conservation remained. Not only was this need not fulfilled by William Morris's founding of the S.P.A.B. in 1877; this action produced a serious breach with a great part of the architectural profession, and for many years offered a bitter and negative heresy-hunt as a substitute for positive union against all forms of destructive agency.

Clearly no opportunity existed then, or could for many years after, to found any new society calling for support from all protagonists of conservation.

It was not, in fact, until 1924 that such a body was launched and even then it was in practice a regional society only, confined mainly to the North of England, centred upon Lancashire and Cheshire. This body was the Ancient Monuments Society, a coming together of two enterprises: one intended to be a national society, the brain-child of the late John Swarbrick; the other a protest movement against the destruction of certain regional buildings. The outcome flourished but for a generation confined almost all its casework to the North. Active devotion to the saving of threatened structures was at all times the key-note of the society's policy, and it was the realization of the urgent nation-wide need for such concentration that in 1952 revolutionized their constitution and activities. The Society's headquarters moved to London, and from 1953 it became effectively the first society devoted to conservation of buildings and their contents of all periods and throughout the country. The very serious need for publicity given to the subject also caused the Society at the same time to found an annual series of transactions, providing an open forum for serious articles on all aspects of conservation.

The first volume of the new series, published in 1953, opened with a note on the general position. It was noted in particular that, in spite of the excellent work of the National Trust and of the then Ministry of Works, what was achieved 'is, in bulk, but a small fraction of what needs to be done.' It was clearly acknowledged that 'there is no virtue in mere age, and constant replacement of the old by the new is a necessity for human well-being and progress.' The Society thus explicitly rejected any desire to keep everything old: 'We do not advocate indiscriminate preservation, but we take up arms against *indiscriminate destruction*. We plead for the retention of what is most worthy . . .' The objects of the Society are succinctly set out in its Rules:—

'The objects of the Society shall be the conservation for the benefit of the nation of places of historic interest, ancient monuments, historic buildings and fine old craftsmanship throughout the whole of Great Britain; to disseminate knowledge of such places, monuments, buildings and craftsmanship, and to stimulate interest therein; to make representations in collaboration with other bodies, or otherwise, to the persons or authorities concerned in order to secure the maintenance of objects of historic interest; and to give guidance and assistance, so far as it is within the power of the Society, to any person or organization with these objects in view.'

Within the first years of the Society's existence in its new form the threat to old buildings became far more acute, in spite of the provisions of the Town and Country Planning Act of 1947 and the listing of buildings then officially begun, under the former Ministry of Housing and Local Government. Other steps taken towards meeting the threat included the founding of the first academic course in the subject, for graduate architects, a Certificate Course in the Preservation and Restoration of Historical Buildings in the Bartlett School of Architecture, at University College, London. Yet the scales were loaded against old buildings, and serious alarm was felt by those who came into close contact with individual cases. The degree of statutory protection afforded was quite inadequate, and various other difficulties militated against a satisfactory solution of the problem on a national scale. An article summarizing the position as it was seen in 1954 is here reprinted (Appendix IV). In certain directions, notably in recent legislation and in completion of the official listing of monuments, there has been distinct progress in the intervening seventeen years; but the position remains far from satisfactory.

In regard to the great majority of the vast number of buildings threatened with destruction, the main burden of protection rests upon private societies and upon individuals with local knowledge. This has always been so in fact, but has now obtained legal recognition under the Town and Country Planning Act, 1968: the Ministry Circular 61/68 on Historic Buildings and Conservation, made under this Act, directs Local Planning Authorities to notify five national bodies as well as the relevant Royal Commission on Historical Monuments of all applications to demolish listed buildings. The bodies concerned: Ancient Monuments Society, Council for British Archaeology, Georgian Group, Society for the Protection of Ancient Buildings, and Victorian Society, are then free to make observations on the proposed demolition. While their observations have no statutory force, they are undoubtedly influential. The amount of work involved, however, in finding local experts with knowledge of individual threatened buildings, and the incidental expense, is very great. Since the loss to the nation would be catastrophic if this private help from experts were not available, there is clearly a case for official subvention of the cost.

Official help, the official provision of funds, and such further official benefits as tax relief on gifts for conservation there must be; but at all times the attitude of the man in the street will remain vital. Only by public outcry can the destructive tendencies of individual spoilers and careless authorities be averted. We have to realize that the battle is never won: the very same buildings saved by one campaign may well be lost a few years later in another. Even monuments that have at last reached the status of world fame have been in the gravest danger. It is now unthinkable that the Walls and Bars of York should not be preserved as a monument almost unique in England, and as one of the greatest parts of the attraction of the city to tourists. Yet it was the Corporation of the City that in 1799 resolved to pull the walls down provided that it had the legal power; it was shown that it had not, but this did not prevent a process of whittling away in which three stone barbicans out of four were removed, as well as three postern gateways and a large section of the walls. The demolitions continued from 1808 to 1832, and further proposals, to destroy Bootham Bar in 1832 and the Walmgate Walls in 1855, were only withdrawn after the most strenuous protest by private societies and local individuals. Thus the threat to the Walls, saved only because Crown permission would have been needed to take them down altogether, lasted for well over half a century, and came from the official custodians of the monuments involved. York now views its walls with pride, but neither this nor any other cause for complacency must lull the public to sleep. Conservation, like everything else worth while, means a great deal of hard work and, now and at all times an unceasing vigilance.

Appendices

APPENDIX I

*Decree of Louis X, Grand Duke of Hesse-Darmstadt, 22 January 1818.
German text as printed by Georg Moller in* Denkmäler der deutschen
Baukunst, *2nd edition (Leipzig, Darmstadt and London, n.d.), 9:–*

*Ludewig, von Gottes Gnaden Grossherzog von Hessen und bei Rhein etc.
etc.*

In Erwägung, dass die noch vorhandenen Denkmäler der Baukunst
zu den wichtigsten und interessantesten Urkunden der Geschichte
gehören, indem sich aus ihnen auf die frühern Sitten, Geistesbildung
und den bürgerlichen Zustand der Nation schliessen lässt, und daher
die Erhaltung derselben höchst wünschenswerth ist, verordnen Wir
Folgendes:

1. Unser Ober-Baukolleg wird beauftragt, alle in dem Gross-
herzogthum Hessen befindliche Ueberreste alter Baukunst, welche in
Hinsicht auf Geschichte oder Kunst verdienen erhalten zu werden, in
ein genaues Verzeichniss bringen zu lassen, wobei der gegenwärtige
Zustand zu beschreiben und die in ihnen befindlichen alten Kunst-
werke, als Gemälde, Bildsäulen und dergleichen mit zu bemerken
sind.

2. Wegen der Ausarbeitung des geschichtlichen Theiles in diesem
Verzeichniss, hat das genannte Colleg diejenigen Gelehrten, welchen
die Geschichte jeder Provinz am bekanntesten ist, zur Mitwirkung
für diesen patriotischen Zweck einzuladen, und sind ihnen zu dem
Ende aus den Archiven die nöthigen Nachrichten mitzutheilen.

3. Die vorzüglichsten dieser Werke, oder die am meisten baufäl-
ligen, sind nach und nach genau aufzunehmen und die Zeichnungen
derselben nebst der Beschreibung in unserm Museum zu deponiren.

4. Unser Ober-Baukolleg wird hierdurch beauftragt, uns das Verzeichniss dieser der Erhaltung oder Abbildung werthgeachteten
Gebäude zur Genehmigung vorzulegen, sich wegen der Erhaltung
und Ausbesserung derselben mit den verschiedenen Behörden in Ver-
bindung zu setzen und Uns darüber die geeigneten Vorschläge zu
machen.

5. Wenn es nöthig scheinen sollte, mit einem oder dem andern dieser Gebäude Veränderungen vorzunehmen oder dieselben ganz abzubrechen, so soll dieses nur mit Vorwissen des erwähnten Kollegs geschehen, und nachdem dasselbe, in den geeigneten Fällen, Unsere höchste Genehmigung eingeholt hat.

6. Wenn bei Nachgrabungen oder andern Veranlassungen Alter-thümer aufgefunden werden, so haben Unsere Beamten dafür zu sorgen, dass dieselben möglichst erhalten werden, und ist davon sogleich die Anzeige an Unser Ober-Baukolleg oder die Direction Unsers Museums zu machen.

7. Den sämmtlichen öffentlichen Behörden wird es zur Pflicht gemacht, für die Erhaltung der in dem oben erwähnten Verzeichnisse bekannt gemachten Denkmäler möglichst zu sorgen, zu welchem Ende dasselbe gedruckt und ihnen mitgetheilt werden soll.

Darmstadt, den 22. Januar 1818.

LUDEWIG.

APPENDIX II

Paper on Restoration drawn up by the Executive Committee of the Society of Antiquaries of London on 29 March 1855, read at the meeting of 3 May, and circulated to all Fellows.

RESTORATION

The numerous instances of the Destruction of the character of Ancient Monuments which are taking place under the pretence of Restoration, induce the Executive Committee, to which the Society of Antiquaries has entrusted the management of its 'Conservation Fund', to call the special attention of the Society to the subject, in the hope that its influence may be exerted to stop, or at least moderate, the pernicious practice.

The evil is an increasing one; and it is to be feared that, unless a strong and immediate protest be made against it, the monumental remains of England will, before long, cease to exist as truthful records of the past. . . .

The Committee strongly urge that, except where restoration is called for in Churches by the requirements of Divine Service, or in other cases of manifest public utility, no restoration should ever be attempted, otherwise than as the word 'restoration' may be under-stood in the sense of preservation from further injuries by time or negligence:— they contend that anything beyond this is untrue in art, unjustifiable in taste, destructive in practice, and wholly opposed to the judgment of the best Archaeologists.'

The paper was circulated over the signature of the President, the fifth Earl Stanhope (1805–1875).

APPENDIX III

The Manifesto of William Morris, setting forth the principles of the Society for the Protection of Ancient Buildings upon its foundation in 1877.

'A Society coming before the public with such a name as that above written must needs explain how, and why, it proposes to protect those ancient buildings which, to most people doubtless, seem to have so many and such excellent protectors. This, then, is the explanation we offer.

No doubt within the last fifty years (since 1827) a new interest, almost like another sense, has arisen in these ancient monuments of art; and they have become the subject of one of the most interesting of studies, and of an enthusiasm, religious, historical, artistic, which is one of the undoubted gains of our time; yet we think, that if the present treatment of them be continued, our descendants will find them useless for study and chilling to enthusiasm. We think that those last fifty years of knowledge and attention have done more for their destruction than all the foregoing centuries of revolution, violence, and contempt.

For Architecture, long decaying, died out, as a popular art at least, just as the knowledge of medieval art was born. So that the civilized world of the nineteenth century has no style of its own amidst its wide knowledge of the styles of other centuries. From this lack and this gain arose in men's minds the strange idea of the Restoration of ancient buildings; and a strange and most fatal idea, which by its very name implies that it is possible to strip from a building this, that, and the other part of its history, of its life that is, and then to stay the hand at some arbitrary point, and leave it still historical, living, and even as it once was.

In early times this kind of forgery was impossible, because knowledge failed the builders, or perhaps because instinct held them back. If repairs were needed, if ambition or piety pricked on to change, that change was of necessity wrought in the unmistakable fashion of the time; a church of the eleventh century might be added to or altered in the twelfth, thirteenth, fourteenth, fifteenth, sixteenth, or even the seventeenth and eighteenth centuries; but every change, whatever history it destroyed, left history in the gap, and was alive with the spirit of the deeds done midst its fashioning. The result of all this was often a building in which the many changes, though harsh and visible enough, were, by their very contrast, interesting and instructive and could by no possibility mislead. But those who make the changes wrought in our day under the name of Restoration, while professing to bring back a building to the best time of its history, have no guide but each his own individual whim to point out to them what is admirable and what contemptible; while the very nature of their task compels them to destroy something and to supply the gap by imagining what the earlier builders should or might have done. Moreover, in the course of this double process of destruction and addition the whole surface of the building is necessarily tampered with; so that the appearance of antiquity is taken away from such old parts of the fabrics as are left, and there is no laying to rest in the spectator the suspicion of what may have been lost; and in short, a feeble and lifeless forgery is the final result of all the wasted labour.

It is sad to say, that in this manner most of the bigger Minsters, and a vast number of more humble buildings, both in England and on the Continent, have been dealt with by men of talent often, and worthy of better employment, but deaf to the claims of poetry and history in the highest sense of the words.

For what is left we plead before our architects themselves, before the official guardians of buildings, and before the public generally, and we pray them to remember how much is gone of the religion, thought and manners of time past, never by almost universal consent, to be Restored; and to consider whether it be possible to Restore those buildings, the living spirit of which, it cannot be too often repeated, was an inseparable part of that religion and thought, and those past manners. For our part we assure them fearlessly, that of all the Restorations yet undertaken the worst have meant the reckless stripping a building of some of its most interesting material features; while the best have their exact analogy in the Restoration of an old picture, where the partly-perished work of the ancient craftsmaster has been made neat and smooth by the tricky hand of some unoriginal and thoughtless hack of to-day. If, for the rest, it be asked us to specify what kind of amount of art, style, or other interest in a building, makes it worth protecting, we answer, Anything which can be looked on as artistic, picturesque, historical, antique, or substantial: any work, in short, over which educated, artistic people would think it worth while to argue at all.

It is for all these buildings, therefore, of all times and styles, that we plead, and call upon those who have to deal with them, to put Protection in the place of Restoration, to stave off decay by daily care, to prop a perilous wall or mend a leaky roof by such means as are obviously meant for support or covering, and show no pretence of other art, and otherwise to resist all tampering with either the fabric or ornament of the building as it stands; if it has become inconvenient for its present use, to raise another building rather than alter or enlarge the old one; in fine to treat our ancient buildings as monuments of a bygone art, created by bygone manners, that modern art cannot meddle with without destroying.

Thus, and thus only, shall we escape the reproach of our learning being turned into a snare to us; thus, and thus only can we protect our ancient buildings, and hand them down instructive and venerable to those that come after us.'

APPENDIX IV

Article 'Old Buildings – Problem and Challenge' by John Harvey, reprinted from the Transactions of the Ancient Monuments Society, *New Series, II, 1954, pages 35–43.*

All concerned with the problem of old buildings, and aware of national and local policy on the subject in recent years, must have been struck by the astonishing – and depressing – gulf between theory and practice. That there is a major problem has been recognised not merely by members of private bodies, but by national legislation and by complementary activity on the part of many local authorities. Much excellent work has been done, but there has been no general realisation of the fundamental principles at stake. To some extent, these principles have even become obscured by the glow of complacency felt at what has already been done. In the last resort, members of Parliament and of the Church Assembly, local councillors and the man in the street, are still thinking of 'Ancient Monuments' as a luxury to be given (in the jargon of our times) a very low priority.

This deep-seated misconception lies behind many losses of irreplaceable buildings, sacrificed not to real necessity, but to an expediency based on a false relative scale of values. Only too frequently buildings are condemned, or their condemnation condoned, by the very bodies legally responsible for preservation, and in the teeth of keen and informed local opposition. Confidence in the efficiency of present measures is repeatedly shaken when important buildings scheduled under the Ancient Monuments Acts are swept away with official sanction; when large numbers of those recently given 'protection' by Statutory Listing are removed from the Lists as soon as there is a conflict with other interests; when really determined vandalism wins all along the line.

Such deplorable results are the effect, not of hypocrisy, but of blindness to the importance of the principle involved, a subconscious relegation of old buildings to a low category in the scale of human values. This scale usually finds material expression in the reduction of each individual case to financial terms: what will preservation cost, either for works of repair or in the modification of some project? In part this is due to survival of the nineteenth-century belief in material progress which has so strongly coloured national education, in part to the spreading sense of man's helplessness in face of his own invention, engendered by the wars and social and economic unrest of our time. What is new is automatically accepted as an improvement, without further question.

That there is no real or consistent policy simply reflects the absence of any philosophy of conservation. Few supporters of protection for ancient buildings and works of art could give a reasoned explanation, nor define the basis of their views. Is then the saving of the old (whether outworn or not) a mere sop to emotion, an affair of sentiment? Even if it were so, it does not follow that preservation would be unjustifiable. But unless we follow St. Bernard of Clairvaux in considering all material things a mere trap for the senses, we need not hesitate in attaching a real value to what possesses both beauty and utility.

The recognition of beauty and utility is highly subjective, but in both qualities there is a relative, if not absolute, scale of values, and few will support the proposition that the more beautiful or useful should be destroyed to give place to the less so. Hence, since it is implicit in such listing as that carried out by the Ministry of Housing and Local Government that the listed buildings do possess these qualities in a high degree, it should be necessary to bring overwhelming evidence of an even higher standard attained by any new proposals which involve their destruction. Evidence of this kind can only be assessed by an independent tribunal, for the present procedure of ministerial enquiry is manifestly unsatisfactory.

Emphasis has commonly, and rightly, been laid upon the aesthetic and amenity values of ancient buildings, but material considerations have generally been overlooked. While some aged construction is unsound, a far greater amount is not merely sound, but has a greater expectation of life than the modern structure which may be put in its place. This is due to two causes: the lavish use of prime materials which was formerly possible; and the high level of craftsmanship attained in the building trade before the development of mechanisation and of large-scale contracting. Medieval buildings in particular witness to the efficacy of provisions for the maintenance of a high standard at a time when the penalty for jerry-building was destruction of the offending work.

England formerly abounded in home-grown hardwoods of the best quality, widespread quarries of good building stone, and a vast number of locally exploited clays producing tiles and bricks. The timber has now disappeared, many of the quarries are exhausted or economically unworkable, and rationalisation in industry has put an end to the supply of sound common bricks and tiles made near the site. The consequently increased rarity of the materials of which our old buildings are made is in itself a reason of the utmost importance for their preservation wherever possible. Indeed, the irreparable loss to the nation caused by the wholesale destruction of work which it is impossible to replace with equally durable materials and workmanship is the most alarming feature of the situation. No nation can afford to waste its accumulated assets in so reckless a manner.

It is more than time that the country awakened to the squandering of its patrimony now in progress, a senseless destruction quite largely due to the people's own elected representatives in local government, and elsewhere inadequately combated by those representatives. The remedy will only come when a national sense of indignation at such waste has been aroused, for nothing short of this can remedy abuses. To arouse this deep and burning indignation is by far the most serious problem for those who already realise the facts.

On a different plane, conservation faces other serious problems of a technical character, some of which relate to the causes of decay, others to the means of maintenance and repair. Two causes of decay are of overwhelming importance: damp, and atmospheric pollution. Against the penetration of buildings by damp the only adequate safeguard is regular maintenance, which in its turn means constant vigilance. It is usually decay due to damp (most frequently in the form of dry-rot) that transforms a sound asset into an unrepairable liability. Hence regular inspection, particularly of roofs and gutters, is the first requirement for all building conservation. This has been recognised in recent provisions for the maintenance of historic churches, but is still too little understood by building owners in general.

While decay due to a wet climate has been present throughout our history, the erosion of building materials in a polluted atmosphere is a relatively modern phenomenon. Public attention has recently been drawn to this, and the creation and rapid extension of smokeless zones provide the only complete solution. In the meantime, vast sums of money are being spent upon palliatives and repairs: sums which ought to be available for other purposes. Since erosion most seriously menaces masonry buildings, the technical problem is primarily one of the treatment and repair of stone. In this field scientific results of great value have been reached through the patient work, carried on for thirty years by the Building Research Station. So far, no substance has been found which will act as a preservative without materially altering appearance, though coating with paint or with whitewash will act as a purely mechanical protection. Among palliatives, the best is undoubtedly cleaning by brushing with water only, or steam-jet, followed by hosing repeated regularly as a measure of normal maintenance. Washing, by removing harmful chemical salts, undoubtedly prolongs the life of masonry and allows original work to be retained for a much longer period before ultimate replacement with new material.

When replacement becomes unavoidable, there is normally a choice between natural and synthetic (plastic) stone. It cannot be too strongly urged upon building owners that the *widespread* use of synthetic materials is a false economy, besides being destructive of the permanent tonal values of the building. Plastic stone can be of real service when its use is limited to the making good of damaged details, where replacement with natural stone would involve the loss of more of the original, and would cause much greater disturbance to the fabric. But the refacing of large expanses of ashlar walling with synthetic material is completely indefensible and should never be accepted as the alternative to a certain degree of irregularity in a weathered and partially repaired surface. Repairs should always be limited to the minimum: in order to preserve as much of the original as possible for the longest possible time; to avoid the serious structural disturbance involved in complete refacing; and to spread the cost of repair. Indeed, it may fairly be laid down that the more closely repairs approximate to regular maintenance, the better they are.

It is a fallacy to suppose that any repair or restoration, however costly, can put a building permanently in order. Experience of the very costly restorations, often amounting to virtual rebuilding, of the last century shows that these were appallingly wasteful, apart from the unnecessary destruction of old work which they involved. In many cases too, the work done was not only wasteful, but structurally inept and badly executed. Among the most serious of the mistakes made in Victorian times are the choice of poor and unsuitable stone, and its use in thin veneers inadequately bonded to the old core. It is noteworthy that certain of the buildings on which most money is now being spent (for example, York Minster and Westminster Abbey), are precisely those upon which most work was done in the nineteenth, and early in the twentieth century.

The correct treatment of old buildings calls for long experience on the part of the architects and the leading craftsmen concerned. The subject cannot be learnt from text-books, useful as are such works as the late A. R. Powys's *Repair of Ancient Buildings*, and the excellent technical treatises and articles on special subjects which have been produced by the Building Research Station and by members of the Ancient Monuments Department of the Ministry of Works. It is, for instance, admitted by research petrologists that no amount of scientific testing of samples can take the place of the personal experience in the choice of sound stone possessed by a well-trained master mason.

Consequently the problem of providing adequate training, both for architect-conservators and for craftsmen, is one of the most serious

difficulties to be faced. The steadily lessening use of traditional materials for new building has, together with general industrialisation,
greatly decreased the number of fully trained craftsmen in the key
trades of masonry, carpentry and plumbing. To a certain extent this
decrease has been offset by the special arrangements made by the
Ministry of Works for training craftsmen, but their numbers are utterly inadequate to cover the needs of the country as a whole. To the
many adverse factors present for a generation and more has now been
added, a disastrous final blow, compulsory National Service. It is not
generally known that the fully trained master craftsman of the type
now so close to dying out, served not merely a minimum apprenticeship of five years, but one of six or seven years with a further three
years as 'improver' or journeyman before he was regarded as qualified.
Furthermore, to obtain the best results, apprenticeship should begin
at 13 or 14, rather than at 15, the present school-leaving age.

The effect of National Service has been felt so severely that it is no
exaggeration to say that the skilled crafts are doomed unless total
exemption is granted. Of the still fairly considerable though fast
diminishing number of apprentices in the building trades, allowed
deferment until the end of a five-year term, hardly any are prepared to
return to a three-years improvership after their period of service. All
attempts to maintain a satisfactory level of craftsmanship are futile unless sufficient inducements are given to encourage apprenticeship, to
enable the passed apprentice to complete his full training, and to provide him with proper employment at an adequate wage. At the present
time the differential rates for highly skilled master craftsmen are so
grossly inadequate that even of the few who can still maintain the
best standards, a number are driven by sheer necessity to abandon
their calling in favour of some less skilled but more remunerative
work.

Dismal as are the prospects in the building crafts, they are hardly
more so than those in the architectural profession. For well over a
generation it has been the practice of most of the schools of architecture in Britain to give only the most perfunctory treatment to history,
and to concentrate upon the use of the latest materials. A thorough
practical knowledge of traditional methods of construction is no longer
a primary requirement, and even the capacity to make accurate measured surveys of old work is very generally lacking. Against such a
background it is clearly impossible to train within a short time a

sufficient number of architect-conservators to deal with the thousands of ancient buildings throughout the country now in need of expert handling. No time is to be lost in putting the education of the conservator on an adequate basis of knowledge and experience.

Here again, incentives are lacking. There must be some guarantee that the work of conservation will be entrusted only to those with the proper training and experience, before entrants to the profession will be likely to undertake the arduous work needed to acquire special qualification. This in turn depends upon the methods of qualifying open to the student, for it is clear that general insistence on specific qualifications can only be based upon acceptance of these as satisfactory. Here it is necessary to consider the type of entrant whom it is desired to attract, as well as the methods by which competence as a conservator can best be attained.

Firstly, it must be recognized that the work of the conservator of ancient buildings demands a very high degree of patience and personal application; it is hardly putting it too highly to describe it as a dedication rather than a career. The work cannot be safely delegated to assistants until they themselves have had long experience. Architectural partnerships or offices of the normal type are seldom well suited to the purpose, and moreover in most cases deal to an overwhelming extent with the production of new buildings. The character of ancient and modern work differs so greatly that a mixed practice of this kind can very rarely be desirable. The conservator should be recognized as a special branch of the architectural profession, not in any exclusive sense, but in a way analogous to the present practice of specialists in town-planning.

Before considering in detail the ideal form which specialised training should take, it is worth studying the methods at present available. These methods are four in number:—

(1) practical experience as an assistant to an architect specialising in work on ancient buildings, or in the Ancient Monuments Department of the Ministry of Works;

(2) practical experience of various kinds organised by the Society for the Protection of Ancient Buildings for holders of their Lethaby Scholarship;

(3) academic and practical training given in the Certificate Course in Preservation and Restoration of Historical Buildings, instituted in 1950 in the Bartlett School of Architecture, London University;

(4) lectures and visits given in the special short courses arranged from 1952 onwards by the York Civic Trust.

All of these apply to architects already qualified, or who, if they have not actually taken final qualifications, are in course of so doing. Of the four methods, the first is that which has produced almost all of those specialists now in practice and, however supplemented by more academic work, the need for such *long-term* practical experience remains essential. It does not, however, lend itself to any form of qualifying test, for which some other provision must be made.

Of the three more intensive types of course offered, that of the S.P.A.B. approaches most nearly to the ideal, consisting as it does of carefully arranged practical experience with different architects on various types of conservation work and surveys, opportunities to inspect craft processes and to attend conferences and lectures on related subjects. It suffers from the very small trust funds available, which limit the awards to a number far too low to have any appreciable effect on the general problem of training. In any case, the special virtue of the system is its highly individual approach, and it is hard to see how it could be extended, even were funds available, to the training of considerable numbers of students.

Short courses of the kind organised at York have the value of being easily attended even by those actually in practice, and it has been found that they have in fact been extensively patronised by relatively senior architects, surveyors and others concerned. As a means of refreshing the conservator's knowledge of up-to-date methods of treatment, courses of this type have great possibilities, but they are obviously quite inadequate as a qualification.

There remains the type of course at present exemplified by that offered at London University. This is, of course, available only to those living or working in the London district, and to provide for the country as a whole, similar courses would have to be instituted at other schools of architecture. Fundamentally, an acceptable formal qualification can only be provided on the basis of some such course and examination, but there is room for extension of the practical requirements before qualification is awarded. A substantial period of working experience of conservation (not less than three years) should be essential. On the other hand, it is already difficult for post-graduate students to undertake the present course. Not only must they attend several evening lectures weekly through some six months of the year, but during the remaining months produce two detailed restoration subjects and a thesis, and spend a fortnight upon a work of repair in progress. These are requirements by no means easy of fulfilment for those already in full-time employment or practice.

It seems clear that such courses would stand on an altogether better footing if they could be spread over a longer period, specialisation beginning during the student's third or fourth year of the full-time course in architecture. This would enable a much greater emphasis to be placed upon the teaching of architectural history and traditional construction, and permit of senior students obtaining full-time practical experience of the right kind during the vacations. Such arrangements would also do a great deal to encourage adequate numbers of the younger generation to take up this study at the right period in their careers.

There should be no insuperable difficulties in effecting such a re-organisation within the framework of the present system of professional education. But it may well be that the speed of events and the progress of the social revolution of the twentieth century may soon call for a more drastic reassessment of values. The architectural profession itself sprang from the ranks of those superior master craftsmen of the twelfth to eighteenth centuries, able to design and supervise the erection of major buildings. The superiority of the craftsmen must have been largely the result of better educational opportunities, but they remained craftsmen in that they all had first-hand experience of the manual skill required in the working of wood or stone. The weak point of the modern architect has always been that he is in the position of a musical composer unable to play a single instrument. It is by no means inconceivable that the progressive decline in the prosperity of the overtaxed professional class may drive its members to take a radically new view of their sons' education and prospects in life. It would be fitting if in some cases this new view were to take the form of apprenticing the professional man's son to one of those skilled crafts now in danger of extinction. Thus the architect might once more become the master craftsman, and the lamented gap between design and execution again be bridged.

The architect and the craftsman are two supports of a tripod, whose missing member is represented by the supplier of materials. Here again very great difficulties are faced, partly because of the exhaustion of certain sources of supply, as already mentioned; partly owing to the prevailing trend towards standardisation and the accompanying growth of the middleman with no personal interest in the raw materials which he handles. To some extent these difficulties can be overcome, and by persistence and tireless pressure have been overcome in favourable cases. Quarries have been reopened, some slight attention is now given to the planting of hardwoods; concerted steps must be taken to find an economic basis for the local brickworks, the plumber who operates his own casting table, the thatcher and the plasterer.

I have painted a gloomy enough picture of the present position. This country faces a challenge, nothing less than the loss of the most tangible part of its traditional heritage. Once the nature of the challenge is realised, and the penalty of failure to meet it, there can be no doubt that it will be met. But our greatest enemy is time: already there has been too long delay, and action must be immediate. To-morrow will be too late.

Bibliographical note

The following list includes only a few books of general scope. For the subject as a whole, see *Conservation of Old Buildings: a select Bibliography*, compiled by John Harvey (1969), obtainable from The Ancient Monuments Society, Publications Office, Boundary Farm, High Legh, Knutsford, Cheshire.

Briggs, Martin Shaw, *Goths and Vandals* (1952)

Brown, G. Baldwin, *The Care of Ancient Monuments* (1905)

Cambridgeshire and Isle of Ely County Council, *A Guide to Historic Buildings Law*, 2nd ed. (1970)

Godfrey, Walter H., *Our Building Inheritance* (1944)

Harvey, William, *The Preservation of St. Paul's Cathedral and other Famous Buildings* (1925)

Kelsall, Moultrie R. & Harris, Stuart, *A Future for the Past* (1961)

Powys, A. R., *Repair of Ancient Buildings* (1929)

Sharp, Thomas, *Town and Townscape* (1968), *The Anatomy of the Village* (1946)

Notes to the text

INTRODUCTION

p. 21 ANTHROPOLOGY, A. M. Hocart, *Kings and Councillors* (1936; new edition by R. Needham, University of Chicago Press, Chicago and London, 1970). The quotations are from the new edition, pp. 41, 43, 250, 251, 253–6.

p. 23 YORK, The former existence of wide greens is evidenced by the dual planning of the streets of Ousegate and Coppergate (east–west) and of The Shambles and Colliergate (north–south), and this is confirmed by early documents.

p. 25 STADTBILD, Brown, *The Care of Ancient Monuments*, 23, 29.

p. 26 ANTIQUARIES, see Joan Evans, *A History of the Society of Antiquaries* (1956).

EUROPE, Baldwin Brown, *op. cit.*, 14.

p. 27 GERMANY, see J. H. Harvey, 'The Origin of Official Preservation of Ancient Monuments' in *Transactions of the Ancient Monuments Society*, N.S., IX (1961), 27–31.

p. 30 GOTHIC, Paul Frankl, *The Gothic*: Literary Sources and Inspirations through Eight Centuries (Princeton University Press, 1960).

WORCESTRE, see *William Worcestre: Itineraries*, ed. J. H. Harvey (Oxford Medieval Texts, 1969).

PETRARCH, Brown, *op. cit.*, 13.

p. 31 CONFUCIUS, *Doctrine of the Mean*, ch. xix. 3; *Analects*, XI.xiii.

HORACE, Epist. I, ep. i, 98, in Neckam, *De naturis rerum*, ed. T. Wright (Rolls Series, 34, 1863), 281.

CHAPTER 1

p. 40 EDINBURGH, etc., Brown, *op. cit.*, 33.

p. 42 VENICE, see Sir Ashley Clarke, 'The Preservation of Venice' in *Transactions of the Ancient Monuments Society*, N. S., XVII (1970), 51–62.

SANTILLANA DEL MAR, A richly illustrated description with text in Spanish, French and English, is Manuel Pereda de la Reguera, *Santillana del Mar y Altamira* (Santander: Editorial Cantabria, 1952 and subsequent editions); cf. *Monumentos Españoles* – Catálogo de los Declarados Histórico-Artísticos (Instituto Diego Velázquez, Madrid, C. S. I. C., II, 1954, no. 918), 552–4.

p. 46 FRENCH SYSTEM, F. Sorlin, 'The French System for Conservation and Revitalization in Historic Centres', in *Conservation and Development in historic towns and cities*, ed. P. Ward (Newcastle-upon-Tyne, 1968), 221–34.

CHAPTER 2

p. 50 ff. Refer to Thomas Sharp, *The Anatomy of the Village* (1946); and A. K. Wickham, *Villages of England* (1932).

CHAPTER 3

p. 74 NEW USES, *New Uses for Old Churches* – Report of the York Redundant Churches Commission (York, 1967); also *Supplementary (Final) Report* (1969), both obtainable from the Church Information Office, Westminster; and S.P.C.K., York.

p. 77 NUMBER OF CHURCHES, *The Preservation of our Churches* (Church Information Board, 1952), 12, 18–19.

CHAPTER 4

p. 90 MODELS, see William Harvey, *Models of Buildings*: How to Make & Use Them (1927).

p. 92 BURGOS, G. E. Street, *Some Account of Gothic Architecture in Spain* (1865, etc.), 27 and footnote.

CHAPTER 5

p. 97 Essential studies are R. J. Schaffer, *The Weathering of Natural Building Stones* (D. S. I. R. Building Research Special Report no. 18, 1932 etc.); and W. J. Arkell, *Oxford Stone* (1947).

CHAPTER 6

p. 116 Standard works are F. H. Crossley, *Timber Building in England, from early Times to the end of the Seventeenth Century* (1951); and W. P. K. Findlay, *Timber Pests and Diseases* (1967).

CHAPTER 7

p. 134 LONDON ASSIZE, The texts of the Assizes of Building of 1189 and 1212 are printed in T. Hudson Turner, *Some Account of Domestic Architecture in England* (1851), 275–83.

YORK, see J. H. Harvey, 'The Fire of York in 1137', in *Yorkshire Archaeological Journal*, XLI, part 163, 365–7.

CHAPTER 8

p. 153 LE MANS, V. Mortet, *Recueil de textes relatifs à l'Histoire de l'Architecture* (Paris, 1911), 165 ff.

CHAPTER 9

p. 159 BOYSE, P. Frankl, *The Gothic*, 380–1.

ST. DENIS, E. Panofsky, *Abbot Suger . . .* (Princeton, 1946), 26–7, 51–2.

CANTERBURY, R. Willis, *The Architectural History of Canterbury Cathedral* (1845), 35–6.

p. 160 GERMAN USAGE, O. Kletzl, *Plan-fragmente aus der deutschen Dombauhütte von Prag in Stuttgart und Ulm* (Stuttgart, 1939), 11.

WELDON, *Registrum Radulphi Baldock* . . . , ed. R. C. Fowler (Canterbury & York Society, VII, 1911), 91–3.

p. 161 NORWICH, W. H. St. J. Hope & W. T. Bensly in *Norfolk Archaeology*, XIV, 110 note.

WINCHESTER COLLEGE, J. H. Harvey quoting bursars' account in *Journal of the British Archaeological Association*, 3rd S., XXVIII (1965), 112 note.

LAUNCESTON, Public Record Office, E.101/461/13.

WOLVESEY, Church Commissioners' documents, 2/3/155836 (now deposited in Hampshire Record Office, Winchester).

p. 162 OUDENBOURG, Migne, *Patrologia Latina*, CLXXIV, col. 1417.

WINDSOR, W. H. St. J. Hope, *Windsor Castle* (1913), I, 63, 80.

HONNECOURT, H. R. Hahnloser, *Villard de Honnecourt* (Vienna, 1935), Pl. 45.

WORCESTER, R. Willis in *Archaeological Journal*, XX (1863), 266–8.

p. 163 CLYVE, see J. Harvey, *English Mediaeval Architects* (1954), 67–8; 'Notes on the Architects of Worcester Cathedral', in *Transactions of the Worcestershire Archaeological Society*, XXXIII (1957), 24.

STRASBOURG, P. Frankl, *The Gothic*, 117.

CAERNARVON, *The Record of Caernarvon* (Record Commission, 1838), 220.

FOUNTAINS ABBEY, R. Gilyard-Beer, *Fountains Abbey* (Ministry of Public Building and Works, 1970), 40.

p. 164 MASTERWORKS, P. Frankl, *op. cit.*, 140–1.

p. 165 TITCHFIELD, *Letters and Papers of the Reign of Henry VIII*, XIII, part i, 749.

p. 166 YORK, *Calendar of Close Rolls, 1296–1302*, 218; *York Civic Records*, ed. A. Raine, notably 4. (Yorkshire Archaeological Society, Record Series, CVIII), 149.

p. 167 MONUMENTS IN CHURCHES, Joan Evans, *A History of the Society of Antiquaries* (1956), 4; M. S. Briggs, *Goths and Vandals* (1952), 36–7.

p. 170 ENGRAVINGS OF ARCHITECTURE, see bibliography in J. Harvey, *Gothic England* (2nd ed., 1948), 194–5.

p. 171 LEGAL DICTUM, '*E vus ne poez ren fere outre le record ke est vostre garant*' (Hereford Eyre, 1292), adopted as a motto by the Bedfordshire Historical Record Society.

WYATT, Joan Evans, *op. cit.*, 207–14.

CHAPTER 10

p. 179 MORRIS, see article by Arthur Waugh in *Encyclopaedia Britannica*, 11th ed. (1910), XVIII, 873; cf. M. S. Briggs, *Goths and Vandals*, 190–1.

p. 180 MORRIS'S PROGRAMME, the real source was Ruskin's famous passage on restoration in *The Seven Lamps of Architecture* (1849):

'Take proper care of your monuments, and you will not need to restore them. A few sheets of lead, put in time upon the roof, a few dead leaves and sticks swept in time out of a water-course, will save both roof and walls from ruin. Watch an old building with an anxious care . . . bind it together with iron where it loosens; stay it with timber where it declines; do not care about the unsightliness of the aid: better a crutch than a lost limb . . .' (chap. VI, The Lamp of Memory, xix).

p. 185 LONDON CONFERENCE, took place on 4 December 1896 (not 1897 as stated by the quotation in Baldwin Brown). I have to thank Miss E. D. Mercer and Mr. A. R. Neate of the Greater London Record Office for this correction.

p. 187 OFFICIAL LITERATURE, mostly listed in *Government Publications Sectional List No. 61: Building*, obtainable free from the Government Bookshops.

p. 194 CONGRESS OF 1904, G. Baldwin Brown, *The Care of Ancient Monuments* (1905), 48.

CHAPTER 11

p. 200 RUSKIN, quoted by Colin McCall in *The Architect*, March 1971 (I, no. 2), 44.

p. 201 DE BIARD, V. Mortet & P. Deschamps, *Recueil de Textes relatifs à l'Histoire de l'Architecture . . . XIIe – XIIIe siècles* (Paris, 1929), 290–1.

WYCLIFFE, in *The Grete Sentens of Curs*, quoted in G. G. Coulton, *Social Life in Britain* (1918 etc.), 490–1.

Index

This index contains all names of persons and places in the text. Attention is drawn to the classified cross-references under the headings: Building parts, Building types, Finance, Materials, Periods, Transport, and Trees. *Italic* numerals refer to plates.